Intellectual Commons and the Law: A Normative Theory for Commons-Based Peer Production

Antonios Broumas

Critical, Digital and Social Media Studies

Series Editor: Christian Fuchs

The peer-reviewed book series edited by Christian Fuchs publishes books that critically study the role of the internet and digital and social media in society. Titles analyse how power structures, digital capitalism, ideology and social struggles shape and are shaped by digital and social media. They use and develop critical theory discussing the political relevance and implications of studied topics. The series is a theoretical forum for internet and social media research for books using methods and theories that challenge digital positivism; it also seeks to explore digital media ethics grounded in critical social theories and philosophy.

Editorial Board

Thomas Allmer, Mark Andrejevic, Miriyam Aouragh, Charles Brown, Melanie Dulong De Rosnay, Eran Fisher, Peter Goodwin, Jonathan Hardy, Kylie Jarrett, Anastasia Kavada, Arwid Lund, Maria Michalis, Stefania Milan, Vincent Mosco, Safiya Noble, Jack Qiu, Jernej Amon Prodnik, Sarah Roberts, Marisol Sandoval, Sebastian Sevignani, Pieter Verdegem, Bingqing Xia, Mariano Zukerfeld

Published

Critical Theory of Communication: New Readings of Lukács, Adorno, Marcuse, Honneth and Habermas in the Age of the Internet
Christian Fuchs
https://doi.org/10.16997/book1

Knowledge in the Age of Digital Capitalism: An Introduction to Cognitive Materialism
Mariano Zukerfeld
https://doi.org/10.16997/book3

Politicizing Digital Space: Theory, the Internet, and Renewing Democracy
Trevor Garrison Smith
https://doi.org/10.16997/book5

Capital, State, Empire: The New American Way of Digital Warfare
Scott Timcke
https://doi.org/10.16997/book6

The Spectacle 2.0: Reading Debord in the Context of Digital Capitalism
Edited by *Marco Briziarelli and Emiliana Armano*
https://doi.org/10.16997/book11

The Big Data Agenda: Data Ethics and Critical Data Studies
Annika Richterich
https://doi.org/10.16997/book14

Social Capital Online: Alienation and Accumulation
Kane X. Faucher
https://doi.org/10.16997/book16

The Propaganda Model Today: Filtering Perception and Awareness
Edited by *Joan Pedro-Carañana, Daniel Broudy and Jeffery Klaehn*
https://doi.org/10.16997/book27

Critical Theory and Authoritarian Populism
Edited by *Jeremiah Morelock*
https://doi.org/10.16997/book30

Peer to Peer: The Commons Manifesto
Michel Bauwens, Vasilis Kostakis, and Alex Pazaitis
https://doi.org/10.16997/book33

Bubbles and Machines: Gender, Information and Financial Crises
Micky Lee
https://doi.org/10.16997/book34

Cultural Crowdfunding: Platform Capitalism, Labour, and Globalization
Edited by *Vincent Rouzé*
https://doi.org/10.16997/book38

The Condition of Digitality: A Post-Modern Marxism for the Practice of Digital Life
Robert Hassan
https://doi.org/10.16997/book44

Incorporating the Digital Commons: Corporate Involvement in Free and Open Source Software
Benjamin J. Birkinbine
https://doi.org/10.16997/book39

The Internet Myth: From the Internet Imaginary to Network Ideologies
Paolo Bory
https://doi.org/10.16997/book48

Communication and Capitalism: A Critical Theory
Christian Fuchs
https://doi.org/10.16997/book45

Marx and Digital Machines: Alienation, Technology, Capitalism
Mike Healy
https://doi.org/10.16997/book47

The Commons: Economic Alternatives in the Digital Age
Vangelis Papadimitropoulos
https://doi.org/10.16997/book46

Intellectual Commons and the Law: A Normative Theory for Commons-Based Peer Production

Antonios Broumas

University of Westminster Press
www.uwestminsterpress.co.uk

Published by
University of Westminster Press
115 New Cavendish Street
London W1W 6UW
www.uwestminsterpress.co.uk

Text © Antonios Broumas 2020

First published 2020

Cover design: www.ketchup-productions.co.uk
Series cover concept: Mina Bach (minabach.co.uk)

Print and digital versions typeset by Siliconchips Services Ltd.

ISBN (Paperback): 978-1-912656-87-5
ISBN (PDF): 978-1-912656-88-2
ISBN (EPUB): 978-1-912656-89-9
ISBN (Kindle): 978-912656-90-5

DOI: https://doi.org/10.16997/book49

This work is licensed under the Creative Commons Attribution-NonCommercial-NoDerivatives 4.0 International License. To view a copy of this license, visit http://creativecommons.org/licenses/by-nc-nd/4.0/ or send a letter to Creative Commons, 444 Castro Street, Suite 900, Mountain View, California, 94041, USA. This license allows for copying and distributing the work, providing author attribution is clearly stated, that you are not using the material for commercial purposes, and that modified versions are not distributed.

The full text of this book has been peer-reviewed to ensure high academic standards. For full review policies, see:
http://www.uwestminsterpress.co.uk/site/publish.

Competing interests: The author has no competing interests to declare.

Suggested citation: Broumas, A. 2020. *Intellectual Commons and the Law: A Normative Theory for Commons-Based Peer Production.* London: University of Westminster Press. DOI: https://doi.org/10.16997/book49. License: CC-BY-NC-ND 4.0

To read the free, open access version of this book online, visit https://doi.org/10.16997/book49 or scan this QR code with your mobile device:

Contents

List of Figures	xi
List of Tables	xi
Preface	xiii

1. Introduction   1

  1.1. The Intellectual Commons at the Forefront   1
  1.2. The Laws of the Intellect and the Commons of the Mind   2
  1.3. World Views Inverted: Fundamental Notions of the Intellectual Commons   3
  1.4. The Moral Aspects of Commons-Based Peer Production   5
  1.5. Towards a Commons-Oriented Jurisprudence   8

2. The Ontology of the Intellectual Commons   11

  2.1. Introduction   11
  2.2. Definitions   11
  2.3. Elements and Characteristics   14
  2.4. Tendencies   18
  2.5. Manifestations   22
  2.6. Conclusion   25

3. Theories of the Intellectual Commons   27

  3.1. Introduction   27
  3.2. The Growth of Academic Interest on the Concept of the Commons   28
  3.3. Rational Choice Theories of the Intellectual Commons: The Commons as Patch to Capital   29
    3.3.1. Main Question and Methodology   29
    3.3.2. The Institutional Analysis and Development Framework   30
    3.3.3. Core Concepts   31
    3.3.4. Critical Evaluation: The Intellectual Commons as Patch to Capital   33

3.4. Neoliberal Theories of the Intellectual Commons:
The Commons as Fix to Capital   35
   3.4.1. Main Question and Methodology   35
   3.4.2. The Intellectual Commons as Component
   to Capital Accumulation   36
   3.4.3. Intellectual Commons and the Restructuring
   of the Corporation and the Market   39
   3.4.4. Critical Evaluation: A Commons Fix for Capital   42
3.5. Social Democratic Theories of the Intellectual Commons:
The Commons as Substitute to the Welfare State   44
   3.5.1. Main Question and Methodology   44
   3.5.2. The Intellectual Commons and Their Potential
   for an Alternative Non-Market Economy   45
   3.5.3. The Intellectual Commons and Their Potential
   for an Alternative Culture and Public Sphere   47
   3.5.4. The Partner State to the Intellectual Commons:
   Planning the Transition   48
   3.5.5. Critical Evaluation: Partnering with the State
   for the Transition to a Commons-Based Society   50
3.6. Critical Theories of the Intellectual Commons:
The Commons as Alternative to Capital   52
   3.6.1. Main Question and Methodology   52
   3.6.2. The Social Intellect as a Direct Force of Production
   and the Death Knell of Capital   53
   3.6.3. The Anti-Capitalist Commons: Commoning
   Beyond Capital and the State   55
   3.6.4. Critical Evaluation: The Commons as Alternative to Capital   57
3.7. Conclusion   60

4. Cultural Commons and the Law from the Renaissance to Postmodernity: A Case Study   63

4.1. Introduction   63
4.2. Cultural Commons and the Law in the Renaissance   64
4.3. Cultural Commons and the Law in Modernity   69
4.4. Cultural Commons and the Law in Postmodernity   77
4.5. Conclusion   85

5. Researching the Social Value of the Intellectual Commons: Methodology and Design   89

    5.1. Introduction   89
    5.2. Research Theory   90
    5.3 Research Method   91
       5.3.1. Constructing the Research Methodology   91
       5.3.2. Building a Research Strategy   92
       5.3.3. Designing the Research   92
       5.3.4. Research Sampling   93
       5.3.5. Carving Out the Method of Data Collection   99
    5.4. Data Coding   100
    5.5. Conclusion   101

6. Social Value of the Intellectual Commons: Dimensions of Commons-Based Value   103

    6.1. Introduction   103
    6.2. The Economic Dimension of Commons-Based Value   103
    6.3. The Social Dimension of Commons-Based Value   105
    6.4. The Cultural Dimension of Commons-Based Value   107
    6.5. The Political Dimension of Commons-Based Value   107
    6.6. General Dimensions of Commons-Based Value   110

7. The Social Value of the Intellectual Commons: Commons-Based and Monetary Value Dialectics   113

    7.1. Introduction   113
    7.2. Commons-Based and Monetary Value Dialectics   113
    7.3. The Comparison between Offline and Online Communities   117
    7.4. Conclusion   118

8. The Social Value of the Intellectual Commons: Conclusions on Commons-Based Value   119

    8.1. Introduction   119
    8.2. Social Value in the Intellectual Commons   119
    8.3. Productive Communal Activity as the Source of Commons-Based Value   120

8.4. The Forms of Commons-Based Value	121
8.5. The Mode of Commons-Based Value Circulation	122
8.6. Crises of Value	125
8.7. Conclusion	127

9. Towards A Normative Theory of the Intellectual Commons — 129

9.1. Introduction	129
9.2. Foundations of the Critical Normative Theory of the Intellectual Commons	129
9.3. Personhood	132
9.4. Work	135
9.5. Value	139
9.6. Community	143
9.7. Basic Elements of an Intellectual Commons Law	150
9.8. Conclusion	153

10. Conclusion — 155

10.1. The Moral Dimension of the Intellectual Commons	155
10.2. The Justification of an Intellectual Commons Law	161
10.3. Concluding Remarks and Political Implications	165
10.4. The Way Forward	166

Notes	169
Bibliography	179
Index	203

List of Figures

2.1	Locating the commons	13
2.2	The elements of the intellectual commons	14
2.3	The dialectics of the intellectual commons	18
2.4	The manifestations of the intellectual commons	24
3.1	Development of the number of published articles on the topic of the commons	28
6.1	Value circulation and value pooling in intellectual commons communities	112
9.1	The normative dimensions of the intellectual commons	132
9.2	A normative model for the intellectual commons	153
10.1	The cycle of moral justification	162

List of Tables

1.1	Top companies by market capitalisation on a global scale	1
2.1	The elements of the intellectual commons	15
2.2	Tendencies and counter-tendencies within the intellectual commons	19
3.1	The intellectual commons as patch to capital	33
3.2	A commons fix for capital	43
3.3	Partnering with the state for the transition to a commons-based society	50
3.4	The commons as alternative to capital	58
3.5	Comparison of theories and approaches	60
4.1	The framework of creativity in the Renaissance	69
4.2	The framework of creativity in modernity	77
4.3	The framework of creativity in postmodernity	84

4.4	The evolution of the creative practice from the Renaissance to postmodernity	85
5.1	Commons-based value circulation in comparison	93
5.2	Intellectual commons communities in times of crisis: The case of Greece	94
6.1	The circuit of commons-based economic value circulation	104
6.2	The circuit of commons-based social value circulation	106
6.3	The circuit of cultural commons-based value circulation	108
6.4	The circuit of commons-based political value circulation	109
6.5	Contested circuit of value in the communities of the intellectual commons	111
6.6	Co-opted circuit of value in the communities of the intellectual commons	111
7.1	The dialectic between commons-based and monetary value circulation	114
8.1	Forms of productive communal activity in the communities of the intellectual commons	120
8.2	Main forms of commons-based value in the communities of the intellectual commons	121
9.1	The moral significance of the commoner	133
9.2	The moral significance of intellectual work	136
9.3	The moral significance of commons-based value	139
9.4	The moral significance of the intellectual commons community	144
10.1	The tendencies, manifestations and moral dimensions of the intellectual commons	156
10.2	The potential of the intellectual commons and their interrelation with capital in literature	159
10.3	The formulae of commons-based value circulation	160
10.4	The methodology of moral justification	162
10.5	The social potential of the intellectual commons	163
10.6	The justification of an intellectual commons law	164

Preface

The current book asserts that the intellectual commons are of social interest, because they have the potential to (i) increase access to information, knowledge and culture, (ii) empower individual creators and productive communities, (iii) enhance the quantity and quality of intellectual production and (iv) democratise creativity and innovation. Morality thus requires the protection of the intellectual commons from encroachment by private enclosures and the accommodation of commons-based practices in the form of a non-commercial sphere of creativity and innovation in all aspects of intellectual production, distribution and consumption.

Throughout its analysis, this book demonstrates that the intellectual commons are a social regime for the regulation of intellectual production, distribution and consumption, which bears moral significance. It is, therefore, argued that the intellectual commons ought to be regulated in ways that accommodate their potential. Its principal thesis is that our legal systems are in need of an independent body of law for the protection and promotion of the intellectual commons in parallel to intellectual property law. Overall, the book provides the fundamentals for a holistic normative theory for the commons of the mind.

Far from dominant Promethean conceptions of authorship, this book has been a collective endeavour in all its aspects. It has been penned by the author's world views, as these have been forged by legal practice and political activity within and beyond communities of common struggle. It has built upon myriad intellectual contributions by other thinkers, academic or not. It has been rendered possible by the author's family commons, to which immense gratitude is owed. It has been shaped by the mentoring of several individuals, above all Christian Fuchs, whose lifetime dedication to critical theory has been a source of inspiration and intellectual mobilisation. Last but not least, every hour spent on this book is hereby dedicated to all those whose creative potential is constantly oppressed and dispossessed by existing laws due to social and economic inequalities.

CHAPTER I

Introduction

1.1. The Intellectual Commons at the Forefront

Nowadays, the epicentre of wealth creation in our societies has rapidly shifted from tangible to intangible assets (Pagano 2014; Zheng, Santaeulalia and Koh 2015). In recent years, technology corporations (in blue in the table below) have overtaken 'traditional' companies in terms of stock market capitalisation.

Top	2001	2006	2011	2016	February 2018
1	General Electric ($406B)	ExxonMobil ($446B)	ExxonMobil ($406B)	Apple ($582B)	Apple ($905B)
2	Microsoft ($365B)	General Electric ($383B)	Apple ($376B)	Alphabet ($556B)	Alphabet ($777.5B)
3	ExxonMobil ($272B)	Total ($327B)	Petro China ($277B)	Microsoft ($452B)	Microsoft ($725B)
4	Citi ($261B)	Microsoft ($293B)	Shell ($237B)	Amazon ($364B)	Amazon ($731B)
5	Walmart ($260B)	Citi ($273B)	ICBC ($228B)	Facebook ($359B)	Facebook ($527B)

Table 1.1: Top companies by market capitalisation on a global scale.
Source: *Visualcapitalist.com*

It is exactly at this cutting edge of wealth creation that people have started to constitute intellectual commons free for all to access, by devising collaborative peer-to-peer modes of production and management of intellectual resources. The surge in new intellectual commons, such as open hardware design, open standards, free software, wikis, open scientific publishing, openly accessible user-generated content, online content licensed under creative

---

How to cite this book chapter:
Broumas, A. 2020. *Intellectual Commons and the Law: A Normative Theory for Commons-Based Peer Production*. Pp. 1–10. London: University of Westminster Press. DOI: https://doi.org/10.16997/book49.a. License: CC-BY-NC-ND

commons licences, collaborative media, voluntary crowdsourcing techniques and activities, political mobilisation through electronic networks and hacktivism, and internet cultures and memes, has revitalised the accumulated knowledge commons of the past, such as language, collective history, tradition, the public domain and past scientific and technological advancements. This kaleidoscope of sharing and collaborative creativity and innovation constitutes our digitised environments not as private enclosures but as shared public space, a social sphere divergent from the one reproduced by the market and the state.

Intellectual commons proliferate at the core of our knowledge-based economies, where capitalist modes of production are supposed to reach their climax of competitiveness and efficiency. This new mode of production, distribution and consumption of intellectual resources emerges in the ruptures and contradictions of capitalist intellectual production and distribution, in all cases where people form self-governed communities of collaborative innovation and produce resources free for all to access. The emergent intellectual commons have the potential to commonify intellectual production and distribution, unleash human creativity through collaboration, and democratise innovation, with wider positive effects for our societies. The law plays a crucial role in the regulation of the contemporary intellectual commons, either by suppressing or by unleashing their potential.

1.2. The Laws of the Intellect and the Commons of the Mind

Intellectual property law constitutes the primal social institution framing and regulating the societal production, distribution and consumption of information, knowledge and culture. It confers legally enforceable powers to private persons to exclude the general public from sharing and collaborating over a significant part of the accumulated information, knowledge and culture of mankind. Backed up by state enforcement, intellectual property rights arise as the social mechanism par excellence for the construction of artificial scarcity over the inherently abundant commons of the intellect. Enclosure through intellectual property law is the foundation of commodity markets inasmuch as sharing constitutes the archetypal practice of the intellectual commons.

The normative approach followed by this book stresses the moral necessity for a set of institutions protecting and promoting commons-based peer production. It argues that the freedom to take part in science and culture ought to become the rule and private rights of exclusivity upon intellectual works the exception to the regulation of intellectual production, distribution and consumption. In this context, the transformative use of intangible resources for non-commercial purposes would remain unrestricted as essential to the participation of the public in science and culture, and relevant forms of private or public non-commercial contractual syndication of sharing, creativity and innovation, such as open licensing, would be recognised and promoted by the law. In addition, the institution of the public domain would be reconstituted in order to include all types of intellectual works considered the fundamental infrastructure for creativity, innovation, social justice and democracy. The protection of the public domain by law would also be proactive, featuring explicit statutory provisions against its encroachment. Finally, exclusive rights upon intellectual works would be granted only for the purpose of providing sufficient remuneration to creators, only to the extent that exclusivity is adequate, relevant and necessary in relation to such purpose and only for time periods deemed necessary for the fulfilment of that purpose.

Contemporary intellectual property laws fail to address the social potential of the intellectual commons. We are, therefore, in pressing need of an institutional alternative beyond the inherent limitations of intellectual property law. The moral significance of the intellectual commons requires the enactment of a distinct and independent body of positive law for their protection and promotion. This law ought to be designed in such a way as to decouple the current conjoinment of intellectual commons and commodity markets under the rule of capital and provide the institutional infrastructure for the exploitation in full of the potential of the intellectual commons for self-development, collective empowerment, social justice and democracy.

1.3. World Views Inverted: Fundamental Notions of the Intellectual Commons

Societies evolve through time according to contending modes of reproduction (Narotzky 1997, 6). Social reproduction is a dual process. It is related, on the one hand, to the circulation and accumulation or pooling of social values and, on the other hand, to the production, distribution and consumption of tangible and intangible resources (De Angelis 2007, 176).

The reproduction of contemporary societies is determined by the dialectic between commodification and commonification. At the negative, dominant pole of the dialectic, commodification is the social process of transforming resources valued for their use into marketable commodities by destroying the communal relations and social values that underpin such use value and management in common (De Sousa Santos 2002, 484; Mosco 2009, 129). Processes of commodification gradually extend commodity market exchange rationality into both public and private life (Mann 2012, 10). At the positive, insurgent pole of the dialectic, commonification is the countervailing practice of transforming social relations, which generate marketable commodities valued for what they can bring in exchange, into social relations, which generate things produced by multiple creators in communal collaboration, openly accessible to communities or the wider society and valued for their use. Commonification can thus be considered the actual movement towards commons-based societies.

At the forefront of commonification, the intellectual commons are conceived as sets of social practices pooling together and managing in common intangible resources produced by sharing and collaboration within and among communities. These practices are at the heart of the contemporary wave of openness in intellectual production, which features such diverse phenomena as open science, open standards, open design, open hardware, free software, open databases, community media, open scientific publishing, online content openly accessible and/or licensed under copyleft licences, alternative cultures, street art, and other forms of non-commercial and/or openly accessible forms of art.

Being an integral part of social reproduction, the intellectual commons are also reproduced according to their dual process, which involves the combination of social activity with both resources and values. On the one hand, they are reproduced according to a specific mode of production, distribution and consumption of intangible resources, termed commons-based peer production.[1] This mode is the dialectical unity of forces and relations of commonification.

Forces of commonification are both subjective and objective. The subjective powers of commonification are the totality of commoners organised in intellectual commons communities. In unison, they constitute the productive power of the social intellect (Fuchs 2014, 30; 2016, 15). The social intellect can be defined as the subjective productive force, producing in community prior and existing information, communication, knowledge and culture through cooperative work and an aggregation of the work of many humans. It consists of our combined and common pooled intelligence, affect, language, skills, experience, creativity, inspiration, inventiveness, ingenuity, talent, insight and imagination, as this is put into action through en masse sharing and collaboration (Marx 1990, 644; 1973, 470). The objective forces of commonification refer to the means of the practice of commonification, upon which subjective forces work and thus come into dialectical interrelation in the productive process. They are further divided between the objects and the instruments of commonification.

Objects of commonification include any resources, tangible and intangible, used as raw input in the process of commonification; these include raw materials and radio spectrum, prior informational resources in the form of data and information, prior knowledge resources in the form of ideas, concepts and meanings, along with prior cultural resources in the form of shared symbols, ethics and norms (Benkler 2003b; Hardt and Negri 2004, 148). The communities of the intellectual commons combine their creative activity with the foregoing resources to produce the outcome of commonification. The instruments of commonification aggregate all the elements of the infrastructure employed by the subjective forces of the social intellect as means of production in the process of commonification, such as language, social structures, networks, databases, machines, equipment, devices, protocols, standards, software, applications and information/knowledge/cultural structures (Dyer-Witheford 1999, 42). The relations of commonification are social relations in each historical context, through which the production, distribution and consumption of common pooled intangible resources are organised. Relations of commonification are manifested in the social relations related to (i) the management of the means of commons-based peer production, (ii) the process of such production, and (iii) the process of distribution and consumption of the outcome of such production (Bauwens 2005; Benkler 2006; Hess and Ostrom 2007b; Rigi 2013; Kostakis and Bauwens 2014; Benkler 2016; De Rosnay 2016).

On the other hand, the intellectual commons are reproduced according to a specific mode of value circulation and value pooling. Social value generally refers to the multiplicity of collectively constructed conceptions of the desirable in each socio-historical context, i.e. dominant and alternative conceptions of the importance people attribute to action (Graeber 2001, 15, 39, 46–47). Commons-based value is the set of alternative conceptions of what constitutes important activity within the communities of the intellectual commons and the conceptions of such activity in society in general (De Angelis 2007, 179). Commons-based values are generated through communal productive practices aimed at certain goals (Graeber 2001, 58–59). Hence, the source of commons-based values is productive communal activity, i.e. unalienated work defined in the widest possible way (De Angelis 2007, 24; Fuchs 2014, 37). Commons-based values circulate in society and challenge dominant perceptions about social value, in particular the dominance of exchange value as the primary, or even exclusive, form of social value and the commodity markets as the primary, or even exclusive, societal value system.

1.4. The Moral Aspects of Commons-Based Peer Production

From an ontological perspective, the intellectual commons can better be conceived as sets of social practices of both pooling common intellectual resources and reproducing the communal relations around these productive practices. They consist of three main elements, which refer to the social practice of pooling a resource, the social cooperation of productive activity among peers and, finally, a community with a collective process governing the (re)production and management of the resource. The intellectual commons have inherent tendencies towards commons-based societies, which, depending on their social context, produce (i) spheres of commonification, (ii) contested spheres of commonification/commodification, or (iii) co-opted spheres of commonification/commodification. Their manifestations in the domains of culture, science and technology provide the core common infrastructures of our culture, science and technology.

The tendencies of the intellectual commons bear moral significance because of their potential for society. Contemporary theories of the intellectual commons investigate this potential in the context of the dominant power of capital. Rational choice theories draw from the work of Elinor Ostrom and deal with the institutional characteristics of the intellectual commons, offering a perspective of complementarity between commons and capital. Neoliberal theories elaborate on the profit-maximising opportunities of the intellectual commons and further highlight their capacities of acting as a fix to capital circulation/accumulation in intellectual property-enabled commodity markets. Social democratic theories propose the forging of a partnership between a transformed state and the communities of the commons and put forward specific transition plans for a commons-oriented society. Finally, critical theories conceptualise the productive patterns encountered within intellectual commons as a proto-mode of production in germinal form, which is a direct expression of the advanced productive forces of the social intellect and has the potential to open alternatives to capital. Each of these four theoretical families offers substantive ethical arguments for the morality of commons-based peer production, which, in combination, formulates a strong normative theory for the intellectual commons.

The evolution of art and culture throughout the ages has fundamentally been based on practices of sharing and collaboration and has always been an inherently collective and communal process. In recent times, though, modern and postmodern processes of commodification in the domains of art and culture have formed a dialectical relation with the emergence and consolidation of copyright law, subjugating the cultural commons in the value system of commodity markets. Hence, from the fourteenth to the seventeenth centuries, the communal elements of artistic and cultural production gave rise to the master artists of the Renaissance. From the eighteenth century until the 1960s, the commodification of the cultural commons led to the apogee of the Promethean artist and the gradual transformation of copyright into intellectual property law. From the 1970s to the 2010s, the decentralisation of the creative practice boosted new forms of cultural commons, while the consolidation of the cultural industries has resulted in the archetype of the celebrity artist as the primal form of commodification.

The historical perspective of the intellectual commons reveals that legal institutions have generally neglected the historical prevalence of sharing and collaboration in the evolution of culture across the ages. Given that law has been dialectically interrelated with society throughout history, both being shaped by dominant modes of social reproduction and shaping legal subjects and social practices, copyright law has quashed the social potential of the intellectual commons, instead of accommodating it. Accordingly, the rules of intellectual property have advanced normative ideologies, which had a transformative effect on the material world towards the commodification of information, knowledge and culture. Historical evidence, thus, shows the discrepancy between the centrality of commons-based production in art and culture and laws overly tilted in favour of the enclosure of intangible resources. Overall, this alternative historical perspective unveils the significance of the cultural commons as the cornerstone of human civilisation and underpins the moral arguments in favour of an intellectual commons law.

The contemporary communities of the intellectual commons generate, circulate, pool together and redistribute to society immense amounts of social value. Commons-based value circulates in specific sequences and circuits of multiple forms across the economic, social, cultural and political spectrum of social activity. These sequences and circuits can be codified into chain-like formulae, which show that weak forms of commons-based value at lower links of the chain result in the absence of commons-based value at the upper levels of circulation and pooling of values. Commons-based values also come into dialectical interrelation with monetary value circuits and the commodity market value system, thus leading to contested or co-opted spheres of commons-based value. The intellectual commons, thus, have the potential to construct alternative modes of value circulation. Nevertheless, commons-oriented communities face severe crises of value owing to their dependence on the dominant value system of commodity markets and the structural power of monetary values as the universal equivalent of value in our societies. Overall, the morality of commons-based value justifies the removal of socially constructed obstacles by positive law, so that the net social benefits of commons-based peer production acquire their full extent.

Taking into account the solid ontological, epistemological, historical and social research findings described above, the critical normative perspective of the intellectual commons highlights their elements and characteristics, which have moral significance, and lays out the fundamentals of an intellectual commons law, which can adequately accommodate their potential. Its critical element lies in the axiom that all forms of domination are fundamentally unethical, because they estrange persons from what they could be and, thus, hinder their potential. Within this framework, the role of law as a social institution is to operate towards the abolishment of domination and the promotion of freedom, equality and democracy. By taking the standpoint of the oppressed, the critical normative approach purports to transform the current discipline of law in all its facets into a science for the negation of the unjust. In terms of methodology, the critical normative theory of the intellectual commons is founded on (i) an explicit orientation towards progressive social transformation, (ii) the dialectics between potentiality and actuality, (iii) the interrelation between structure and agency, and (iv) the moral significance of the dimensions of the intellectual commons. In terms of structure, such a theory justifies the ethical value of personhood, work, value and community in the context of the intellectual commons, by providing sets of arguments from all lines of moral justification, whether deontological and political or consequentialist and utilitarian. In terms of substance and potential, the normative theory of the intellectual commons proposes the basic tenets of an intellectual commons law, which basically concern the proactive protection and expansion of the public domain and the recognition of an enhanced freedom to take part in science and culture for non-commercial purposes.

1.5. Towards a Commons-Oriented Jurisprudence

The purpose of this book is to lay down the foundations for the moral justification of the intellectual commons and to provide an integrated normative model for their protection and promotion. In this context, the book's main question is: why are the intellectual commons morally significant and how should they be regulated so that their social potential is accommodated? The foregoing main question of the book is further articulated in detail in the following five sub-questions:

- Which are the elements, characteristics, tendencies and manifestations of the intellectual commons and their potentials for society?
- Which are the main theories regarding the social potential of the intellectual commons and how are the intellectual commons in these theories perceived to be related to the dominant power of capital?
- How have the cultural commons been shaped across history and, in turn, how have they shaped society?
- How is social value generated, circulated, pooled together and redistributed within and beyond the communities of the intellectual commons? What relationship is there between commons-based and monetary values?
- Which elements and characteristics of the intellectual commons have moral significance and which ought to be the fundamentals of an intellectual commons law that will adequately accommodate their potential?

The book is structured into ten chapters. Each chapter examines the intellectual commons from a different discipline and perspective. The second chapter of the book analyses the ontology of the intellectual commons. The third chapter introduces the main trends in theory that have been formulated in relation to the analysis of the intellectual commons. The fourth chapter deals with the interrelation between the cultural commons and the law from a historical perspective, concentrating mainly on Anglo-American and Continental European history. Chapters 5–8 formulate together a coherent research project on the circulation and pooling of social value in the context of the intellectual commons. The ninth chapter relies on the ontological, epistemological, historical and social research conclusions of the previous chapters of the book in order to produce a critical normative theory of the intellectual commons.

Overall, the eight chapters of the main body of the book are integrally related to each other and together form a consistent analysis of the intellectual commons and their interrelation with morality. The general structure of the study follows a scheme of gradual escalation from the empirical to the normative, starting from the ontological and epistemological analyses of the intellectual commons, proceeding to their historical and sociological examination and concluding with their normative evaluation. The second (ontological) and third (epistemological) chapters thus open the way for the historical research in the fourth and the social research in the fifth to eighth chapters and, thus, offer a solid theoretical base for the normative justifications of the ninth chapter.

This book contributes in multiple ways to the current level of knowledge on the intellectual commons and their normative aspects. The second chapter of the book offers a dynamic ontology of the intellectual commons, by conceiving of them as communal practices of sharing and collaboration with the potential to become the dominant mode for the regulation of intellectual production, distribution and consumption. The chapter begins by identifying the inherent elements and characteristics of the intellectual commons, building upon relevant work on the field (Ostrom and Lessig 2002b; Boyle 2003; Hess and Ostrom 2003; Benkler 2006; Linebaugh 2008; Bollier and Helfrich 2015). It proceeds by pointing out their tendencies and manifestations in the context of their dialectical interrelation with capital and commodity markets. This chapter is an analysis of the elements of personhood, work, value and community within the intellectual commons, which bear moral significance. It thus constitutes the ontological basis for the normative theory of the intellectual commons developed in the study.

The fourth chapter of the book narrates the history of culture from the prism of the intellectual commons. It thus shifts the focus of analysis from the enclosures of intellectual property law to the significance of intellectual sharing and collaboration across history. Further developing arguments of legal historians over the evolution of copyright (Nesbit 1987; Hesse 1990; Jaszi 1991; Rose 1993; Woodmansee 1984, 1994; Drahos and Braithwaite 2002; Bracha 2004, 2008; Deazley 2004; Coombe 2011), this chapter unfolds the argument that, despite their prominence, in recent historical periods socialised creativity and inventiveness have been framed by copyright laws in a way that has suppressed the social potential of the intellectual commons, instead of accommodating them.

Chapters 5–8 unveil an integrated theory of commons-based value. Elaborating on anthropological theories of value (Graeber 2001; De Angelis 2007), these chapters exhibit the pluriversity of value in the realm of intellectual activity. Accordingly, they support the view that the dominant value system of commodity markets is countered by the alternative mode of commons-based value circulation. The sequences and circuits of commons-based value are, then, analysed in detail, codified according to specific formulae of circulation and counter-examined vis-à-vis monetary values. The chapter concludes by pointing out the unsustainability of value flows from commons-based towards monetary value circuits and the need for counter-balancing flows to avert value crises in intellectual commons communities.

The ninth chapter of the book establishes the foundations of a holistic normative theory of the intellectual commons as a social totality. According to such a theory, the intellectual commons are held to be important from a normative perspective, because they bear moral aspects of personhood, work, value and community in their practices. This chapter transforms well-known deontological and consequentialist justifications of the public domain (Hettinger 1989; Litman 1990; Samuelson 2003; Benkler 1999, 2004, 2006; Drahos 2016; Dusollier 2011; De Rosnay and De Martin 2012; Geiger 2017) into a coherent and integrated normative model for the moral justification of the intellectual commons as a social totality. It thus concludes by asserting the morality of the enactment of an intellectual commons law in relative independence from intellectual property law, which should embody statutory rules for the protection and promotion of the intellectual commons.

Overall, this book follows a multi-disciplinary approach as a means to include in its analysis the multiple forms of the intellectual commons, the wide variations between them and the diversity of their social contexts. Throughout its analysis, the intellectual commons are viewed as contested terrains of domination and resistance and modes of regulation are examined to achieve their potential in advancing freedom, equality and democracy. In this context, the fragmentary manifestation of the intellectual commons is considered the direct effect of their domination by capital. Therefore, this study distances itself from liberal theorisations, which invest in fragmented case studies of social phenomena related to the intellectual commons. Instead, it relies on their conception as social totalities in dialectical interrelation with their societal context.

CHAPTER 2

The Ontology of the Intellectual Commons

2.1. Introduction

In essence, the intellectual commons are social practices of both pooling intangible resources in common and reproducing the communal relations around these productive practices. They are related to terrains of mainly intellectual, as demarcated from those of chiefly manual, human activity. They are constituted as ensembles of power between contending social forces of commodification and commonification. In this respect, intellectual commons are formulated as crystallisations of the sublation of the opposing forces referred to above, subject to correlations of power both within their boundaries and in their wider social context.

This chapter formulates a processual ontology of the intellectual commons, by examining the substance, elements, tendencies and manifestations of their being. The first part of the chapter introduces the various definitions of the concept. Its second part focuses on the elements that constitute the totalities of the intellectual commons. Its third part emphasises their structural tendencies. Finally, the fourth and last part of the chapter deals with the various manifestations of the intellectual commons in the domains of culture, science and technology.

2.2. Definitions

The concept of the commons is today most commonly defined in connection to resources of a specific nature. In her seminal work, Ostrom conceives of the commons as types of resources – or, better, resource systems – which feature certain attributes that make it costly (but not impossible) to exclude

---

How to cite this book chapter:
Broumas, A. 2020. *Intellectual Commons and the Law: A Normative Theory for Commons-Based Peer Production.* Pp. 11–25. London: University of Westminster Press. DOI: https://doi.org/10.16997/book49.b. License: CC-BY-NC-ND

potential beneficiaries from appropriating them (Ostrom 1990, 30). Hess and Ostrom thus broadly describe the commons as a resource shared by a group of people, which is vulnerable to social dilemmas (Hess and Ostrom 2007a, 4; Hess 2008, 37). Following the same line of thought in relation to intangible resources, the same authors stress the importance of avoiding the confusion between the nature of the commons as goods and the property regimes related to them (Hess and Ostrom 2003, 119). According to this approach, information and knowledge are socially managed as common pool resources owing to their inherent properties of non-subtractability and relative non-excludability. These two attributes of common pool resources make them 'conducive to the use of communal proprietorship or ownership' (Ostrom and Hess 2008, 332). Yet, resource-based approaches run the danger of reifying the commons and downgrading their social dimension.[2]

On the other hand, property-based definitions equate the social phenomenon of the commons with collective property in contradistinction to private and public property regimes (Lessig 2002b, 1788; Boyle 2008, 39; Mueller 2012). Indicatively, Derek Wall writes that the '[c]ommons can be seen as a particular category of property rights based on collective rather than state or private ownership' (Wall 2014, 6). In the intellectual realm, James Boyle labels the commons of the intellect 'property's outside' or 'property's antonym' (Boyle 2003, 66). Along the same lines, Jessica Litman considers that the intellectual commons coincide with the legal concept of the public domain, which she juxtaposes with intellectual property: 'The concept of the public domain is another import from the realm of real property. In the intellectual property context, the term describes a true commons comprising elements of intellectual property that are ineligible for private ownership. The contents of the public domain may be mined by any member of the public' (Litman 1990, 975).

Alternatively, relational/institutional approaches define the commons as sets of wider instituted social relationships between communities and resources. As Helfrich and Haas state, '[c]ommons are not the resources themselves but the set of relationships that are forged among individuals and a resource and individuals with each other' (Helfrich and Haas 2009). Linebaugh adds that '[c]ommons are not given, they are produced. Though we often say that commons are all around us – the air we breathe and the languages we use being key examples of shared wealth – it is truly only through cooperation in the production of our life that we can create them. This is because commons are not essentially material things but are social relations, constitutive social practices' (Linebaugh 2008, 50–51). Hence, according to relational/institutional approaches, the commons can be defined as 'a social regime for managing shared resources and forging a community of shared values and purpose' (Clippinger and Bollier 2005, 263) or even an 'institutional arrangement for governing the access to, use and disposition of resources', in which 'no single person has exclusive control over the use and disposition of any particular resource'

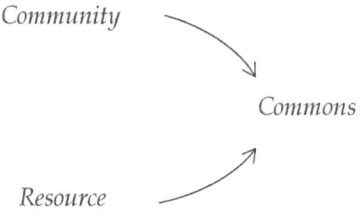

Figure 2.1: Locating the commons.
Source: Author

(Benkler 2006, 60–61). In conclusion, relational/institutional approaches pinpoint that commons refer neither to communities nor to resources, but instead to the social relations and structures which develop between the two.

At an even higher level of complexity, processual definitions pinpoint the dynamic element of the commons. According to processual approaches, commons are defined as fluid ensembles of social relationships and sets of social practices for governing the (re)production, access to and use of resources. In contrast to resource-based or property-based definitions, the commons are not equated with given resources or to the legal status emanating from their natural attributes, but rather to social relations that are constantly reproduced (Bailey 2012). Furthermore, in contrast to relational/institutional approaches, the commons do not coincide with but are rather co-constituted by their institutional elements. According to the processual approach, the commons are a process, a state of becoming, not a state of being. Therefore, they could best be described as a verb, i.e. the process of 'commoning' (Linebaugh 2008, 50–51). Hence, in contrast to analytical definitions, processual approaches refer to the ontology of commoning not as a common pool resource but as the very process of pooling common resources (Bollier and Helfrich 2015, 76).

Nonetheless, the process of commoning is not only restricted to the (re)production of the resource. On the contrary, throughout this process the community itself is constantly reproduced, adapting its governance mechanisms and communal relationships in the changing environment within and outside the commons. According to such an 'integrated' approach, commoning should be viewed in its totality as a process that produces forms of life in common, a distinct mode of social co-production (Agamben 2000, 9).

The intellectual commons are commons related to intellectual, instead of manual, activity and intangible, instead of tangible, resources. They refer to sets of social practices characterised by sharing and collaboration among peers in a community. Such practices extend from the stage of production up to the stages of distribution and consumption. At the stage of production, intangible resources are generated through peer sharing and collaboration and managed in an equipotential manner by communities of producers. At the stage of distribution, intangible resources are shared and used either openly or subject to conditions, which primarily involve share-alike and/or non-commercial licensing. At the stage of consumption, the transformative use of intangible resources results in derivative works, which, depending on the licensing status of the original resource(s), are often shared under the same copyleft provisions, thus closing the virtuous circle of commons-based peer production.

The term 'intellectual commons' has been deemed more appropriate to represent the subject matter of this study, instead of other terms such as 'information' or 'knowledge commons' or even 'commons-based peer production'. On the one hand, terms, such as 'information' or 'knowledge commons' imply that the commons are conceived as resources, falling into the fallacy of reifying social relations. On the other hand, commons-based peer production does not refer to the commons themselves but rather to the mode of how the commons are reproduced through time. The term 'commons-based peer production' also implies that distribution and consumption do not fall within the scope of such reproduction. By contrast, the term 'intellectual commons' is grounded on a conception of the commons as social relations, in which human communities interrelate with intangible resources, the latter only being the object of such relationship. Most important, this term implies that intellectual activity is the source of value and the motivating force behind the reproductive cycle of the intellectual commons.

2.3. Elements and Characteristics

The intellectual commons are produced by the interrelation between their subjective and objective elements. The subjective element is twofold, consisting on the one hand of the collective actors and on the other hand of the communal structures of commoning. The objective element consists of the intangible resources that are used as input for commons-based peer production. The products of the sublation between the objective and subjective elements of the intellectual commons are again twofold. Obviously, practices of commoning yield more information, communication, knowledge and culture.

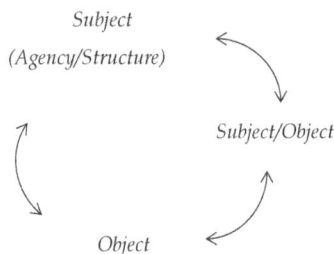

Figure 2.2: The elements of the intellectual commons.
Source: Author

	Elements		
Characteristics	Object (resource)	Subject/agency (productive activity)	Subject/structure (community/institution)
	Non-excludability	Non-monetary incentives	Rules of self-governance
	Non-rivalry	Voluntary participation	Communal ownership rules
	Zero marginal costs of sharing	Self-allocation of productive activity/ consensus-based coordination	Access rules
	Cumulative capacity	Self-management	Communal values

Table 2.1: The elements of the intellectual commons.
Source: Author

Hence, intangible resources are both object of the dialectical process and outcome of the sublation. This characteristic distinguishes the intellectual commons from other types of commoning. Yet, the dialectical process constantly reproduces and evolves itself, its social bonds being both medium and outcome of the process. Rather than being analysed as separate from one another, the objective and subjective elements of the commons should be viewed as forming an inseparable and integrated whole (Bollier and Helfrich 2015, 75).

As far as their objective element is concerned, the intellectual commons are primarily related to the (re)production of intangible resources, in the form of data, information, communication, knowledge and culture (Benkler 2006; Frischmann, Madison and Strandburg 2014, 3). Practices of commoning in relation to tangible resources are characterised by resource attributes of relative non-excludability and of rivalrousness (Ostrom and Ostrom 1977). In particular, the exclusion of individuals from the use of common pool resources through physical or legal barriers is relatively costly, and any resource units subtracted by one individual are deprived from others (Ostrom 1990, 337). As a corollary, such resources are susceptible to problems of congestion and overuse and can even be open to the risk of destruction, matters that have to be dealt with by commoners through sophisticated and adaptable governance technics, if commons upon these resources are to last and thrive. On the other hand, intangible resources have the status of pure public goods in the strict economic sense (Samuelson 1954). First of all, intangible goods share the attribute of non-excludability with common pool resources, only that in the case of the former such non-excludability is absolute rather than relative (Hess and Ostrom 2007a, 9). Furthermore, they are non-rivalrous in the sense that their consumption does not reduce the amount of the good available to others (Benkler 2006, 35–36). In addition, information, communication, knowledge and culture have been known to bear a cumulative capacity (Foray 2004, 94; Hess and Ostrom 2007a, 8). In the words of Thomas Jefferson, 'one new idea leads to another, that to a third, and so on through a course of time until someone, with whom no one of these ideas was original, combines all together, and produces what is justly called a new invention' (Jefferson 1972, 686). According to this approach, the very process of creativity and inventiveness essentially involves standing on the shoulders of the intellectual giants of the past, as Newton famously confessed.[3] Finally, intangible resources enjoy near-zero marginal costs of sharing among peers, in the sense that the cost of their reproduction tends to be negligible (Arrow 1962, 623; Benkler 2006, 36–37). The partly intransitive attributes mentioned above, i.e. non-excludability, non-rivalry, zero marginal costs of sharing and cumulative capacity, which characterise the objective element of the intellectual commons, are not found in types of commoning based on tangible resources.

Regarding their subjective agency element, intellectual commons are reproduced according to a commons-based peer mode of intellectual reproduction, which significantly differentiates itself from the dominant mode, based on capital and commodity markets (De Angelis 2007, 36). Communal relations between peers are characterised by voluntary participation, the self-allocation of tasks and autonomous contribution to the productive process (Soderberg and O'Neil 2014, 2). Participation in the productive process is motivated less by material incentives and more through bonds of community, trust and reputation (De Angelis 2007, 190; Benkler 2004, 2016). Coordination is ensured 'by the utilization of flexible, overlapping, indeterminate systems of negotiating difference and permitting parallel inconsistencies to co-exist until a settlement behavior or outcome emerges' (Benkler 2016, 111–112). Eventually, such relations tend to be based on sharing and collaboration between commoners, who join their productive capacities together as equipotent peers in networked forms of organisation (Bauwens 2005, 1). Even though the degree and extent of control may vary, the productive process, available infrastructure and means of production tend to be controlled by the community of commoners (Fuster Morell 2014, 307–308).

In relation to their subjective structural element, the intellectual commons arise whenever a community acquires constituent power by engaging in the (re)production and management of an intangible resource, with special regard for equitable access and use (Bollier 2008, 4). In this sense, there can be no commons without a self-governing community. Rules of self-governance include both rules for the management of the productive process and rules of political decision-making. On the one hand, self-management rules determine the general characteristics of the mode of production/distribution/consumption of the resource, the choices over the design of the resource and the planning of the productive process, and the criteria for the allocation of tasks and the division of labour. On the other hand, political decision-making determines the collective mission or goal of the process, the membership and the boundaries of the community, the constitutional choices over the mode of self-governance, the participation of individual commoners in the decision-making process, the interaction between commoners, the adjudication of disputes and the imposition of sanctions for rule violation. In addition, the intellectual commons are regulated by ownership and access rules. Ownership rules determine the property status of both the means of production and the resources produced. Access rules regulate the appropriation and use of resource units (Ostrom 1990, 32). Access can be open to all or managed and limited to certain individuals or usages (Mueller 2012, 42). Property rights are bundles of access, contribution, extraction, removal, management/participation, exclusion and alienation rights, thus conferring different types of control over resources vis-à-vis persons and entities other than their right-holder (Hess and Ostrom 2007b, 52). Contrary to the monolithic form of private or public property, ownership in the realm of the intellectual commons comes in multiple forms by taking full advantage of the nature of the institution of property as a bundle of rights. Ownership of communally managed and communally produced resources bestows the rights to regulate access and use. Access rules generally aim to sustain and guarantee the communal mode of resource management and to avert exhaustion through commodification. They constitute the constructed boundaries between the realm of the intellectual commons and the sphere of commodity markets. Hence, ownership and access in the intellectual commons are inextricably linked. Furthermore, the intellectual commons are established as communities of shared values, oriented towards communal cohesion and reproduction through time (Clippinger and Bollier 2005, 263). Values, such as reciprocity, trust and mutuality among peers, are not confined to one-to-one relations. Rather, they develop and are set in circulation both within and among commoners' communities. Communal values are very important for the well-being of the intellectual commons, since their circulation and accumulation contribute to the construction of group identities and the consolidation of reciprocal patterns of commoning. Yet, communal values within the sphere of the intellectual commons also function in contradistinction and as alternatives to circuits of dominant monetary values. There is an underlying confrontation between alternative and dominant value spheres, which is connected with practices of commoning and processes of commodification (De Angelis 2007). Intellectual commons communities reveal a wide diversity of institutional practices, which evolve through time in correspondence to the vulnerabilities to enclosure or under-production of the relevant resource and the social dilemmas faced by the community during the course of sustaining each specific commons (Hess 2008, 37).

As with any other type of social institution, intellectual commons control and, at the same time, empower the activity of their participants. Nevertheless, they significantly differ from state or market regulation of people and resources, since they constitute social spheres in which institutions are immanent in, rather than separate from, the reproduction of the community.

2.4. Tendencies

The commons of the intellect are fundamentally characterised by their orientation toward self-governance and open access to their productive output. Yet, in societies dominated by capital, intellectual commons unfold themselves neither as wholly open nor as entirely self-governed. Instead, openness and self-governance are tendencies that emerge from the essential properties encountered in the social relations of commoning. In particular, the degree of openness and self-governance in each community of commoners is determined by the specific outcomes of the dialectics between the intellectual commons and dominant forces/relations in each social context. In this view, institutions in the sphere of the intellectual commons are the result of the interaction between the intellectual commons and the objective conditions of their environment. Such a perspective also leaves ground for counter-influencing agency/structure dialectics between the resulting institutions in the sphere of the intellectual commons, their generative elements and their social context. Hence, in capitalism, structures of commoning are inherently contested and contradictory terrains of social activity, which are constantly reproduced in a non-linear manner on the basis of the dialectics mentioned above but also counter-influence their environment. Outcomes of the sublation between the intellectual commons and dominant forces/relations in the social context can be classified into two distinct spheres of reproduction: contested spheres of commonification/commodification and co-opted spheres of commonification/commodification.

The dialectics within the reproduction of the intellectual commons exhibit certain tendencies and counter-tendencies (see Table 2.2), which emanate from their essential characteristics and the essential characteristics of the wider social context. In particular, due to the attribute of non-excludability, intellectual commons are less vulnerable to 'crowding effects' and 'overuse' problems and relatively immune to risks of depletion (Lessig 2002a, 21). Therefore, practices of commoning in relation to intangible resources have

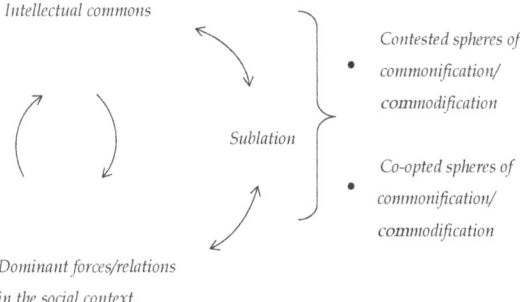

Figure 2.3: The dialectics of the intellectual commons.
Source: Author

The Ontology of the Intellectual Commons   19

Characteristics of commoning (commons-based peer production)	Tendencies (forces of commonification)	Sublation (subject/object dialectics)	Counter-tendencies (forces of commodification)	Characteristics of commodification (capitalist mode of production)
Non-excludability	Open access	Commonification ↔ commodification	Monetized access	Enclosure
Non-rivalry/zero marginal costs of sharing	Sharing	Pooling of common resources ↔ private accumulation of resources	Market allocation	Fixity
Cumulative capacity/non-monetary incentives/voluntary participation	Collaboration	Commons-oriented relations of production ↔ market competition and oligopolies	Antagonism	Monetary incentives
Self-allocation of productive activity/consensus-based coordination	Self- and collective empowerment	Self-management of the productive process ↔ hierarchical management of the productive process	Alienation	Command
Communal value sphere	Circular reciprocity	Work in collaboration/waged labour	Labour as commodity/exploitation	Market value system
Communal ownership	Self-governance	Consensus-based decision-making ↔ hierarchical decision-making	Domination	Private/state ownership

Table 2.2: Tendencies and counter-tendencies within the intellectual commons.
Source: Author

the potential to be structured as open access commons on their demand side, i.e. 'involving no limits on who is authorized to use a resource' (Ostrom 1990, 335–336; Hess and Ostrom 2007b, 48). This of course does not happen in a deterministic manner but only on the condition that the relevant subjective forces of commonification effectively reinforce their corresponding tendencies. In such cases, the consumption of the resource is regulated as openly accessible to anyone. Examples of open access intellectual commons include our common cultural heritage and the public domain. Yet, intellectual commons are also subject to opposing forces in the social context, manifested in legal institutions and technological infrastructures of enclosure, which tend to socially construct information, communication, knowledge and culture as artificially scarce, to monetise access and, eventually, to commodify them (Hess and Ostrom 2007a, 5). Accordingly, the characteristics of non-rivalry and zero marginal costs of sharing observed in relation to intangible resources tend to encourage patterns of sharing among creators, which may result in the pooling of common resources, on the condition that forces of commonification are also set in motion. Conversely, institutions and technologies in the social context enable the fixation of intellectual works in the form of commodities and, thus, make them susceptible to market allocation and private accumulation (Cohen 2007, 1195). Sharing is a fundamental characteristic, which distinguishes commons from commodity markets or other systems of private resource accumulation (Madison, Frischmann and Strandburg 2010a, 841). Therefore, the degree of sharing tolerated by the sublation of the opposing tendencies mentioned above gives evidence about the degree of their relative independence or co-optation by market logic.

The dialectics that give birth to the sphere of the intellectual commons are framed by additional characteristics and tendencies, the social determination of which is even more extensive than the partly intransitive attributes of intangible resources. In particular, the importance of non-monetary incentives within the realm of the commons and the participation of commoners on a voluntary basis combined with the partly intransitive characteristic of the cumulative capacity of intangible resources weave relations within the productive process, which generate collaborative tendencies among peers. By contrast, the dominance of monetary incentives in the wider social context reproduces antagonistic relations. The countervailing tendencies mentioned above impact both the patterns of commoning within intellectual commons communities and the relations among them, pushing towards either commons-oriented peer relations of production or market competition, accumulation of market power and oligopolies. Furthermore, the characteristics of self-allocating tasks and consensus-based coordination in the productive practices of commoning promote the self- and collective empowerment of commoners. On the other hand, hierarchical command of labour in the productive practices, which dominate the social context, generates alienation of creative individual workers. The sublation between the two juxtaposing spheres shifts the productive practices of the intellectual commons either towards self-management or towards hierarchical management. Intellectual commons should also be examined as alternative communal value spheres reproduced at the margins of dominant market value systems. Whereas markets circulate social power in the form of monetary values and labour in the form of commodity through decentralised bilateral transactions, communities of commoning are based on circuits of circular reciprocity among peers. Interrelations between the two value spheres generate relations of production within the intellectual commons, which may range widely between the two extremes of collaborative work among peers and exploited waged labour. Finally, the communal or private/state ownership of the infrastructure and means of commoning is critical for the degree of self-governance and domination encountered in each intellectual commons community and eventually determines its mechanisms of political decision-making, i.e. whether such mechanisms will be consensus-based or hierarchical. In conclusion, intellectual commons generally share the characteristics mentioned in the preceding section. Nonetheless, the extent and quality of those characteristics in each case of commoning are ultimately determined by the dialectics between forces and relations of commonification/commodification. Hence, the more an intellectual commons community dynamically transforms its practices and orients itself away from the contested to the co-opted sphere of commonification, the less extensive and qualitative its characteristics of open access, self-management and self-governance will be, and vice versa.

At the same time, the intellectual commons feature certain tendencies, which are attributed to their inherent characteristics, both objective and subjective. Compared to other types of commoning based on tangible resources, the tendencies of the intellectual commons towards open access, sharing and collaboration are also supported by partly intransitive characteristics. Hence, whereas in the general category of the commons these tendencies are produced solely on the basis of the subjective element, in the context of the intellectual commons they arise from a combination of their objective and subjective characteristics. Nevertheless, the establishment of either open access commons-based sharing and collaboration, or commodified spheres of intellectual activity based on private monopolies and antagonism or hybrid commonified/commodified social forms is ultimately a socially constructed outcome determined by the dialectics constituting the sphere of the intellectual commons vis-à-vis the sphere of commodity markets. They are related to tendencies and counter-tendencies that may be realised or remain unrealised. The intellectual commons embody the potential to unleash in full the creative and innovative powers of the social intellect, yet their future remains open, subject to struggles for social change within their sphere and in the wider social context.

2.5. Manifestations

Intellectual commons ascribe to practices of social reproduction in relation to primarily intellectual human activity. Intellectual work manifests itself in the form of data, information, communication, knowledge and culture.

Information refers to collections of data meaningfully assembled 'according to the rules (syntax) that govern the chosen system, code or language being used' (Floridi 2010, 20). It is a combination of data and intellectual work, which embodies human interpretation. Therefore, in order to be accessible and comprehensible, any assemblage and transformation of data into information must comply with a socially constructed and shared system of semantics. Furthermore, the process of assembling information by the pooling together of data is in itself based on patterns of sharing and collaboration. Since the accumulation of factual data and its collaborative assimilation into information constitute the foundation for knowledge production, robust commons of information are a precondition for all modes of intellectual production, distribution and consumption. The information commons include the vast realm of non-aggregated data and information, which has been collected, processed, accumulated and stored across history by humanity as a result of sharing and collaboration among many individuals. It also includes the aggregated data and information about nature, human history and contemporary society that has not been enclosed either directly or indirectly by virtue of patent, copyright and database laws or by technological means and, therefore, lies in the public domain.[4]

Knowledge is the assimilation of information into shared structures of common understanding (Machlup 1983). It is a social product generated on the basis of objects of a transitive dimension, i.e. prior knowledge produced by society, and objects of an intransitive dimension, i.e. structures or mechanisms of nature that exist and act quite independently of humans (Bhaskar 2008, 16). With the term 'social', reference is given to the fact that the production of knowledge is essentially a process of cooperation among several individuals which is structured in dynamic sub-processes of cognition, communication and cooperation (Fuchs and Hofkirchner 2005). The accumulated knowledge of mankind constitutes the intellectual basis of social life. The building blocks of human knowledge are produced and managed as commons, according to socially constructed rules that prohibit any kind of exclusionary conduct.[5] Hence, discoveries about physical phenomena and laws of nature, abstract ideas, principles and theories, and mathematical symbols, methods and formulae are managed as open access commons pooled together by the cooperative activity of the scientific community, past and present. All in all, the core of scientific knowledge is generally managed as commons, advanced through sharing and collaboration among peers in a community.[6] The knowledge commons also consist of technological inventions, which fall short of patentability, because they do not fulfil the criteria of novelty, non-obviousness/involvement of an inventive step, and social utility/susceptibility of industrial application. Broadly speaking, this includes the accumulated technological advancements of the greatest part of human history, i.e. inventions (i) that were conceived before the existence of patent laws, (ii) that were communicated to the public but have not been filed for patent protection by their inventors, (iii) whose patent rights have expired, or (iv) that have been invalidated by litigation. Furthermore, technologies in use, whether protected by private monopolies or not, lead to further innovation and invention though practices of maintenance, repair and modification shared among the communities of their users (Edgerton 1999, 120; Von Hippel 2005). In addition, the knowledge commons include all types of 'traditional knowledge'. The latter refers among others to the know-how, practices, skills and innovations developed within and among communities though patterns of sharing and collaboration in a wide variety of contexts, such as governance, agriculture, science, technology, architecture, arts and crafts, ecology, medicine and biodiversity (WIPO 2012). Finally, the development of packet-based electronic communication systems and advanced information technologies in the form of the internet and the World Wide Web have greatly facilitated the sharing of knowledge between peers along with commons-based peer modes of production based on collaboration.

Communication refers to a socialised process of symbolic interaction between human subjects, through which meaning is exchanged. Therefore, being more than the transmission of data, communication is in essence the social production of meaning that constitutes social relationships (Mosco 2009, 6, 67). The communication commons primarily consist of the assemblage of linguistic elements, which constitute our common code of communication. They also comprise any other form for the transmission of meaning between individuals, such as body techniques and patterns of behaviour (Mauss 1973; Williams 1983, 90; Sahlins 2013). Furthermore, the contemporary commons of communication include the natural and technological infrastructure of electronic communication networks, such as open spectrums and open standards. Overall, the common infrastructure of communication functions as the basis for the development of culture, which is also in itself a system of symbols.

Cultures are unities of symbolic systems reproduced by means of interpersonal human communication (Cuche 2001, 87). Culture includes the fundamental elements of socialisation that are necessary for life in common, i.e. the a priori of human society. It is essentially a socialised process based on sharing and collaboration and a collective project in constant flux. The cultural commons refer to shared ethical, moral, religious and other value systems (Mauss 1973; Williams 1983, 90; Sahlins 2013). They also include common traditions, habits and customs, religious or secular belief systems, interacting world views and shared conceptions about social life in general. In addition, the cultural commons consist of common aesthetic systems and styles, artistic and cultural techniques, practices, skills and innovations, along with artistic and cultural expressions of folklore, such as folk art, arts and crafts, architectural forms, dance, performances, ceremonies, handicrafts, games, myths, memes, folktales, signs and symbols. Last but not least, when we talk about culture, we refer not only to its contemporary form but also to cultural heritage and collective historical narratives handed down from one generation to the next (Burke 2008, 25). The cultural commons therefore include the public domain. Intellectual works in the public domain, i.e. those not protected by copyright or unbundled from exclusionary private rights, include works created before the existence of copyright, those of insufficient originality for copyright protection, works whose copyright has expired or is otherwise inapplicable owing to invalidation by litigation, along with government works, works dedicated by their authors to the public domain and works that are licensed by their authors under conditions that are oriented towards open access.[7] De facto cultural commons, which develop beyond the boundaries of law, have also been facilitated by contemporary information and communication technologies through the unauthorised sharing or mixing of copyright-protected works in digitised environments.

Regardless of their form, data, information, communication or culture are manifestations of intellectual activity. In all cases where they are subject to communal modes of governance and shared access or lie in the public domain, such intangible resources fall within the intellectual commons. The latter encompass the totality of information, communication, knowledge and cultural commons of our societies. The intellectual commons are thus the general category of the commons, which embodies our collective and shared, past and present, intellectual activity in all its forms and manifestations.

Figure 2.4: The manifestations of the intellectual commons.
Source: Author

2.6. Conclusion

Intellectual commons are the great other of intellectual property-enabled markets. They constitute non-commercial spheres of intellectual production, distribution and consumption, which are reproduced outside the circulation of intangible commodities and money (Caffentzis 2013, 253). Yet, intellectual commons are not just an alternative to the dominant capitalist mode of intellectual production. On the contrary, they provide the core common infrastructures of intellectual production, such as language, non-aggregated data and information, prior knowledge and culture. In addition, they constantly reproduce a vast amount of information, communication, knowledge and cultural artefacts as common pool resources. It is the compilation of these intellectual infrastructures and resources with the productive force of the social intellect, subjected to the rule of capital, that constitutes the foundation of the capitalist mode of intellectual production. As De Angelis pinpoints, 'every mode of doing needs commons' (De Angelis 2007, 243). Capitalist modes of producing intellectual goods are inescapably dependent on the commons. Nonetheless, such dependence is not mutual. Forces of commonification can materialise their potential to unleash socialised creativity and inventiveness without the restraints of capital.

The current chapter has offered a processual ontology of the intellectual commons, not only by focusing on the essential elements and characteristics that constitute their being but also by elaborating on the tendencies and manifestations that form their becoming and reveal their social potential. The next chapter continues with the epistemological perspective of the intellectual commons. It elaborates on the main theories of the intellectual commons and their relation with capital. In combination, both chapters have the purpose of providing an integrated perspective of the subject matter of the book. Furthermore, the conclusions of these chapters are inextricably linked with the normative perspective of the intellectual commons, because they provide sufficient bases to ethically justify their protection and promotion as institutions with inherent moral value and beneficial outcomes for society.

CHAPTER 3

Theories of the Intellectual Commons

3.1. Introduction

Over the past twenty years, theorising about the intellectual commons has undeniably become a popular activity, not only among scholars who deal with the dialectics between information/communication technologies and society but also among the wider scientific community. This chapter introduces the main theoretical trends that have been formulated in relation to the analysis of the intellectual commons and their relation with capital.

In this context, four families of theories are distinguished on the grounds of their epistemological foundations, their analytical tools with regard to social actors, social structures and the dynamics between them, their normative criteria and, finally, their perspectives on social change. Rational choice theories draw from the work of Elinor Ostrom and deal with the institutional characteristics of the intellectual commons, offering a perspective of complementarity between commons and capital. Furthermore, neoliberal theories elaborate on the profit-maximising opportunities of the intellectual commons and further highlight their capacities of acting as a fix to capital circulation/accumulation in intellectual property-enabled commodity markets. In addition, social democratic theories propose the forging of a partnership between a transformed state and the communities of the commons and put forward specific transition plans for a commons-oriented society. Last but not least, critical theories conceptualise the productive patterns encountered within intellectual commons as a proto-mode of production in germinal form, which is a direct expression of the advanced productive forces of the social intellect and has the potential to open alternatives to capital. In conclusion, the four theoretical frameworks are compared, with the aim of formulating a strong theory of the intellectual commons.

How to cite this book chapter:
Broumas, A. 2020. *Intellectual Commons and the Law: A Normative Theory for Commons-Based Peer Production*. Pp. 27–62. London: University of Westminster Press. DOI: https://doi.org/10.16997/book49.c. License: CC-BY-NC-ND

3.2. The Growth of Academic Interest on the Concept of the Commons

A search for the topic 'commons' in articles indexed in the Social Sciences Citation Index (SSCI) since 1968[8] shows a huge rise of academic interest in the commons in social sciences in recent years.[9] In the figure below, one can observe that there was a relatively low academic article output about the commons in the period 1968–1987 (250). Yet, the years 1988–1997, during which Elinor Ostrom published her seminal work *Governing the Commons* (Ostrom 1990), constitute a turning point, in which theoretical analysis of the commons began to gather attention (479). Then, between 1998 and 2016, the number of articles on the topic rose exponentially (4,203). In the period 2008–2016 in particular, the article output about the commons reached an average of 347 per year.

Commons and their theorisations have not come coincidentally to the forefront of academic attention. This circumstance is an empirical indicator of a rising interest in social sciences for sets of social relations for the management of resources that develop beyond the state and/or the commodity markets. Most likely, such a rise may be an effect of the social and ecological crises, which are in themselves repercussions of the deep contradictions encountered in these two prevalent institutions governing our lives in common.

Yet, in relation to the intellectual commons, other factors may also apply. Today, the epicentre of wealth creation in our societies has rapidly shifted from tangible to intangible assets. Intellectual production is more than ever considered

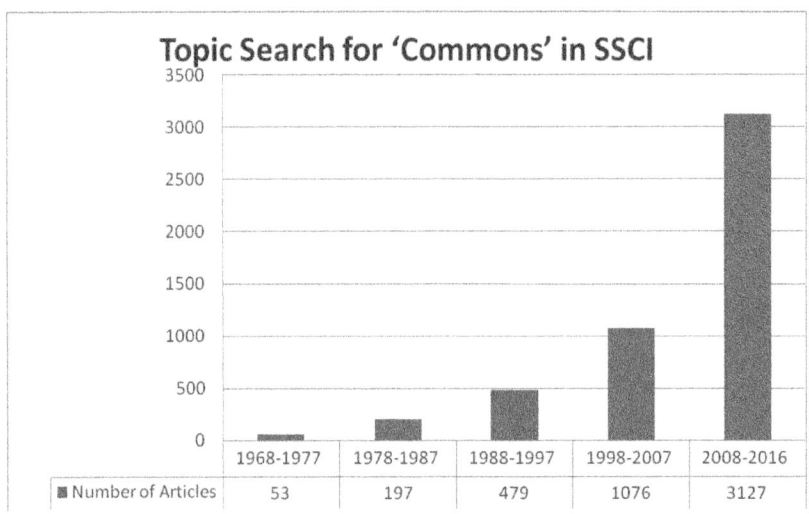

Figure 3.1: Development of the number of published articles on the topic of the commons.
Source: Social Science Citation Index

to be the engine of social progress. As a result, the focus of business, policy-making and civil society has accordingly shifted to the regulation of intellectual production/distribution/consumption. Moreover, rapid techno-social developments have led to the convergence of media and communications in a single network of networks based on packet-switching technologies, making the internet the archetypal communication medium of our times. It is exactly at this cutting edge of technological progress and wealth creation that people have started to constitute intellectual commons free for all to access, by devising collaborative peer-to-peer modes of production and management of intellectual resources (Bollier and Helfrich 2015, 76).

3.3. Rational Choice Theories of the Intellectual Commons: The Commons as Patch to Capital

3.3.1. Main Question and Methodology

Rational choice theories of the intellectual commons deal with the ways that individuals come together, establish communities and institute rules for the sustenance of intellectual resources or for the pursuit of desired outcomes on the basis of sharing and equality (Ostrom 1998; Hess and Ostrom 2007b, 42). In this light, rational choice theorists also examine how stakeholders in an interdependent situation self-organise in order to avoid social-dilemma situations within intellectual commons communities, such as phenomena of free-riding, shirking or opportunistic behaviour (Ostrom 1990, 29). Ultimately, they search for the reasons that lead to the success or failure of resource production/management systems within the sphere of the intellectual commons in order to synthesise appropriate frameworks that will ensure long-term viability (Frischmann, Madison and Strandburg 2014, 11). Even though they belong to the field of collective action theory, in contrast to other traditions in the field, rational choice theories pay tribute to the previously neglected social phenomena of the commons as institutional sets for the governance of resources that are distinct from market- or state-based institutions (Ostrom 1990, 1, 40–41).

In relation to methodology, such theories emphasise the clarity and precision of definitions, concepts and arguments used, where they establish connections between them through rules of formal logic (Russell 1945, 834). Clarity is underpinned by strong empirical research, which interrelates to theoretical abstraction through a dialectical back-and-forth process between theory and practice. Overall, rational choice theories tend to evaluate the intellectual commons according to consequential criteria, focusing on the degree of efficiency that the institutions of the intellectual commons exhibit with regard to the provision of positive outcomes for general social utility (Ostrom 1990, 193, 195–205; Frischmann, Madison and Strandburg 2014, 36–37). In terms of agency, rational choice theorists commence from a rational individualistic conception of human actors. Nevertheless, they consider individuals as having complex motivations, which cannot be reduced to monetary incentives, whereas their productive activity is expected to be shaped both by economic and social factors (Ostrom 1990, 183). Rational choice theorists thus arrive at the conclusion that innovators are essentially placed in interdependent situations, in which they are able to develop inclinations to reciprocity through the use of reason, as long as they have faith that their contribution will be reciprocated (Benkler 2002, 369).[10] In this context, *Homo reciprocans* is considered to be the productive unit of the commons, who, while still serving her own interests, chooses to cooperate with the other members of the community in order to collectively pursue common long-term interests (De Moor 2013, 94). Hence, social structures emerge from the bottom up in the form of patterns of interactions, often crystallised in social norms.

3.3.2. The Institutional Analysis and Development Framework

Rational choice theories were initially developed by Ostrom and her collaborators for the scientific analysis of the natural commons. These theories were consolidated in a detailed theoretical framework, termed institutional analysis and development (IAD). The method of research followed by IAD scholars has progressively escalated from the thorough analysis of empirical phenomena to clear-cut theoretical conceptions about their qualities and causal interrelations. In particular, as a first step, the resource characteristics, community attributes and communal rules of the commons under investigation are examined. Next, the focus of analysis shifts to the action arena of the commons, along with its actors and action situations. Then, patterns of interaction among actors and the outcomes of commoning are elicited. Finally, abstract evaluative criteria are extracted in order to draw more general conclusions about the elements that contribute to the equity, efficiency and sustainability of commons' institutions (Hess and Ostrom 2007a, 6).

In relation to the natural commons, Elinor Ostrom distilled eight design principles as evaluative criteria for robust, long-enduring, common pool resource institutions on the basis of a large set of empirical studies (Ostrom 1990, 90–102):

1. Clearly defined boundaries in place.
2. Rules in use, well matched to local needs and conditions.
3. Participation of individuals affected by rules in the modification of these rules.
4. Respect of the right of community members to devise their own rules by external authorities.
5. A system for self-monitoring members' behavior in place.
6. A graduated system of sanctions in force.

7. Access of community members to low-cost conflict-resolution mechanisms.
8. Nested enterprises, i.e. appropriation, provision, monitoring, enforcement, conflict resolution, and governance activities organized in a nested structure with multiple layers of activities.

In the process of bringing intellectual commons under the lens of the IAD framework, rational choice theorists commence their argumentation by establishing an analogy between the natural environment and the public domain (Boyle 1997, 2008). According to this analogy, just as ecosystems are shared resources necessary for our sustenance and well-being, intellectual resources in the public domain constitute our commonwealth and the basis for our future cultural and scientific advancement. Therefore, it is important to preserve the public domain from enclosure in a similar way that we strive to protect the natural environment from degradation. Yet, unlike ecosystems, which are given by nature, intellectual commons are created from scratch. Hence, social arrangements within the intellectual commons are not only dedicated to the 'preservation' of the resource through egalitarian sharing mechanisms; they also purport to establish the appropriate social terrain for its sustainable reproduction (Frischmann, Madison and Strandburg 2014, 16).

3.3.3. Core Concepts

Intellectual resources are as a rule non-rivalrous and non-excludable, feature zero marginal costs of sharing and bear a cumulative and aggregate capacity. Yet, intellectual resources are not produced out of thin air. Depending on the type of the resource, their production presupposes the existence of an appropriate material infrastructure, such as construction facilities, electronic communication networks and micro-electronics-based equipment in the case of the digital commons (Hess and Ostrom 2007b, 47). The ownership status and mode of governance of these secondary material resources often heavily influence the architecture of the intellectual commons as a whole (Fuster Morell 2014, 285).

Intellectual commons are also formulated around communities of commoners, who contribute to, use and manage the resource, and govern its infrastructure and its productive process. The main building blocks of these communities are on the one hand a commonality between their members, which relates either to their cultural or scientific interests or their expertise (Frischmann, Madison and Strandburg 2014, 16), and, on the other hand, the spur to contribute to a commonly shared goal of creative/innovative content. The capacity of the producer, consumer and/or decision maker may be either dispersed to all the members of the community or concentrated to distinct groups within the community (Hess and Ostrom 2007b, 48). Consumers in their own capacity play a significantly less important role than producers in the realm of the intellectual commons and normally have limited or no direct rights in the decision-making mechanisms of the community. Alternatively, decision makers come as a rule from the group of producers, without meaning that these two groups necessarily coincide. Finally, participation in intellectual commons communities is contributed on a voluntary basis. This characteristic may result in hierarchical relations between resource-poor and resource-rich participants or even the de facto exclusion of the former from the community (Fuster Morell 2014, 286).

Governance arrangements within the intellectual commons are imprinted on the applicable rules-in-use of the community. Rules-in-use are conceived as shared normative understandings between commoners, which shape the behaviour of the latter in the action arena and have the capacity to produce specific patterns of interaction and outcomes though monitoring and sanctioning mechanisms in cases of noncompliance (Crawford and Ostrom 2005). Depending on their importance and hierarchical relation with each other, rules-in-use are categorised in three levels of regulation: operational (day-to-day level), collective choice (policy level) and constitutional (allocation of power level) (Hess and Ostrom 2007b, 49). Rational choice theorists generally tend to apply Ostrom's eight design factors in order to evaluate the robustness of different cases of intellectual commons (Fuster Morell 2010; Frischmann, Schweik and English 2012). In relation to the first of these factors, boundary setting rules, it has been persuasively argued that boundaries in the information environment are necessarily social and cultural, rather than spatial, constructs (Madison 2003). On the one hand, access to common pool-produced intellectual resources is regulated by communal norms or legal rules or a combination of the two. Copyleft licensing is the most common example of this type of rule. On the other hand, communally enacted licences also determine the boundaries of the community, as assent to them constitutes the main prerequisite for participation (Frischmann, Madison and Strandburg 2014, 34). Accordingly, other design factors, such as participatory decision-making arrangements, monitoring mechanisms, conflict-resolution processes and nestled enterprises, are found in many robust, long-enduring intellectual commons communities, showing that the central suppositions of the IAD framework are also applicable to a certain extent to the realm of creativity and innovation (Madison, Frischmann and Strandburg 2010b).

Rules-in-use are in dialectical relationship with action arenas, as both interrelate, act and counter-act and, eventually, shape one another. Incentives of participants in action situations are particularly important for the determination of patterns of interaction (Hess and Ostrom 2007b, 54). Outcomes of commons-based peer production are proposed to be classified according to the binary logic of enclosure/access to produced resources (Hess and Ostrom 2007b, 58). Finally, Hess and Ostrom suggest the following criteria for the evaluation of registered outcomes, which apparently enrich the strictly consequentialist cost/benefit approach of the IAD framework with deontological evaluations of the common good (Hess and Ostrom 2007b, 62):

1. increase of scientific knowledge,
2. sustainability and preservation of resources,
3. participation standards,
4. economic efficiency,
5. equity through fiscal equivalence, and
6. redistributional equity.

3.3.4. Critical Evaluation: the Intellectual Commons as Patch to Capital

The main argument of rational choice theorists is the thesis that intellectual commons are relevant today as objects of research, because they significantly contribute under certain conditions of institutional efficiency to the advancement of art and science and should, therefore, be utilised by policymakers as a complement to state and/or market regulation of intellectual production, distribution and consumption.

A critical approach to rational choice theories of the intellectual commons should first start from their methodology and, then, extend to their content and outcomes. The quest for objective and value-free knowledge through inductive methods of research, which characterises rational choice theories, inevitably bears the shortcomings of positivism. As far as the goal of objectivity is concerned, observations of the empirical reality of the intellectual commons are fatally theory-laden and, as a result, framed from the given social context, in terms of both the socially preconstructed meanings of the semantics used to describe them and the theoretical presuppositions and motivations of the observer. As far as the ideology of value-free science is concerned, the choices of rational choice theorists regarding the objects of their analysis, their core elements and interrelations and, finally, the stated goals of their theoretical endeavours are also laden with specific values that correspond to or contend with dominant or subversive value systems in our societies. Finally, the

Epistemology	Rational choice institutionalism
Agency	Individual(s) in interdependent relations
Structure	Patterns of interactions
Internal dynamics	Bottom-up emergence
External dynamics	n/a
Normative criteria	Consequential
Social change	The commons as patch to capital

Table 3.1: The intellectual commons as patch to capital.
Source: Author

persistence on an analysis of the intellectual commons as precisely defined, with clear-cut boundaries, internally consistent, reduced to their components and interconnected with iron causal laws may end up with a static and fragmentary perception of reality, subjugated to the incapacity of grasping processes of becoming.

These methodological choices have an impact on the form and content of rational choice theories. In terms of the internal dynamics of the intellectual commons, rational choice theorists fail to recognise that the public goods character of intellectual resources is not only based on their intangible traits but also in part socially determined, being nowadays more and more under pressure by legal and technological enclosures. Furthermore, they disregard the fact that the commons ultimately refer to social relations in the context of communities and that the formulation of the commons in history has not been confined to non-rival resources. Accordingly, human agency within the rational choice framework remains inescapably confined to a methodological individualism and to a transaction cost-based approach that conceives of individuals as engaging with the intellectual commons in order to maximise their personal benefits, even if such benefit is recognised to relate with the establishment of relations of reciprocity (Bardhan and Ray 2006, 655, 660–661; Macey 2010, 763). Thus, the IAD framework fails to fully grasp the shared ethics, values, goals, narratives and meanings that hold communities of the intellectual commons together, tending to reduce them to their functionalist, procedural and consequential aspects (Bailey 2013, 109). By focusing on individual action as the means to explain how social institutions develop and how social change takes place, rational choice scholars inevitably conceive of commoners primarily as extractors of resource units or free-riders of the efforts of others, and competition is again elevated at central stage. As a result, the institutional forms of the commons are mainly conceived by rational choice theorists as shaping behavioural patterns more by putting fetters on and less by empowering social action and enabling sharing and collaboration.

Yet, the main shortcoming of rational choice theories is their reluctance to place the social phenomena of the intellectual commons within social tendencies, contradictions and antagonisms, which determine the contemporary assemblage of social totality (Macey 2010, 772–774). Such theories diminish the interrelation of the intellectual commons with capital to a simplistic conception of either co-existence or complementarity. By approaching the intellectual commons from a utilitarian perspective, rational choice theorists evaluate these social phenomena in comparison to state intervention or intellectual property-enabled markets solely according to the criterion of utility maximisation (Wright 2008, 236). Hence, intellectual commons are held to be more effective modes of organisation in social contexts where they outcompete the state or the market. In this theoretical exercise, asymmetries of power between the dominant capitalist mode of intellectual production/distribution/consumption and the insurgent sphere of the intellectual commons, along with the consequent asymmetries of access to investments, income and infrastructure and of favourable or inimical frameworks of law/litigation are not taken into account. In addition, the impact of commodification over commons-based peer production and the public domain and the clash and struggles within intellectual commons communities and in wider social groups between opposing value practices are generally neglected in favour of a more conciliatory ideological conception of society free from contradictions and antagonisms (De Angelis and Harvie 2014, 287). Most important, the utilitarian perspective of rational choice theories falls prey to the dominant perspective over the common good, which inextricably connects the maximisation of social utility with the proliferation of private property, capitalist markets and private monetary incentives. Inevitably, values proliferating within and through the sphere of the intellectual commons that are found at the margins of the current state of social reproduction, such as access, sharing, collaboration, self-government and individual and collective empowerment, tend to be ranked lower in the utilitarian calculus of rational choice theories and their positive social outcomes tend to be downgraded in comparison to dominant conceptions of the common good.

3.4. Neoliberal Theories of the Intellectual Commons: The Commons as Fix to Capital

3.4.1. Main Question and Methodology

Neoliberal theories of the intellectual commons have as their foundation the orthodoxy that markets are the most appropriate mechanisms to maximise net social benefits (Mankiw 2014, 150–151). From this perspective, neoliberal theorists examine the ways in which the intellectual commons are accommodated by the capitalist mode of intellectual production, with the aim of providing proposals that best serve market needs. Along these lines, they engage in an analysis of the alternative organisational patterns and value systems of the intellectual commons and research their potential for creativity and innovation in order to provide useful tools for their monetisation. Finally, they search for appropriate restructuring policies for business patterns, capitalist markets and for-profit corporations that will efficiently exploit this potential. In dealing with their object of analysis, neoliberal thinkers mainly draw from neoclassical economics and other disciplines that are compatible with its basic tenets, such as law and economics and public choice theory. In relation to methodology, neoliberal theories are strongly inclined to evaluate the intellectual commons according to either a pragmatic consequentialism or an openly utilitarian cost/benefit analysis in strong connection with the promotion of markets and the accumulation of capital.

The philosophical anthropology of neoliberal theories generally implies a conception of commoners that is methodologically individualistic (Macpherson 1964, 1973). In relation to social structures, neoliberal theorists opt for a reductionist methodology. According to this perspective, explanations about the intellectual commons are reduced to explanations in terms of facts about the individuals composing them (Bentham 1948, 126; Mill 1858, 550; Hayek 1948, 6; Hayek 1955, 37–38; Popper 1961, 135). Social order emerges in spontaneous form from the bottom up through the autonomous and decentralised matching of individual intentions and expectations (Hayek 2013, 34–52). The most efficient mechanism of such a spontaneous order of allocating resources is the invisible hand of the free and competitive commodity market (Stiglitz 1991, 1). Within markets, the pursuit of individual private interests leads to greater wealth for all and a more effective distribution of labour (Botsman and Rogers 2010, 41).

Projecting this methodology to the realm of the intellectual commons, neoliberal theorists consider the ensemble of social relations within the communities of the intellectual commons to be collections of individuals who exercise their freedom of creativity and innovation according to their own preferences and without external interference. In the process of commons-based peer production, commoners pool together their private property rights over their individual intellectual works through private contracts in order to extract pleasure or other forms of personal utility (Benkler 2006, 230). As a result, neoliberal thinkers tend to conceive the structures of the intellectual commons as markets, wherein individuals meet and earn social capital and/or personal pleasure in exchange for putting their skills to work for a mutually agreed cause (Raymond 1999). In general, the arrangements within the intellectual commons and in their relation with the market are framed in terms of individual free choice and business opportunities. In this context, an efficient social order emerges by spontaneity from the bottom up, as long as the state does not interfere to unsettle the balance.

3.4.2. *The Intellectual Commons as Component to Capital Accumulation*

Neoliberal theorists have been quick to grasp the potential of the resurging intellectual commons for human creativity and business profitability. In their business manifesto, Don Tapscott and Anthony Williams enthusiastically welcome us 'to the world of Wikinomics where collaboration on a mass scale is set to change every institution in society' (Tapscott and Williams 2006, 10). In a similar manner, in an earlier online version of his own book-length call to the brave new world, Charles Leadbeater again greet us 'to the world of We-Think', where '[w]e are developing new ways to innovate and be creative en masse. We can be organised without an organisation. People can combine ideas and skills without a hierarchy' (Leadbeater 2008). Even *Time* magazine confirmed this rising new fashion in 2006 by naming as its 'Person of the Year' the creative 'You'.

New terms have been coined to describe the exciting dynamics of the digital era. Even in 2004, at the O'Reilly Media Web 2.0 Conference, Tim O'Reilly and Dale Dougherty talked about the emergence of Web 2.0, a second phase of the World Wide Web, which is characterised by the abundance of user-generated content and online content platforms that facilitate peer-to-peer sharing and collaboration and, ultimately, empower internet users (O'Reilly 2005). In its relation to the market, O'Reilly has later clarified that the whole idea and the success of Web 2.0 is based on 'customers [...] building your business for you'.[11] Inspired by Alvin Toffler's idea that the information age will blur the boundaries between production and consumption and give rise to the 'prosumer' (Toffler 1980, 265), Tapscott and Williams have elaborated on the model of prosumption as an important new way through which businesses are putting consumers to work, calling it 'the lifeblood of the business', which leaves entrepreneurs with no choice but to 'harness the new collaboration or perish' (Tapscott and Williams 2006, 13, 43, 125–127). In their vision about prosumption, they have further explained that 'leisure becomes a form of work. A huge amount of creative work is done in spite, or perhaps because, of people not being paid' (Tapscott and Williams 2006, 6). Hence, prosumers are included in the productive process as fundamental component, and the market is no longer a space where supply and demand meet but has rather become inseparable from the productive process as the actual 'locus of co-creation (and co-extraction) of value' (Prahalad and Ramaswamy 2004, 5).

Other commentators have added an even more insightful dimension in the debate, claiming that the business technique of prosumption reconstructs the very agency of consuming masses in ways more prone to exploitation by exchanging new consumer freedoms and a feeling of empowerment with the right of corporations to expropriate consumer creativity and innovation (Zwick, Bonsu and Darmody 2008, 185). Along these lines, it has been argued that, by invoking the personal autonomy of commoners to freely share ideas and collaborate, corporations become capable of overcoming their hierarchical top-down and inflexibly bureaucratic structures of organisation, of transcending their boundaries and of developing more appropriate means to unleash collective capacities for creativity and innovation. In this context, for-profit entities that grasp the zeitgeist of the information age not only become leaders of the new mode of intellectual production but also renew the fractured social contract upon which conventional modes of work and production are established (Leadbeater 2008, 88–90). Therefore, Charles Leadbeater rightly pinpoints commons-based peer production as having the potential to offer 'a way for capitalism to recover a social – even a communal – dimension that people are yearning for' (Leadbeater 2008, 91).

The proliferation in the networked information economy of social and business patterns relative to the productive processes described above have led Botsman and Rogers to introduce the term 'collaborative consumption' so as to describe social arrangements in which communities of individuals pool together and share privately owned products and services with the help of contemporary information and communication technologies (Botsman and Rogers 2010). Drawing from the concept of crowdsourcing, defined by Jeff Howe as the 'act of taking a job traditionally performed by a designated agent (usually an employee) and outsourcing it to an undefined, generally large group of people in the form of an open call' (Howe 2006), Botsman and Rogers have coherently demonstrated the potential of emerging patterns of online collaboration for the satisfaction of individual needs and the promotion of collective goals, as diverse as co-sharing scarce resources, producing intellectual goods in commons-based peer mode, building business models upon the intellectual commons and even acting together for the resolution of social problems as important as climate change (Botsman and Rogers 2010, 59). From such a perspective, engagement with collaborative consumption not only secures a small income but also transforms participants into 'microentrepreneurs' and has a positive cumulative effect on their social capital (Botsman and Rogers 2010, xvii, 180). Businesses that base their profitability on communities of collaborative consumption are successful on the condition that they view themselves not as rulers 'but more as hosts of a party helping to integrate new members with the rest of the community' (Botsman and Rogers 2010, 204). Acting as the definite community builders of the information age, such corporations actually own and architect the online platforms and tools, which both facilitate the horizontal peer transactions of collaborative consumption and encourage relations of trust and reciprocity among participants (Botsman and Rogers 2010, 91).

In this nexus of social relations, corporations are not just looking for unpaid work to be exploited. Instead, they invest in the construction and management of entire communities of resource sharing, sociality, collaborative creativity and innovation (Botsman and Rogers 2010, 204). The main object of profit extraction is the information and communication produced by the matrix of social relationships continuously weaved within online communities.[12] Ownership of the platform and the related infrastructure, which underpins the community, bestows access and control over the data produced by the networked social exchange of its users. Sociality itself in the fixation of data becomes a form of commodity and a source of profit. 'Prosumption', 'value co-creation', 'collaborative consumption' and the 'sharing economy' are concepts that illuminate the emerging mutations in the relations of intellectual production. Hence, the most important technique for business ventures to develop in order to surpass the profitability of competitors in this context is how to monetise the community and embed the powers of the social intellect into the structures of the capitalist market (Bollier 2008, 238).

The exploitation of the free labour of prosumers and the monetisation of online collaborative communities are two significant elements that synthesise the dynamic relation between the intellectual commons and capital. A third mode, in which the intellectual commons are employed as component to capital accumulation, is in market competition between corporations. Neoliberal theorists have pointed out two main ways in which such instrumentalisation of the intellectual commons takes place. First of all, the intellectual commons are utilised as a tool by single enterprises to leverage their position in market competition. The most famous example of this type of relationship between the intellectual commons and a for-profit corporation is the relationship between IBM and the free software community (Lessig 2002a, 71). In 1998, IBM began supporting the Apache and Linux free software communities and granting to the latter compatibility with its hardware. As this collaboration gained momentum, IBM reaped the benefits, by gradually improving its position vis-à-vis its main competitors (Tapscott and Williams 2006, 79–83).

The utilisation of the intellectual commons as a means to alter the competitive structure of markets has also taken a more collective form. In various recorded cases, alliances of non-dominant actors have pooled together and shared resources for their industries in order to pre-empt the ability of competitors to control assets of strategic importance for the development of the market (Merges 2004a). According to this view, the development of many market consortia and patent pools, especially in biotechnology and open source software, where pooled intellectual resources are managed as commons between the members of the market alliance, is the outcome of this process (Madison, Frischmann and Strandburg 2010b, 692). This has led Milton Mueller to claim that '[t]he commons as an institutional option is rarely implemented as the product of communitarian compacts or a sharing ethic. It is more likely to be an outcome of interest group contention' (Mueller 2012, 40–41). Neutralisation of strategic assets might even take place in relation to a single market actor. Indicatively, Tapscott and Williams report that, with the release of 15,000 human gene sequences into the public domain in 1995, the pharmaceutical giant Merck 'pre-empted the ability of biotech firms to encumber one of its key inputs with licensing fees and transaction costs' (Tapscott and Williams 2006, 166–167).

3.4.3. *Intellectual Commons and the Restructuring of the Corporation and the Market*

Since monopolisation is in the nature of intellectual property, its contentious relationship with market competition has been a well-recorded issue of interest both in theory and in policy planning (WIPO 2012; OECD 2013). It has been claimed that intellectual property-enabled markets encounter static inefficiencies in the allocation of information, knowledge and culture. In the long run, they may also generate dynamic inefficiencies in the production of new information, knowledge and culture (David 1993, 28). In particular, monopolies over prior art and knowledge give right-holders the power to tax innovative competitors for gaining access to them (Kapczynski 2010, 28). When such private monopolies are instituted as extensively broad, they essentially raise significantly high barriers to entry for new entrants in markets (Greenwald and Stiglitz 2015, 276). In addition, the saturation of knowledge-based sectors of the economy by the proliferation of private enclosures increases the costs of examining the prior level of knowledge and art and may also stifle innovation by transforming inventiveness into a process of walking in a minefield (Heller 2008, 66). Yet, the multiplication and increased breadth of intellectual property rights may even have long-run repercussions in the structures of markets. Intellectual resources of strategic importance for sectors of the economy acquire the significance that the means of production have in the production of material goods. The ownership of crucial means of production in a market ultimately determines its structure. Private control by incumbent stakeholders over intellectual resources of strategic importance may effectively hinder or even foreclose newcomers from entering and acquiring competitive position in a market (Levin et al. 1987, 788). The powers conferred by such monopolies may also lead to a gradual displacement of competitors and to market concentration.

By expanding the public domain and facilitating access to prior information, knowledge and culture, vibrant intellectual commons communities are a social force that has the potential to counter the dynamic inefficiencies produced by the unbalanced enclosures of intellectual property-enabled markets over competition (Lessig 2002a, 6–7; Boyle 2003, 63–64). Hence, a commons-oriented regime of governance at the cutting edge of technology and in the new modes of cultural production may be required as a fix to the rigidity of dominant intellectual property regimes in order for corporations to take full advantage of the rapidly shifting conditions in intellectual production/distribution/consumption.

Apart from lowering barriers to entry and facilitating access to prior intellectual assets in knowledge-based sectors of the economy, the intellectual commons are also implemented as a strategic tool for the aversion of market failures that have been characterised as tragedies of the anti-commons (Heller 1998). Such conjunctures occur when too many market players hold and exert partly or wholly overlapping rights of exclusion against each other over a strategic resource, so that no party finally acquires an effective right of use (Hunter 2003, 506). These failures in the optimisation of social utility constitute the tipping point where the social relation of property becomes a fetter to forces of production (Mueller 2012, 45). They are regularly encountered in the networked information economy, where productivity depends on prior art and knowledge and operates in a cumulative manner (Lemley 1997; Heller and Eisenberg 1998; Heller 2008). The proliferation and excess of intellectual property rights tends to fragment control over existing intellectual resources (Hess and Ostrom 2007a, 11). In this light, fixing the failures of monopolies through the construction of intellectual commons over strategic assets, while keeping market competition around them, is viewed as a method to combine the best of both worlds and achieve optimum social utility (Mueller 2012, 60). Examples where state and market institutions coordinate to produce intellectual commons in order to avert tragedies of the anti-commons over strategic intellectual assets include standard-setting entities, joint ventures for research and development, informational databases and patent pools (Tapscott and Williams 2006, 178–179; Madison, Frischmann and Strandburg 2010b, 692; OECD 2013, 22).

As far back as 1945, Friedrich von Hayek claimed that knowledge is a resource unevenly distributed in society (Hayek 1945). In the context of the collective intelligence of post-industrial intellectual commons communities, Pierre Levy wrote: '[n]o one knows everything, everyone knows something, all knowledge resides in humanity' (Levy 1997, 20). To make matters even more complicated, the distributed force of the social intellect does not exist in static form within the individual minds of creators/innovators; instead, it is unleashed by a dynamic process of intellectual sharing and collaboration. In order to correspond to the challenges mentioned above, commercial enterprises in knowledge-based sectors of the economy restructure their organisational patterns in order to coordinate and pool together the productive forces of the social intellect. This ambitious aim has a corrosive effect not only on the hierarchical top-down structures of the corporation but also on its boundaries with society. As Tapscott and Williams put it, '[i]n an age where mass collaboration can reshape an industry overnight, the old hierarchical ways of organising work and innovation do not afford the level of agility, creativity, and connectivity that companies require to remain competitive in today's environment. Every individual now has a role to play in the economy, and every company has a choice—commoditize or get connected' (Tapscott and Williams 2006, 31). Permeability vis-à-vis the distributed innovative powers of society is achieved by various means, all of them involving the engagement of actors located outside the organisational structures of the corporation (Chesbrough 2003, xxiv). Outsourcing creative work to the crowd is one among the many corporate methods of capturing the productive value of the social intellect, which cannot be supplied in-house. The aggregation of distributed individual talent and knowledge is conducted on privately owned project platforms, which are focused on the management of creative labour supply. The platform design enables open recruitment, meritocratic ranking and self-selection of tasks (Lakhani and Panetta 2007). Commercial innovation management platforms also borrow the organisational patterns of task modularity, granularity and diversity, which are observed in the institutions of intellectual commons communities. Such platforms have grown enough to influence well-established practices of conventional corporate research and development and to press managers to open up their business models to the innovative power of the crowd. Innocentive, one of the most prominent examples, boasts 40,000 solved scientific problems and $40 million in posted awards for its 365,000+ workforce from nearly 200 countries.[13]

The impact of the intellectual commons on corporate structures has not been confined to the elaborated ways of outsourcing innovation to the crowd. A deeper corporate restructuring seeks to embrace the potential of the intellectual commons by combining the market with the community. In Leadbeater's vision, '[t]he most exciting business models of the future will be hybrids that blend elements of the company and the community, of commerce and collaboration: open in some respects, closed in others; giving some content away and charging for some services; serving people as consumers and encouraging them, when it is relevant, to become participants' (Leadbeater 2008, 91). In this peculiar hybrid, the engine of 'collaborative consumption' and the 'sharing economy' is the community and the lifeblood flowing within its circuits is trust (Botsman 2012). The mere role of the corporation is to enable and empower 'decentralized, and transparent communities to form and build trust between strangers' (Botsman and Rogers 2010, 91). In practice, this contribution usually concerns the provision of material infrastructure, which requires an expensive and concentrated capital base to be produced and can rarely be provisioned by communities themselves (Benkler 2016, 102). According to another less materialistic view, market mechanisms and commercial enterprises generally provide to intellectual commons communities the instruments of regulation and management that are necessary for their well-being and cannot be provided internally (Ghosh 2007, 231). This type of management is however relatively 'soft' to leave enough space to individuals to decide for themselves the terms of interacting and collaborating with each other and, thus, become innovative through individual empowerment (Lakhani and Panetta 2007).

Hence, corporations and markets have the unique opportunity to embrace and harness the potential of the intellectual commons for collaborative creativity and innovation by orchestrating the forces of self-organisation thriving within their communities (Tapscott and Williams 2006, 44). In this market/ commons hybrid scheme, social power is not only circulated and accumulated via the monetisation of the community. Ownership of the communal infrastructure, on the one hand, separates commoners from the means of reproducing their sociability and controlling their collaborative productivity and, on the other hand, gives owners the power to govern production and determine its final goals (Andrejevic 2011, 87–88).

3.4.4. Critical Evaluation: A Commons Fix for Capital

Neoliberal theorists conceive of the intellectual commons not as human communities but as networked markets of exchange among self-interested individuals and between individuals and corporations. According to the neoliberal view, their decentralised structure and capacity for individual self-empowerment render the intellectual commons an ideal terrain for human creativity and innovation. What attributes value to the intellectual commons is their potential for intellectual productivity, which under certain circumstances may even supersede the innovative capacities of the corporation (Benkler 2002, 377). First, commercial enterprises can benefit by capturing their social value with various business techniques. Furthermore, they can be utilised as a vehicle to restructure markets in order to make them more competitive and well-functioning, whereas, on the other hand, they can be employed as a tool to avert serious market failures and gridlock effects. Therefore, neoliberal theorists recommend that the positive organisational aspects of commons-based peer production be either assimilated by the dominant mode of capitalist intellectual production or appended as a component to it.

The main contribution of neoliberal theories in relation to the analysis of the intellectual commons is the fact that they bring to our attention the various ways through which capital dialectically relates with the intellectual commons. Nevertheless, the neoliberal theoretical endeavour projects this dialectical relation in a simplistic and ideologically biased manner, which tends to obfuscate or even neglect more critical aspects of the whole process. In this respect, the alleged co-existence between the intellectual commons and capital is emptied from its obvious contradictions. Even though it illuminates the manifold ways through which the circuits of capital extract value from the sphere of the commons, it fails to pinpoint that such a subsumption of the intellectual commons is not without repercussions, as communal resources, values and their systems, which are consumed by private for-profit activities, constantly undercut the energy and dynamics of intellectual commons communities and degrade their potential for creativity and innovation. Ultimately, neoliberal thinkers do not pose the question of who holds the power within the sphere of the intellectual commons. Hence, asymmetries of power between commoners and corporations are concealed by the use of terms such as 'co-creation' and 'co-existence'. Control

Epistemology	Methodological individualism
Agency	Isolated individual(s)
Structure	Market
Internal dynamics	Bottom-up emergence
External dynamics	Co-optation of commons by capital
Normative criteria	Utilitarian
Social change	The commons as fix to capital

Table 3.2: A commons fix for capital.
Source: Author

over infrastructure and the powers it confers to its owners is considered either a benevolent contribution or a new type of social corporate responsibility, or even another proof that private profit motivation and market mechanisms maximise social utility. And the governance of the intellectual commons by capital is apprehended as necessary regulation that cannot be supplied internally.

To sum up, neoliberal perspectives approach the intellectual commons as a fix to capital, both by exploiting commons-based peer production as a component to capital accumulation and by utilising the productive force and organisational capacity of intellectual commons communities as a means to restructure commodity markets and corporate forms and avert their failures. Critical theorists have generalised this tendency in the contentious relation between capital and the commons, claiming that the commons are nowadays employed in manifold ways as fix to the failure of capital to ensure social reproduction (De Angelis 2012) and that they constitute neoliberalism's 'plan B' to reorganise and expand capital accumulation in order to overcome its inherent crises of social and ecological devastation (Caffentzis 2010).

3.5. Social Democratic Theories of the Intellectual Commons: The Commons as Substitute to the Welfare State

3.5.1. Main Question and Methodology

Social democratic approaches of the intellectual commons employ political economic methodologies to analyse the dynamic relations that unfold between the commons, the market and the state, with the aim of proposing reconfigurations of these relations, which will best serve social welfare (Kostakis and Bauwens 2015). Social democratic theorists believe that the intellectual commons have the potential to bring us to freer and more egalitarian societies, characterised by an abundance of intellectual resources (Rifkin 2014). Nevertheless, according to their views, existing institutional arrangements suppress this potential and should be changed (Arvidsson and Peitersen 2013, 136–137), in particular by the deliberate transformation of the state into a state in partnership with the commons (Restakis 2015). In relation to methodology, such theories follow a relational analysis of social structures. Emphasis is thus given to the revelation of the dialectical interrelations that develop between the institutions of the intellectual commons and the mechanisms of intellectual property-enabled markets. Overall, social democratic theorists tend to employ deontological criteria for the evaluation of the intellectual commons by examining the possibilities for positive reforms within the framework of existing social arrangements (Bauwens 2015, 13).

Contrary to individualistic perceptions of agency, the main presupposition for social democratic theories is that individuals are to a major extent constituted by the various communal relations of which they are part (Chang 2014,

193). It follows that individual agency is shaped by social structures, which at the same time frame and empower individual activity (Giddens 1984). Commoners construct and constantly reproduce and evolve the productive communities of the intellectual commons, while at the same time these communal structures and institutions constrain and enable sharing and collaboration, leading to the emergence of new properties. While they share the view of rational choice theorists of the intellectual commons that human behaviour is determined by a multiplicity of incentives (Benkler 2002, 369; 2006, 462; Kostakis and Bauwens 2014, 40), social democratic theorists claim that the element of reciprocity is the foundation of social life, emerging within the social matrix as the determinant characteristic of the behaviour of socially integrated individuals (Bauwens 2015, 67–69). Embedding norms of reciprocity and cooperation in social systems and structures hence creates a virtuous cycle of reinforcing the behaviours that need to be promoted and plays a major role in achieving intended social changes (Benkler 2011, 161–162).

According to social democratic perceptions, the gradual accumulation of commons-oriented reforms, primarily through state intervention, is the most appropriate road to commons-based societies. In Michel Bauwens's words, the social democratic set of proposals 'is the next great reform of the system, the wise course of action, awaiting its P2P "neo-Keynes", a collective able to translate the needs of the cooperative ethos in a set of political and ethical measures. Paradoxically, it will strengthen cognitive capitalism, and strengthen cooperation, allowing the two logics to co-exist, in cooperation, and in relative independence from one another, installing a true competition in solving world problems' (Bauwens 2005).

3.5.2. *The Intellectual Commons and Their Potential for an Alternative Non-Market Economy*

Social democratic intellectuals stress the potential of the intellectual commons for individual and collective empowerment, the democratisation of intellectual production, the decentralisation of social power and the enrichment of the public sphere. They are thus keen on highlighting the fundamental role of public institutions in social reproduction and the connection of the idea of the public with the intellectual commons. Even though the modern idea of the public is strongly connected with the state, social democratic thinkers are quick to identify the sphere of the commons as a public realm, which is not owned by the state. As Tommaso Fattori describes it, fundamental goods for social reproduction should 'not belong to market actors nor are they at the disposal of governments or the state-as-person, because they belong to the collectivity and above all, to future generations, who cannot be expropriated of their rights' (Fattori 2013, 260–261). In relation to intellectual resources, social democratic thinkers reimagine the information networks, the public domain, fair use rights and the intellectual commons primarily as a space free from unwarranted interventions by the market and the state (Lessig 2006; Wu 2010, 306). Unencumbered access to such an intellectual public space is considered fundamental for exercising individual freedoms crucial for self-empowerment and democracy, primarily the freedom of expression (Netanel 2008). Freedom in this space, in the sense of freedom to create and innovate, also entails that its building blocks are insusceptible to excessive control by powerful market players, thus safeguarding its public character from concentrated powers, i.e. a public character not in the sense of state ownership and provision but in the sense of the commons (Wu 2002, 2010). Hence, the intervention of law in this context is to 'protect the integrity of individual and social autonomies' against the power of the market or the state (Teubner 2013, 114).

Apart from policies that protect and safeguard the sphere of the intellectual commons, social democratic theorists advocate the deliberate promotion of a distinct non-commercial commons sector in the networked information economy, alongside the private and the public sector. According to their views, in contradistinction to private monopoly rights, centralisation and competition characterising intellectual property-enabled markets, the non-commercial commons sector propels the freedom and autonomy of participants 'by operating on principles of access, decentralisation and collaboration' (Fuster Morell 2014, 280). Furthermore, the sets of practices thriving within the intellectual commons have already constructed an economy parallel to the corporate one, which allegedly generates culture, innovation and, generally, social wealth in ways based on sharing and collaboration that are not encountered in corporate environments (Benkler 2004). Based on self-production and self-management of resources by both formal and informal communal institutions, this mode of economic organisation outcompetes market- or state-based modes in terms of democratic participation and decision-making in the economy (Benkler 2002, 2006). Simultaneously, it gives the opportunity to overcome, at least to a certain extent, power inequalities between order-givers and order-takers observed in corporate forms of organisation (Benkler 2003a, 1249). Furthermore, certain theorists maintain that the mutualisation of intellectual resources within the commons-based mode of peer production comes along with processes of mutualisation of material resources and the rise of a distinct cooperative economy of material resources (Restakis 2010, 2015). Finally, the intellectual commons provide information and communication infrastructures vital for the exercise of democratic rights and liberties in a self-governing and transparent manner. Hence, the more the building blocks of our networked information environment are reproduced by commons-based peer production, the better it is ensured that the power of citizens in this sphere of activity is not overcome by the power of corporations and states (MacKinnon 2012, xxi).

Overall, social democratic thinkers favour the consolidation of a commons sector in the networked information economy on normative grounds, claiming that such a power shift will promote individual and collective empowerment, democratise the economy and society, contribute to social justice and increase overall social welfare. Nevertheless, social democratic theories fork when it comes to the interrelation between the intellectual commons and capital. On the one hand, liberal-minded thinkers believe that a synergistic symbiosis between the sectors of the commons and the market is attainable, on the condition that an equitable balance is struck between the two (Bollier 2007, 38). On the other hand, political economists believe that such a harmonious symbiosis is not possible, proposing instead the implementation of commons-oriented policies on behalf of the state so as to establish a level playing field for the alternative non-market economy of the commons (Bauwens and Kostakis 2015). According to their views, the relation between netarchical capital and the intellectual commons is not viable in the long term, because the value captured from commoners is not redistributed to them, as is the case, no matter how unevenly, with wage labour.

3.5.3. *The Intellectual Commons and Their Potential for an Alternative Culture and Public Sphere*

Social democratic intellectuals believe that the intellectual commons have the potential to become part of the solution to the current crisis of liberal representative democracies, by reconfiguring power relations and, correspondingly, by democratising our culture, public sphere and polity. The political potential of the intellectual commons lies to a large extent on their capacity to empower 'decentralised individual action' (Benkler 2006, 3). In this context, a more participative and transparent process of making culture has a democratising impact on the world of ideas and symbols, which constitutes the cultural base of our societies, while at the same time it encourages critical thinking and creativity (Fisher 2001, 193).

In the networked information environment, individual and collective participation in cultural production is enabled by (i) the lower cost of engaging in cultural production, which has led to wide social diffusion of the means of such production, in terms of both equipment and software, (ii) the provision of easier, wider and more equal access to the mass of prior cultural achievements archived at the World Wide Web on a non-commercial openly accessible basis, (iii) the facilitation of knowledge sharing, cultural exchange and collaboration between creators through contemporary information and communication infrastructures, and (iv) the increased technical capacity of remixing prior art into new forms of cultural expression (Benkler 2006; Lessig 2008; Broumas 2013, 430). On this basis, Benkler has proposed that commons-based peer production gives birth to a new folk culture, which is not only more open, participatory and transparent than industrial cultural production but also has the potential to acquire critical mass and challenge dominant norms, standards and patterns of the industrial cultural production system (Benkler 2006, 277).

Apart from the cultural domain, political implications of the intellectual commons also extend to the transformation of both the public sphere and the modes of social mobilisation and political organisation. In the industrial era, the public sphere was characterised by the accumulation of communication power in the hands of powerful commercial corporations (Habermas 1989). In the informational era, an alternate mode is emerging alongside the dominant relations of managing communication, which is based on mass self-communication (Castells 2009, 55). Widespread social practices in the networked media environment are organised in the form of decentralised and horizontal information dissemination and deliberation among individuals (Benkler 2006, 215–219). Furthermore, horizontal communication networks formulate nodes around participatory media structures, which facilitate and coordinate the dissemination of alternative messages and meanings (Lievrouw 2011). Even though the asymmetries of communication power between corporate mass media and horizontal networks of communication persevere, these two distinct poles in the contemporary public sphere are dialectically interconnected (Castells 2008, 90), with the latter having developed the capacity to circulate news, opinions and ideas at the social base, to contribute to social awareness over the exertion of arbitrary state/corporate power and to counter-influence dominant agenda-setting patterns.

Accordingly, the properties of contemporary information and communication technologies are reshaping the political mobilisation, organisation and action of the twenty-first century at the grass roots. With regard to the interrelation between communication processes and social movements, Manuel Castells claims that 'the characteristics of communication processes between individuals engaged in the social movement determine the organizational characteristics of the social movement itself: the more interactive and self-configurable communication is, the less hierarchical is the organization and the more participatory is the movement' (Castells 2012, 15). The dialectics between contemporary information and communication technologies and grass-roots political activity influence both social mobilisation and political organisation. On the one hand, such technologies constitute an important element of the information and communication infrastructure, which enables and, simultaneously, frames horizontal political coordination, mobilisation and physical aggregation of protestors through the decentralised dissemination of messages across mobilised masses. On the other hand, they empower and, at the same time, condition networked forms of organisation inside the social movements within and beyond borders (Juris 2008).

3.5.4. *The Partner State to the Intellectual Commons: Planning the Transition*

Social democratic thinkers argue that the present configuration between the state, the market and civil society works only at the service of capital and to the detriment of the intellectual commons (Bauwens and Kostakis 2015). Hence, the consolidation of a commons sector in the economy and, subsequently, the transition to a commons-oriented society is claimed to be only possible under the establishment of a partnership between the state and the social sphere of the intellectual commons and the commons in general (Bauwens and Kostakis 2015; Bauwens, Restakis and Dafermos 2015).

Elaborating on Cosma Orsi's approach (Orsi 2005, 2009), Bauwens and Kostakis define the partner state as 'a state form for the transition period towards a social knowledge economy, in which the resources and functions of the state are primarily used to enable and empower autonomous social production' (Bauwens and Kostakis 2015). Unlike the market state, the partner state form has the mission of both safeguarding the sphere of the intellectual commons and facilitating the mode of commons-based peer production, while, at the same time, promoting social entrepreneurship and participatory politics (Bauwens and Kostakis 2015). Hence, whereas the present market state is only at the service of property owners and profit-oriented economic activities, the partner state also empowers the commons-oriented social forces of civil society and the social solidarity economy (Orsi 2009, 42; Bauwens and Kostakis 2015). In the dialectic relationship between the state and the intellectual commons, the strengthening of civil society is expected to initiate a reversal of the current tendency to shift power from nation states to the forces of capital and an exodus from the socially and ecologically unsustainable political economy of globalised capitalism (Restakis 2015, 99). In the partner state framework, relations between the state, the market and the commons are reconfigured in order to produce a 'triarchy' that preserves and combines the positive aspects of each sector for social welfare and ecological sustainability (Bollier and Weston 2013, 262). In this context, the partner state acquires the role of the arbiter, who ensures 'an optimal mix amongst government regulation, private-market freedom and autonomous civil-society projects' (Bauwens and Kostakis 2015).

According to social democratic theories, the partner state becomes the central planner for the transition to a commons-oriented society. In this respect, specific sets of policies have to be carved out with the core aim of establishing institutions that guarantee that the social value produced and circulated by practices of commoning is not appropriated by capital but rather accumulated again in the sphere of the intellectual commons (Bauwens 2015, 53). This virtuous cycle of value circulation/accumulation is expected to make an alternative political economy possible and pull intellectual commons communities out of the margins and to the centre of the economy (Bauwens and Kostakis 2015). A commons-oriented political economy of the social intellect consists of interrelated layers of economic activity, all of which are underpinned by positive state policies. At its core are the intellectual commons communities and their coordinating institutions, which usually take the form of special purpose foundations and other non-profit entities (Bauwens 2015, 32). Its periphery, where capital-intensive activities take place, especially in relation to the production of material goods or labour-intensive services, is occupied by social and solidarity cooperatives, which are connected together by bonds of reciprocity and mutuality. Finally, its relation with the market is configured by the rise of an ethical entrepreneurship, which is mobilised by 'generative forms of ownership' and 'open, commons-oriented ethical company formats' (Bauwens and Kostakis 2015). The partner state facilitates and co-funds this ecosystem of ethical economy (Restakis 2015, 113).

3.5.5. Critical Evaluation: Partnering with the State for the Transition to a Commons-Based Society

Overall, social democratic approaches employ political economic tools for the examination of the intellectual commons, emphasise their interrelations with the political economic totality and its structures and merge on affirmative reformist proposals for the restructuring of existing social institutions (see Table 3.3 below). In particular, such theories are characterised by their transcendent perspective towards existing arrangements of the networked information society and by their transitive approach in favour of emancipatory and ecologically sustainable social change. Their basic tenet is that the mode of commons-based peer production has deeply influenced the evolution of the networked information economy and can also be implemented in wider sectors of social reproduction. Therefore, the intellectual commons have the potential to bring about significant changes to society as a whole in favour of social justice, individual/collective empowerment and democracy. As a result, social democratic theorists strive to delineate specific plans for a transition to a commons-based society. In their approach, they call for a shift beyond the classic discourse over the power balance between the state and the market and, instead, focus on the ways that the state and the market can enable, facilitate and empower civil society arrangements, which are reproduced around and within the intellectual commons.

Epistemology	Political economy
Agency	Social individual(s)
Structure	Productive community
Internal dynamics	Bottom-up/top-down emergence
External dynamics	Co-existence of commons with capital
Normative criteria	Deontological (reformist)
Social change	The commons as substitute to the welfare state

Table 3.3: Partnering with the state for the transition to a commons-based society.
Source: Author

Social democratic theories, especially when founded on liberal philosophical premises and rational choice methodologies, often cross the thin line that separates dialectical thinking over the interrelation between society and technology from one-dimensional techno-deterministic approaches of the intellectual commons. Nevertheless, the tense relation between the intellectual commons and capital cannot be obfuscated by ideologically laden perspectives about the alleged inevitability of the technological revolutions. As Yochai Benkler has aptly commented about the potential of the intellectual commons and the social forces that obstruct its realisation, '[t]he technology will not overcome [the industrial giants'] resistance through an insurmountable progressive impulse. The reorganisation of production and the advances it can bring in freedom and justice will emerge, therefore, only as a result of social and political action aimed at protecting the new social patterns from the incumbents' assaults' (Benkler 2006, 15). Apart from straightforward technological determinism, certain strands of social democratic theory are also criticised on the basis of over-emphasising the realm of the networked information environment and the digital commons with regard to transformative politics (De Angelis and Harvie 2014, 288–289). By disregarding the interdependencies between the intellectual commons and the material realm, social democratic theorists fall in certain cases prey to cyber-optimism and underestimate the wider power shifts that need to take place for a commons-based society to emerge.

Yet, a more penetrating critique of social democratic theories should reveal the deep contradictions regarding their idea about the essence of the bourgeois state and its dialectics with capital and the intellectual commons. The social democratic proposal for the possibility of co-existence between the sphere of the commons and capitalist markets through the establishment of cycles of additive value between the two fails to grasp the deeply contested nature of the relation between commons and capital. In its current phase of development, capital operates as a voracious colonising force, which constantly invades realms of life in common for the purpose of growing and reproducing its monetary value (De Angelis 2007, 6). Capitalist penetration in previously untouched fields of cultural and communicational activity takes the form of a surging commodification, as is evident in the various genres of postmodern culture (Jameson 1991). In a social terrain dominated by commodity markets, social value is primarily circulated and accumulated in the form of money and through the exploitation of labour. In such a terrain, forces of intellectual commoning are incapable of outcompeting forces of commodification, owing to the fact that the former base their sustainable reproduction on non-monetary values. Therefore, no matter how extensively the intellectual commons counter-influence the processes of capital circulation/accumulation in the networked information economy, commons-based peer production is constantly co-opted in multiple ways as component to the dominant mode of capitalist intellectual production/distribution/consumption.

Apart from the vulnerabilities and failures of the notion of the intellectual commons as co-existing with capital, the social democratic conception of the partner state is also in itself a contradiction. The contradictory essence of the state as the condensation of competing social forces precludes the materialisation of a specific socio-historical state form that will partner with the commons. Instead, state policies regarding the commons are and will in the future be the specific contradictory outcome of the contention between the dominated social force of the commons and the dominant social force of capital each time at work. The ideal-type of the partner state obscures the contradictory and antagonistic elements of the process towards a commons-oriented society, the latter being a possibility dependent ultimately on social struggles rather than technocratic solutions. The concept of a state in partnership with the commons and, hence, deliberately promoting decommodification strategies collides with the contemporary transformation of the state into a 'competition state', which acts within the golden straightjacket of neoliberal globalisation as a 'collective commodifying agent' of social life (Cerny 1997, 267). By claiming that this market-enabling role of the state can be completely reversed, without revealing the complex dialectics within social antagonism, which can render this colossal reversal possible, social democratic theorists of the partner state obfuscate more than they illuminate.

3.6. Critical Theories of the Intellectual Commons: The Commons as Alternative to Capital

3.6.1. Main Question and Methodology

Critical approaches search for the elements of the intellectual commons that have the potential to abolish all forms of domination and exploitation and exhibit tendencies towards a state of non-domination, a stateless and classless society. Critical theorists posit commons-based peer production within the wider social antagonism between the dominant force of capital and the countervailing forces of commoning. Furthermore, following Marx, they consider the intellectual commons to be part of the real movement of communism constantly at work at the base of contemporary capitalist society, which abolishes dominant social relations and creates the new world (Marx 1970). Without any ground for conciliation between the two opposing forces, the mission of critical intellectuals is to elaborate on the ways that the intellectual commons and the commons in general can be armoured in their dialectic relation with capital, so as to acquire anti-capitalist dynamics and transcend the current ensemble of social relations.

In relation to methodology, critical theories follow a critical political economic approach to the commons as systems of social forces/relations embedded into the antagonisms of capitalism. Dialectical relations between the intellectual commons and capital are considered to develop as internalisations of characteristics of one element to the unity of the other. The unity in diversity of such elements and their interrelations constitutes an interconnected social totality, which is replete with inherent contradictory tendencies (Fuchs 2011, 21). Furthermore, critical theories are materialistic in the sense that they analyse the processes of resource distribution, circulation and accumulation taking place within the dynamic interrelation between the intellectual commons and capital. Holding that, in this context, social change is ubiquitous and that the understanding of its processes plays a key role for shaping the future, critical theories engage in a processual ontology of social structures, viewing the latter as sets of processes of social (re)production (Mosco 2009, 127–128).

From a critical perspective, agency is an analytical category posited in the wider context of antagonism between social forces and classes. In this context, commoners do not confine themselves in one-to-one relations of reciprocity but circulate dominant or alternative social values along wide cycles of reciprocity formed around communities (Hyde 2007, 19). In this respect, existing societal objects frame subjective action, enabling dominant patterns of social activity and suppressing alternative potentialities, whereas individuals and collectivities choose to reproduce existing structures or go against the current and establish alternative structures, keeping history perpetually open to change (Bhaskar 2008, 144; Fuchs 2011, 61). Within the intellectual commons, there are both knowledge structures and social relations/organisations/institutions as structures, which constrain and, at the same time, enable commoners in specific ways, aligned to either dominant or subversive orientations. In this context, commons-based peer production is considered a mode of intellectual production, through which meanings, perceptions, truths, knowledge and culture are produced as alternatives to their hegemonic counterparts. Therefore, the intellectual commons are conceptualised as having properties that attribute to them the potential to provide intellectual and cultural bases for social reproduction against and beyond capital.

3.6.2. *The Social Intellect as a Direct Force of Production and the Death Knell of Capital*

In the third volume of *Capital*, Marx characterises the intellectual commons as the end product of universal labour, on the basis that '[all scientific labour, all discovery and all invention] depends partly on the co-operation of the living, and partly on the utilisation of the labours of those who have gone before' (Marx 1992, 199). In the *Grundrisse*, Marx describes that in the apogee of its development capital articulates fixed capital (machines) and living labour (workers) in such a way that it gives birth to the general intellect as a direct force of production. Marx defines the general intellect as the 'universal labor of the human spirit' (Marx 1992, 114), 'general social knowledge', 'the power of knowledge, objectified' or 'the general productive forces of the social brain' (Marx 1973, 705, 706, 709). According to the Marxian approach, machines are conceptualised as 'alien labour merely appropriated by capital' (Marx 1973, 701), whereas their constituting technologies are the outcome of work of the human brain (Marx 1973, 706). In this phase, capital gradually dispenses of direct human labour by means of machination and transforms the entire production process into 'the technological application of science' (Marx 1973, 699). What then capital appropriates is '[the individual worker's] general productive power, his understanding of nature and his mastery over it by virtue of his presence as a social body – it is, in a word, the development of the social individual which appears as the great foundation-stone of production and of wealth' (Marx 1973, 701). Hence, in the age of the general intellect the intellectual commons become the ultimate source of capital's profit (Marx 1992, 114).

The emergence of the general intellect is a social transformation, which takes place within capitalism and in the direction of totally subsuming the creative powers of the human brain and body under the processes of capital circulation/accumulation. Nonetheless, in one of his unexpected dialectical twists of thought, Marx alleges that the same transformation, which brings capital to the apex of its social power, also 'works towards its own dissolution' in four ways (Marx 1973, 700). On the one hand, the replacement of living labour by machines is expected to decrease profit rates, since only human labour is perceived to have the capacity to produce value (Caffentzis 2013, 139–163). On the other hand, the diminishing dependence of capital on workers sets on fire the relation of wage labour, which holds capitalist societies together. 'Post-operaist' thinkers go so far as to elicit from Marx's writings the idea that value produced by 'immaterial labour' is by its nature beyond measure, rendering the Marxian law of value redundant and forcing capitalist markets into severe crisis (Hardt and Negri 1994, 9, 175; 2000, 209, 355–359; 2004, 140–153). Finally, the necessity of human supervision over the objective dimension of the general intellect, i.e. the technoscientific systems at work in production, gives rise to a subjective social force that has the potential to transcend private property relations through sharing and collaboration. Hence, the rise of the general intellect gives birth, albeit still in spermatic form, to an alternative commons-based proto-mode of production (Fuchs 2014, 170). The new society begins to form itself within the shell of the old.[14]

Critical theorists believe that the advent of the networked information society induces transformations in the relations of production, which contribute to the emergence of the general intellect as the principal productive force of our age (Fuchs 2014, 151). The exponentially increasing usage of information and communication technologies and their machinery in the process of production indicate the extent to which general social knowledge has become a direct force of production, having significant spillover effects on most terrains of social (re)production (Dyer-Witheford 1999, 221). Focusing on the subjective pole of Marx's concept of the general intellect, i.e. living labour, certain intellectuals of the autonomist Marxist camp claim that the generation of the productive force of the general intellect and the generalisation of 'immaterial labour' in the global workforce has led to the emergence of 'mass intellectuality'. The latter is a set of cognitive, technical, cultural and affective competencies and organisational capacities widely dispersed in the workforce, which constitutes the 'know-how' for the operation of post-Fordist production (Virno 1996, 265). By reaching the stage of the general intellect, the development of productive forces thus unveils an anti-capitalist subjectivity of labour, which autonomously constructs alternative processes of 'self-valorisation', i.e. production of use value, which escapes its commodifying cycle into exchange value and, at the same time, production of proletarian class consciousness and organisation (Hardt and Negri 1994, 282).

To sum up, 'post-operaist' thinkers, such as Hardt and Negri, assert that the emergence of the general intellect in capitalist production gives birth to a new revolutionary vanguard. Instead of the industrial proletariat of the Leninist era, the subversive subjectivity of our times is the social cyborg workers' association, which supervises the technoscientific bases of post-Fordist production. As the degree of the socialisation of labour at the core of high-tech capitalism is exponentially increased, 'post-operaist' thinkers believe that 'a kind of spontaneous and elementary communism' at the base of society unfolds itself (Hardt and Negri 2000, 294). Hence, we potentially enter an era in which, as Marx vividly described, '[t]he death knell of capitalist private property sounds. The expropriators are expropriated' (Marx 1990, 929).

3.6.3. *The Anti-Capitalist Commons: Commoning Beyond Capital and the State*

From a critical perspective, the intellectual commons constitute 'a sublation of the mode of the organization of the productive forces' within capitalism, rather than a proper full-fledged post-capitalist mode of production (Fuchs 2014, 170). The emerging contradiction between the forces and relations of production clearly observed today in the form of the resurgent commons may, as has happened repeatedly in the past, just as well lead to the sublation of capital to a superior level of organisation and the consolidation of its powers over societies, instead of pointing towards an exodus from its domination (Tronti 1972). Therefore, in relation not only to the particular case of the intellectual commons but also to wider social change, the opportunity to move beyond capitalist societies is ultimately determined by the shift of co-relations of power brought about through social struggles and political organisation (Hardt and Negri 2009, 150). In Nick Dyer-Witheford's words, the radical potentials of the commons 'can be actualised, not according to any automatic technology determinist progression, but only via struggles about not just the ownership but the most basic design and architecture of networks, struggles that have to be not only fought, but fought out in detail, with great particularity' (Witheford 2006).

By holding that capital has subsumed social reproduction in its entirety, certain 'post-operaist' thinkers inescapably view patterns of commoning as exclusively reproduced by the antinomies of the capitalist mode of production. It suffices to discover and promote the subversive tendencies unleashed by such contradictions in order to fully grasp and mobilise the revolutionary potential of the commons. From this perspective, capital is perceived to produce its opposition within its own sphere of reproduction, by socialising immaterial labour and, consequently, generalising 'communism' at the social base. Following such a reasoning, it should not come as a surprise that the forces of anti-capitalist commoning are exhorted to 'push through Empire to come out the other side' (Hardt and Negri 2000, 218). In this context, a distinct line of critical theorists has been claiming that the commons are generated 'outside' and against the capitalist system, albeit facing internal contradictions owing to the dialectical relation between the forces of commoning and the dominant force of capital. For Massimo De Angelis, the commons constitute spheres of social reproduction, which are mutually exclusive and in constant confrontation with capital. These spheres are reproduced on the basis of circulating and accumulating alternative value practices beyond the value practices of money accumulation, commodity circulation and profit-maximisation. The beginning of history beyond capital, if realised, will only take place when societies overcome the 'law of value',[15] which reduces everything to capital's measurement, and posit the values of commoning as dominant (De Angelis 2007, 135, 150, 247). For Caffentzis and Federici 'commoning' is a social practice, which constitutes the organising base for human communities since their inception and, therefore, predates the state and capital forms of governance and power. They conceive of anti-capitalist commons as 'autonomous spaces from which [we] reclaim control over our life and the conditions of our reproduction, and [...] provide resources on the basis of sharing and equal access, but also as bases from which [we] counter the processes of enclosure and increasingly disentangle our lives from the market and the state' (Caffentzis and Federici 2014, 101). For the commons to acquire anti-capitalist tendencies and fulfil their emancipatory potential, they will have to transcend intellectual production and spread to the material realm. Furthermore, they need to be embedded in self-governed communities, which in themselves will also have to be characterised by non-commodification of their outputs and by the socialisation of both the means of their reproduction and the centres of their decision-making (Caffentzis and Federici 2014, 102–103).

In contrast to social democratic theorists, who address their proposals for commons-oriented planning to state officials, critical intellectuals choose instead to provide their analysis of the commons to the service of radical social movements. According to their views, any potential commons-oriented transformations cannot involve the seizure but rather the overcoming of the neoliberal market state from the bottom up by a social counter-power based on the commons. Fully aware of the crucial role of the state both in the enclosures of the pre-capitalist commons and in the new wave of enclosures currently in effect, critical thinkers strongly support the view that the power shift needed for the commons to thrive can only become possible by a social force in autonomy from the state and any political vanguards attached to it, albeit in a dialectical relationship of disjunctive synthesis with political forces in government that are in favour of commons-oriented policies (Hardt and Negri 2012). The circulation of the resurgent powers of commoning gradually breaks the barriers of the intangible and extends to the material realm through the formulation of hackerspaces, FabLabs, community wireless communication networks, open design commons, open hardware, decentralised desktop manufacturing and peer-to-peer community energy systems (Dyer-Witheford 2006; Kostakis, Niaros, Dafermos and Bauwens 2015).

In conclusion, critical theorists believe that the contemporary battles for the defence and diffusion of the commons, whether taking place in the intellectual or the material realm, are an integral part of a wider reconception of class struggle and social antagonism, which also includes the power to be able to refuse wage labour and the power to gain control over the means of production and subsistence (Caffentzis 2013, 249). They predict that the class struggles of the twenty-first century will be centred on the generation or destruction of the commons. According to Žižek, the contemporary struggles for the commons constitute struggles for the collective survival of humanity from its annihilation. Therefore, capitalist enclosures of the commons create the social conditions for the establishment of wider coalitions between different social agents on the basis of shared communist perspectives (Žižek 2008, 420–429; 2010, 212–215). In this respect, two alternative futures loom for humanity: '[e]ither: social movements will face up to the challenge and re-found the commons on values of social justice in spite of, and beyond, […] capitalist hierarchies. Or: capital will seize the historical moment to use them to initiate a new round of accumulation' (De Angelis 2009).

3.6.4. Critical Evaluation: The Commons as Alternative to Capital

In relation to the criteria applied in this analysis, critical approaches are distinguished from the other three families of theories in that they conceptualise the intellectual commons as contested terrains of domination and resistance in juxtaposition to capital (see above). In general, critical intellectuals engage in an examination of the ways that the intellectual commons can be exploited by corporations in order to (re)produce relations of domination and oppression or employed by society for the advancement of freedom, equality and democracy. Consequently, such theories hold a strong prescriptive/normative approach to social arrangements, openly embracing the aim of radical social change

Epistemology	Critical political economy
Agency	Social intellect
Structure	Community of struggle
Internal dynamics	n/a
External dynamics	Commons/capital antagonism and sublation
Normative criteria	Political (subversive)
Social change	The commons as alternative to capital

Table 3.4: The commons as alternative to capital.
Source: Author

for the transition to commons-based societies. In this context, the commons are viewed as unified social processes and relations, which exhibit continuity between the realms of the manual and the intellectual. In juxtaposition to the other three approaches, critical thinkers perceive the intellectual commons as posited within social antagonism between the forces of labour and capital and consider that position as largely determinant of their essence and their future. Hence, the focus of their analysis is centred on the specific crystallisations of such power relations within the ensembles of intellectual commons themselves, the antinomies of these crystallisations and their elements that have an anti-capitalist potential and should be promoted in the transition to commons-based societies.

Owing to their subversive approach, critical theories of the intellectual commons reveal vulnerabilities of an essence different to those exhibited in the other three families of commons theories analysed above. In terms of methodology, the majority of critical thinkers do not spend much energy supporting their intuitions with adequate empirical evidence. Furthermore, the intellectual commons and capital are often Manichaeistically conceived as polar opposites in their dialectic relationship, even though dialectical schemata between the two almost never take such simplified forms of direct juxtaposition and conflict. In addition, structuralist epistemological influences within certain critical viewpoints result in deterministic tendencies and a very thin conception of social subjectivity as casuistically generated by structural dynamics with limited capacity to counter-act. Indicative of such tendencies is the intuition of Hardt and Negri that the key to 'com[ing] out the other side' of capitalism is ultimately not the emancipatory potential of the forces of commonification but rather the internal contradictions of capital, which have to be pushed all the way through to their full materialisation in order for meta-capitalist societies to come into being (Hardt and Negri 2000, 218). Finally, post-structuralist influences lead certain intellectuals to introduce fuzzy terminologies, which are open to ideological regression. In this sense, 'immaterial' labour literally cannot exist, since even the most intellectually based labour materialises in specific forms (Caffentzis 2013 176–200).

Methodological vulnerabilities are inevitably reflected in the content of critical theories. The often Manichaean conception of social antagonism as solely taking place between the forces of labour and capital and the need to engage in a radical critique of existing social arrangements pushes critical intellectuals to focus more on the dominant pole of the dialectic (capital) and much less on alternatives embodied in the commons. As a corollary, critical perspectives of the intellectual commons generally fail to problematise over issues of collective action, organisation, coordination and consolidation related to communities of commoning and to engage in informed discourses regarding their shortcomings. Hence, political economic analysis centred on the intellectual commons themselves is rather scarce. On the other hand, no matter how much the categories of production and labour are conceptually stretched to cover all aspects of social activity and include them within the schemata of critical political economy, such an analytical framework still falls short of fully grasping the actuality of dynamics between contemporary forces and relations of social power. The conceptualisation of all social activity as reduced to the concept of labour is more attached to the reality pursued by capitalist dynamics rather than to anti-capitalist alternatives, thereby acting as a co-opted imaginary contributing to the commodification of ever more terrains of social activity.

The forking of critical theories over the debate of informationalism is also susceptible to ideological regression in relation to both of its expressions. In particular, the assumption that the informational forces of production have acquired centrality within social antagonism is as much an ideologically constructed perspective as the assumption that capitalist relations of production have remained exactly the same since their extensive penetration by the use of information and communication technologies. A more balanced approach should research and identify the specific changes that have taken place in production, distribution and consumption and the potentials that they open for anti-capitalist alternatives (Fuchs 2014, 151). The same balance should be kept in relation to conceptions about the ways that radical social change can take place. Both hypotheses on the subjective element of social counter-power – that it is solely produced either by the structural contradictions of capital or by social struggles – are ideologically loaded. Structural dynamics frame and condition collective social subjects but subversive subjectivities are ultimately forged within and through struggles, where their substratum, i.e. communal relations of solidarity and collaboration and alternative value systems, can actually come in to effect. Therefore, attempts to invent de novo political vanguards and propose roadmaps of transition to post-capitalist societies run counter to the historical experience of the past two centuries.

3.7. Conclusion

Far from forming a coherent and systematic theoretical body, theories of the intellectual commons offer a diversity of approaches to the object of their analysis. The following table compares the four distinct theoretical families analysed in this study and reveals the advantages and the shortcomings of each theoretical approach, thus providing insight on which element of each theory could appropriately contribute to a 'strong' theory of the intellectual commons.

In order to acquire substance and achieve impact, a strong theory of the intellectual commons should hold a critical perspective over existing social arrangements. Therefore, it ought to have solid normative foundations, not confined within the limitations of the status quo in the field but rather oriented towards what the current state of affairs should become. In this context, the normative horizon of such a theoretical endeavour stretches to nothing short of the realisation of the radical potential of the intellectual commons to fully unleash the productive forces of the social intellect. In addition, a strong theory of the intellectual commons should in principle analyse social phenomena not in isolation but rather within their social context and, hence, touch issues related to the interrelation between the intellectual commons and the social totality.

In this light, the fundamental choices regarding the categories of a strong theory of the intellectual commons ought to mindfully harvest the most appropriate elements of each theoretical approach according to the following criteria:

	Rational choice theories	Neoliberal theories	Social democratic theories	Critical theories
Epistemology	Rational choice institutionalism	Methodological individualism	Political economy	Critical political economy
Agency	Individual(s) in interdependent relations	Isolated individual(s)	Social individual(s)	Social intellect
Structure	Patterns of interactions	Market	Productive community	Community of struggle
Internal dynamics	Bottom-up emergence	Bottom-up emergence	Bottom-up/top-down emergence	n/a
External dynamics	n/a	Co-optation of commons by capital	Co-existence of commons with capital	Commons/capital antagonism and sublation
Normative criteria	Consequential	Utilitarian	Deontological (reformist)	Deontological (subversive)
Social change	The commons as patch to capital	The commons as fix to capital	The commons as substitute to the welfare state	The commons as alternative to capital

Table 3.5: Comparison of theories and approaches.
Source: Author

- Epistemology – The methodological choices that feature both a critical perspective and an examination of the intellectual commons as nested within the social totality are better represented in political economic approaches. Nonetheless, even such approaches tend to limit their scope of analysis within production. The social phenomena of the intellectual commons extend to modes of distribution and consumption and, along with production, transform forces and relations of wider social power. Hence, a strong theory of the intellectual commons needs an expansive and fundamentally transformed analytical framework, which will focus on social power itself and take into account the reproduction of society in its entirety.
- Agency and structure – Notwithstanding the importance of commoners as individual actors, reductionist individualist methodologies constantly fail to provide sufficient explanations for the bottom-up reproduction of the intellectual commons. Circular reciprocity encountered in robust productive communities and socio-wide modes of intellectual production/distribution/consumption pushes towards a shift from an exclusively individual to a collective conception of agency, taking also into account the presence of social forces. Along the same lines, structures ought to be dialectically analysed as contested terrains and processes in constant flux, where social forces interrelate, collide and lead to syntheses.
- Dynamics – Taking into account the influence of agency and structure in social systems, an inclusive analysis of the intellectual commons should view them as evolving through processes of both bottom-up and top-down reproduction. Nevertheless, such an analysis is partial if not accompanied by an exploration of the dynamics developed between the sphere of the intellectual commons and the social totality. Dominant social forces/relations decisively influence intellectual commons communities, and the latter counter-influence the former. The dialectics between the intellectual commons and capital impact both the processes of commoning and the wider social processes of reproducing the intellectual bases of society.
- As far as normative evaluations and their reflection on social change is concerned, the specific outcomes of the sublation between the intellectual commons and capital, as described by neoliberal and social democratic theorists, provide guidance as to which policy choices are each time implemented or omitted and which policy aims are each time promoted or rejected. Therefore, a strong theory of the intellectual commons should abstain from obfuscations in the form of technological or social determinism, search for the choices made and the forces backing them in the context of the intellectual commons and elaborate on proposals that fully exploit their potential in terms of the powers of the social intellect.

In alignment with the aim for a strong theory of the intellectual commons, heterodox theorists converge in their proposals to reinvent the rules that govern our networked information economies, by reforming intellectual property laws and by inventing policies that accommodate and embrace commons-based peer production. Hence, an integrated approach is gradually being formulated for a commons-oriented social and political programme capable, among others, of constructing an institutional ecology for the intellectual commons.

Nevertheless, the engagement with theoretical ventures over the intellectual commons needs to be attentive to the fact that the radical transformations mentioned above cannot be pushed forward purely by theorising. Instead, they presuppose tectonic shifts in the co-relations of power between incumbent economic forces and the emerging commoners' movements. Therefore, our transition to commons-based societies may only come as a result of social and political action. As the commons cannot be separated in their tangible/intangible expressions, in this project no division of labour between its intellectual and socio-political manifestations is possible. Participants can only be commoners of the mind as much as of the soul and body.

The current chapter has given an overall view of contemporary theories of the intellectual commons. Such theories have been evaluated from the standpoint of their approach to social change, which is represented by their conception of the social potential of the intellectual commons and their interrelation with capital. Critical tenets from each theory are utilised in the framework of the current study as the bedrock for the moral justification of an intellectual commons law. The next chapter offers a theorisation of the intellectual commons across history, by unfolding the evolution of the regulation of cultural commons from the Renaissance to postmodernity. Its aim is to examine in parallel, on the one hand, the importance of the commons for art and culture and, on the other hand, the discrepancy of their treatment under positive law. Given that, the purpose of the next chapter is to raise the argument for alternative modes of regulation, which will accommodate the potential of the intellectual commons in the digital age.

CHAPTER 4

Cultural Commons and the Law from the Renaissance to Postmodernity: A Case Study

4.1. Introduction

Throughout history, humanity's cultural endeavours have been characterised by collective practices of sharing and collaboration. From the advent of civilisation to the age of information and communication networks, the greatest achievements of art have resulted from collaborative creativity among many minds working together in community. Our cultural heritage, upon which any new cultural advancements are based, operates as an immense common pool resource, accumulated through the ages by the collective intellectual efforts of past generations. In general, cultural commons constitute the bedrock of human civilisation and lie at the core of socio-cultural reproduction.

Nonetheless, the greater the role that sharing and collaboration play in creativity, the more the prevalent perceptions and social institutions disregard their existence. Dominant historiographies of art primarily focus on the role of the individual, the commodity market and copyright law in modern and postmodern processes of intellectual production. Such perceptions of our past and present reinforce structural tendencies towards the enclosure and commodification of cultural resources. An alternative historical narrative from the perspective of the cultural commons aims to raise awareness of the fundamental role of the cultural community and the practices of sharing and collaboration in human creativity/inventiveness. Such a narrative brings the cultural commons and their importance for the contemporary networked information economy to the forefront of our attention.

The previous two chapters have revealed the ontological and epistemological perspectives of the intellectual commons. The present chapter unveils a

---

How to cite this book chapter:
Broumas, A. 2020. *Intellectual Commons and the Law: A Normative Theory for Commons-Based Peer Production*. Pp. 63–87. London: University of Westminster Press. DOI: https://doi.org/10.16997/book49.d. License: CC-BY-NC-ND

historical narrative of the communal, cooperative and sharing characteristics of artistic and cultural production, distribution and consumption. Viewed as a productive process, culture is in any historical era based on units of collaboration and structures of sharing. Furthermore, artistic expression is framed and conditioned by the structures that dominate its wider socio-historical context. These primarily refer to: (i) structures controlling access to resources and infrastructure necessary for the reproduction of the creative process, (ii) structures controlling the social diffusion and circulation of works of art, and (iii) legal institutions. Finally, the creative process is heavily influenced by dominant social perceptions regarding the role of the author within artistic production. Such a narrative does not approach its object of analysis, i.e. the forces and structures of the cultural commons, as clear-cut historical manifestations of a certain ideal-typical abstraction. Instead, it seeks for the historical manifestations of information, knowledge and cultural sharing and collaboration, which persistently pervade the reproduction of the cultural bases of society, and their penetration by countervailing forces and structures of enclosure, antagonism and control. The chapter is structured in three main parts, which, in the context of the cultural commons, consecutively examine the history of creativity and the evolution of its regulation as the outcome of the clash between forces of commonification and commodification. The current historical analysis commences from the Renaissance, which signifies the rise of the master artist and the emergence of commodity markets in art and culture, and stretches up to postmodern times. The chapter concludes with general observations and findings elicited from the historical tendencies revealed in its main body.

4.2. Cultural Commons and the Law in the Renaissance

During the Renaissance, folk art produced within cultural communities was central in the creative process. Furthermore, workshops embedded in cultural communities were the main units of artistic production (Hauser 1999, 18). Nevertheless, the fifteenth century was marked by a shift of demand for the employment of skill and the participation of renowned individual artists in art works (Baxandall 1972, 23). Traditional hierarchies within the workshop were thus gradually reconstructed on the basis of skill, with the talented artist elevated at the centre as master of the productive process and the cooperating craftsmen acting as 'assistants'. In reality, however, art works were produced through the collective work of multiple craftsmen. Even though art works produced in workshops were normally signed by their masters, many of them were a product of collaboration between the master and his assistants and pupils (Tummers 2008, 38). All in all, artistic production remained a chiefly cooperative process until the nineteenth century (Heinich 2001, 112). In the context of authorship, the copying, collating and reworking of preceding forms, methods, styles and techniques dominated the creative process. Authors built their creative contributions in close relation to prior works of authorship in their genre (Woodmansee 1994, 17). Likewise, in relation to music, the great composers of classical music systematically borrowed from each other and appropriated the folk music of their era (Meconi 2004).[16] From such a perspective, the archetype of the Renaissance artist is William Shakespeare. Rather than being the epitome of original genius, Shakespeare was not the actual originator of the plots of most of his plays. Instead, he could best be described as a 'reteller of tales', undoubtedly a brilliant one, whose tales were evidently derived from history, mythology, folk culture and prior art (Rose 1993, 122).[17]

In the Renaissance, artisanship was organised in guilds, as in the Middle Ages. Nevertheless, the diffusion and expansion of commerce across borders and the subsequent emergence of mercantile capital led to transformations in intellectual production and distribution (Zukerfeld and Yansen 2016, 211). Medieval guildship was formalised, consolidated and solidified, while the guild form of organisation was also expanded to trade groups emerging within artistic distribution, such as those of printers and publishers. The guild system became interrelated with political institutions through the ratification of its internal rules by public authorities, their enforcement by state sanctions and the granting of privileges by the ruling aristocracy to its members (Merges 2004b, 12). Hence, throughout the Renaissance the source of regulatory power over the creative practice gradually shifted from the guild and the Church to the political authority and from social/associative norms to state laws. In addition, the sixteenth century marks the dawn of the modern institution of the academy. The rise of the academy and the university in arts and science signifies a break with the tradition of keeping knowledge secret, which thrived under the control of religious institutions and guilds, and promotes the transformation of knowledge into a universal commons (David 2005), produced on the basis of a communistic ethos (Merton 1979). The academy was founded as an educational institution for the tutelage of new entrants in the artisanship (Pevsner 2014, 44–47). Thereafter, the institution of the academy gradually became a central mechanism in the framing of sharing artistic knowledge and in the control over the orientation and evolution of creative practice.

In the Renaissance, patronage emerged as a novel structure of power within the reproduction of the creative practice, setting the outer limits of its expression (Wackernagel 1938). Members of the aristocracy and the upcoming wealthy bourgeoisie channelled their accumulated social surplus to the reproduction of artistic activity in the form of financial aid, material resources and social privileges to their protégés. In exchange, they received symbolic power bestowed by the aesthetic value of the works of art, which were produced through their aid. Even the feudal state was engaged in acts of patronage, which took the form of honoraria, i.e. financial grants or stipends as rewards to esteemed artists within its jurisdiction for their service to the state (Rose 1993, 17). As a corollary, the emerging figure of the patron gave rise to the master, a thin upper class of artists, which distinguished itself from guilded artisanship in terms of both creative innovation and financial rewards. Works of art produced through the patronage system greatly reflected in their form and content the interests and world views of the social classes, to which patrons belonged (Antal 1986). Patrons intervened heavily in the productive process to the extent of ordering the colours to be used and the form of the figures depicted (Baxandall 1972, 11).

The sixteenth century signified groundbreaking technological and social transformations in the reproduction of artistic activity. By 1500, the emerging forces of capital had adapted the printing press to the needs of mass production and, thus, transformed the fixation of works of authorship into a great industry (Febvre and Jean-Martin 2010, 186–187). Whereas social perceptions of books as divine gifts insusceptible to absolute private appropriation persevered from the prior age of book barter (Davis 1983, 87), the social diffusion of books was being rapidly metamorphosed into a large-scale commodity market. From the sixteenth century onwards, the capitalist printer/publisher became the dominating mediator in the field of artistic production, distribution and consumption. In the late Renaissance, the tendencies of commodification were also reinforced by the gradual demise of the feudal system and the rise of a wealthy class of merchants and small industry owners, who increased demand and correspondingly expanded the nascent commodity market of art (Bourdieu 1993, 112–113). As a result, a parallel commodified system of distribution appeared alongside the social reproduction of culture as an inclusive part of community life through folk culture, folk art and the exchange of artefacts in local markets, which covered everyday cultural needs. Such a market of commodities rendered possible the exchange of fixated art between buyers and sellers of creative activity and stabilised the private appropriation of cultural artefacts.

The impact of mercantile capital and the subsequent commodification was not only confined to the transformation of social relations and the shift of social power in the production, distribution and consumption of art. Forces of commodification in combination with ideological forces also changed social perceptions over the relation of the artist with her work. The Protestant reformation and its demands for individual responsibility, self-discipline on earth and the non-dogmatic studying of the holy books accentuated the ethical value of personal autonomy. The authority of established communal entities, such as the Church, the municipality and the commons, were brought into question, whereas emergent political and economic institutions, such as the nation state and the commodity market, gained in importance. As the concept that social reproduction could be more efficiently governed by the autonomous economic activity of citizens under the rule of centralised nation states acquired political representation, law and politics gradually shifted their point of reference to the individual (De Moor 2013, 85). Hence, an amalgam of political centralisation and economic liberalization set in motion by social transformations in late Renaissance societies began to weaken communities and strengthen individualism. These changes had a radical impact on the social perceptions regarding artistic activity. The rise of the master marked the beginning of a process of differentiation between the social status of artisanship, which was considered to belong to the domain of manual work, and art, which was perceived as intellectual and spiritual work of a higher social value (Becker 2008, 353–354). In the late Renaissance, the rising social value of originality in art works increased the importance of creative innovation in the productive process. As a result, in the seventeenth century the individual artist started to be viewed as the main source of artistic production and her creative contribution as crucial for any kind of artistic activity (Hauser 1999, 23).

In terms of regulation through social norms, the relation between publishers and authors was determined by the custom of the honorarium, according to which publishers offered financial rewards to authors, whose works they printed and traded. Honoraria often took the form of contracts between publishers and authors. Yet, even though authors were considered to own private property rights over their unpublished manuscripts as physical objects, such rights did not extend to the texts engraved on them (Rose 1993, 9). Hence, instead of being founded on common law or statute, honoraria were gradually developed as trade norms grounded on the necessity to sustain the material reproduction of authors and, accordingly, literary production and the publishing industry. Overall, the honorarium was a normative and economic institution not backed by state sanctions, which, like patronage, served the aim of the physical reproduction of authors' works.

In terms of regulation through law, the feudal state intervened at the mediatory level of distribution, in order to achieve censorship and control of the creative expression and, secondarily, in order to correspond to powerful private interests and regulate art trade (De Sola Pool 1983, 16–17). State regulation of the creative practice thus took the form of state-granted privileges to individuals or collectivities. Such privileges were chiefly issued by the sovereign as horizontal concessions to printer/publisher guilds for the regulation of book trade and the competition with neighbouring feudal states (Goldstein 2003, 33–34). Only in exceptional and rare cases were privileges assigned as vertical benefits to individual artists for their services to the well-being of the community (Bugbee 1967, 45; Rose 1993, 10). Privileges were exclusive monopoly rights to print works of authorship for limited periods of time within the geographical jurisdiction of the sovereign entity granting the privilege. They were granted on an ad hoc and case-by-case basis and as a discretionary policy choice of the sovereign, as opposed to general standardised legal rights under the rule of law 'conferring a uniform set of entitlements whenever predefined criteria were fulfilled' (Bracha 2004, 180–181).

The flourishment of commerce in the region of Venice boosted the economic role of private property and, gradually, gave birth to the institutional imaginary of private enclosures over intangible goods. The first privilege, which was issued in 1469 by the Venetian Senate, was actually a predecessor of the institution of patents, since it conferred the monopoly over the art of printing itself for a term of five years to the German printer John of Speyer, the person who introduced the printing technology to the city (Mandich 1960, 381). Only five years later, on 19 March 1474, the institutional practice of granting privileges in the Republic of Venice was consolidated in the enactment of the Venetian Patent Statute. Being a triumph of mercantile capital, the latter constituted not only the first patent institution in the world but also the first statute that in general granted monopoly rights over products of the intellect. In the sixteenth century, variations of the Venetian printing privileges spread to most European states with significant printing industries, such as the Netherlands and Germany. Yet, it was chiefly in England that privileges were gradually transformed into an integrated system of industrial regulation and censorship implemented by the guild and sanctioned by the sovereign. Even though the Crown continued to assign printing patents on a separate basis, in 1557 the royal charter of incorporation granted to the Stationers' Company, i.e. the publishers' guild of London, the monopoly on book production (Rose 1993, 12). According to the by-laws of the guild, once one of its members asserted ownership of a text, no other member was entitled to publish it within the territory of England (Paterson 1968 46–64). Through state enforcement the guild was thus able to administer the distribution of works of authorship, indirectly determine power relations between authors and publishers, and orient the creative practice towards the logic of the commodity market. The monopoly over book printing was combined with censorship of the creative practice. From the Injunctions of 1559 to the Licensing Act of 1662, with the exception of the Interregnum, all books had to be licensed by the state before entering into circulation, and the Stationers were legally empowered to seize unauthorised books and bring offenders before authorities. As Paul Goldstein has written, '[t]he Stationers got the economic rewards of monopoly; in return, the Crown got from the Stationers a ruthlessly efficient enforcer of the censorship' (Goldstein 2003, 33–34).

In conclusion, the Renaissance artist was an artist in collaboration with preceding and contemporary creators and a collator of prior and contemporary cultural artefacts. Both the form and the content of works of art was greatly determined by dominant social perceptions and the influence of powerful actors in artistic production, distribution and consumption. The artist was still considered an artisan, yet the demand for aesthetic value created a new class of master artists with upgraded social status. In parallel, the rise of the book trade begun to shift perceptions over the commodification of knowledge, as art was for the first time seen as a source of valorisation by the nascent forces of capital. The combination of printing technology and industrialisation raised the need of sovereigns to control and censor printed works of authorship. These two fundamental factors led to the introduction of state licences for printing and to the granting of private monopolies over the printing of works of authorship. In accordance with the foregoing

Unit of collaboration	Structures of sharing	Forces controlling access to resources	Structures controlling distribution	Perception of the author	Normative framework
Workshop, individual artist as contributor to the creative process	Guilds, academies	Patron, publisher (after the sixteenth century)	Exchange markets/ commodity markets	Artisan, master	Honorarium, privilege

Table 4.1: The framework of creativity in the Renaissance.
Source: Author

analysis, the above table summarises the main elements framing creativity during the Renaissance.

4.3. Cultural Commons and the Law in Modernity

The era of modernity is characterised by the prevalence of the perception of the Promethean artist,[18] i.e. the perception of artists as exceptionally creative individuals, who 'craft out of thin air, and intense, devouring labor, an Appalachian Spring, a Sun Also Rises, a Citizen Kane' (Goldstein 1991, 110). In modernity, individualistic perceptions over the creative process became naturalised and their dominance was projected as the natural state of art and culture throughout history (Foucault 1979, 141, 159). Nevertheless, the notion of the Promethean artist ran counter to the inherently collective and collaborative character of the creative process, which persevered in all artistic forms throughout modernity. Contrary to the Promethean ideal-type, art continued to be the outcome of knowledge sharing and collaboration between multiple creators, past and present. Folk art produced within communities continued to be the cultural base and the source of inspiration whence artists and creative industries derived the raw materials for their creative practice. Popular musical traditions, such as folk, jazz and rock, emerged and grew as artistic commons of sharing and adaptation within communities of musicians in constant dialogue to wider cultural communities (Seeger 1993; Hobsbawm 1961). In addition, both the artistic personality of individual authors and their works of art were strongly influenced by the socio-historical context of modernity. Thus, artistic production in modernity not only reflected the social conditions of its era (Lukács 1974; Weber 1958) but also contributed to the reproduction of the modernistic project towards conventional or alternative trajectories (Klingender 1947; Adorno 1991, 1992, 2002). Pablo Picasso can be considered more than anyone else to be the archetype of the modern artist owing to his multifarious talent and immense influence on the evolution of the visual arts. Yet, far from adhering to the ideal-type of the Promethean artist creating out of thin air, Picasso systematically appropriated shapes, styles and techniques from prior artistic traditions, such as tribal art,[19] and was clearly influenced from great artists of the past, such as Velazquez, Goya and Rembrandt, and from his contemporary fellow artists, such as Henri Toulouse-Lautrec, Paul Cézanne and Edvard Munch. Furthermore, Picasso collaborated with Georges Braque in the co-evolution of the art movement of cubism (Lucie-Smith 1986, 34). In addition, Picasso is considered the inventor of constructed sculpture and co-inventor of collage, both of them artistic techniques that are mainly based on the appropriation of existing material objects and their composition and transformation into works of art. In his words, '[w]hen there's anything to steal, I steal' (Picasso 1993, 53). Finally, in contrast to the social perception of the Promethean artist creating in introspective isolation, Picasso was allegedly a social and political being and, therefore, social events and political beliefs left an indelible mark upon his art and personal life.

The rise of the social perception of the Promethean artist coincided with a contrasting cooperative tendency in the actual relations of artistic production. Modern art was characterised by the reinvention of collective productive practices, centred on the art movement and the creative factory. As the development of individual artistic consciousness and the social emphasis on originality gradually destabilised prior nuclei of production, such as the artisanal workshop, individual artists begun to establish novel modes of sharing, pooling together and reworking the achievements of their creativity. In modernity, creative innovation was thus reinvented as a collective endeavour and the art movement became its main vehicle. As a result, the metamorphoses of art during the nineteenth century and the first half of the twentieth century were strongly determined by individual artists participating in wider art collectivities and movements with common genres, styles and techniques (Lucie-Smith 1986). The artistic and literary movements of neoclassicism, romanticism, realism, impressionism and post-impressionism revolutionised nineteenth-century art. The surge of collective artistic activity during the first half of the twentieth century ignited more than 70 major art movements, such as Fauvism, German expressionism, cubism, futurism, the Vienna and Paris schools, realism, Dada, surrealism and Bauhaus. Circulation of knowledge among artists was taking place both by the formal means of exhibitions and by informal means, i.e. in artists' workshops and in artistic and literary public meeting places (Rittner, Scott-Haine and Jackson 2016). To exchange views and ideas, share knowledge and collaborate towards current artistic problems and common causes, the nineteenth-century Parisian bohèmes met at Café Guerbois (Tinterow and Loyrette 1994, 314), Italian futurists at Le Giubbe Rosse, Gilli and Caffè Paszkowski in Florence (Livorni 2009) and Dadaists at the Cabaret Voltaire in Zurich (Sandqvist 2006). Geographical proximity played a major role in the establishment of art groups that collaborated in the production of common projects and exhibitions, such as the Dutch neoplasticist 'De Stijl', the German expressionist 'Die Brucke' and 'Der Blaue Reiter' and the Moscow avant-garde 'Jack of Diamonds'. Often, these shared world views were expressed and shaped by acts of self-determination in the form of art manifestos, such as Gustave Courbet's 1855 realist manifesto, Jean Moréas's 1886 symbolist manifesto, Filippo Tommaso Marinetti's 1909 futurist manifesto, Albert Gleizes's and Jean Metzinger's 1912 'Du Cubiste', Kazimir Malevich's 1915 suprematist manifesto, Ugo Ball's 1916 Dada manifesto and André Breton's 1924 surrealist manifesto. Apart from the commonality of forms and styles, the collective and socialised character of modern artistic production was also evident in the common identity that art movements constructed and represented, which either overtly or tacitly functioned in the form of an avant-garde of radical critique and renewal in relation to the artistic and social status quo of their era (Poggioli 1968, 16–41; Jencks 1990).

Modernity was characterised by the Industrial Revolution and the subsequent transition from the domination of mercantile to industrial capital. As a result, by the end of the nineteenth century and, especially, during the twentieth century various fields and practices of artistic production were transformed into full-fledged industries. In these industries, creativity was practised collectively and begun to approximate the factory-form of organisation (Adorno and Horkheimer 2002, 94–96). Owing to the unique characteristics of the resource of creative labour, which was the most important input in its productive process, the creative factory was since its inception an idiosyncratic factory-form based on the innovativeness of labourers rather than the formulaic manual repetition of artistic expression encountered in the earlier unit of the ancient and medieval workshop. A combination of technological, social, economic and cultural factors, such as the invention of film and television, the establishment of a middle class in the global North, the rise of consumerism, increased leisure time and levels of literacy and the mediation of entertainment by the commodity market expanded the commodification of art and established the basis for the mass production of symbolic goods and services (Hesmondhalgh 2002). In this context, individual artistic practice was first professionalised (Bourdieu 1995, 54–55) and then set within a wider organisational framework of industrialised cultural production based on the cooperation between multiple artists, the rationalised division of creative labour and the pooling together of talent and creativity under the rule of capital (Becker 2008, 2). Within the creative factory artists were transformed into wage labourers subject to the extraction of surplus value, the intellectual property of art works produced was as a rule automatically transferred to employers by virtue of statutory provisions and their extensive reproduction and distribution led to the mass consumption of commodity art and the rise of popular culture (Miege 1979, 1989; Garnham 1990). As a corollary, the consolidation of the creative factory resulted in an increased socialisation of the productive process of art, albeit one in which artistic expression was framed and conditioned by novel social powers and hierarchies.

Throughout modernity, already-established structures of cultural sharing, such as the academy and the guild, faced significant challenges, whereas novel structures emerged, such as the exhibition, the library and the museum. The consolidation of art commodity markets and the industrialisation of cultural production under the rule of capital undermined the workshop form of production and displaced the erstwhile dominant artisan guilds. The eighteenth century signified the domination of art by academic dogma (Pevsner 2014, 173). The royal academies in France and England became the incumbent institutions for the regulation and control of artistic activity by the state. Nevertheless, the academisation of art and the inherent hostility of the academic system against innovation and change constructed a rigid framework for the freedom of artistic expression. Such rigidity was disputed and surpassed, on the one hand, by artists themselves through the development of art movements, such as romanticism, which countered dominant academic perceptions about art, and, on the other hand, by the dynamism of art commodity markets. After the end of the seventeenth century academies in various countries began to organise public art exhibitions. In France, the members of the Académie des Beaux-Arts organised such non-commercial exhibitions, called 'salons', so as to circumvent the self-imposed prohibition of exhibiting their works for sale. Even though prizes were insignificant,[20] awards for artists competing in salons opened access to the art commodity market (White and White 1965, 27–43). In the nineteenth century, salons acquired an international aspect through their interaction with the novel institution of international industrial expositions. As an institution freely open to the public and widely popular, salons became the main structures for the social diffusion of visual arts and the popularisation of dominant and alternative aesthetics. Artistic and literary perceptions and modes of sharing were also determined by public museums and libraries. Museums emerged in the fifteenth century from the desire of wealthy patrons and art collectors, such as the Medici family in Florence, to emphasise their superior social status by opening their private collections to the public (Hooper-Greenhill 1992, 24, 47–49). Yet, the museum acquired its modern public form only in the late eighteenth and early nineteenth centuries with the opening of the Louvre museum to the public by the 1789 revolution. The museums became institutions central for the sharing of historical knowledge and, subsequently, for popular cultural education (Bennett 1995, 19–20). Open access to cultural heritage and knowledge was also facilitated during the nineteenth century by the transformation of libraries into public institutions, i.e. institutions freely open to the public and funded by public or non-profit sources.[21] The humanitarian and democratic ethos of the time strongly pushed towards the universal free access of the citizenry to information, knowledge and literature (Ditzion 1947). As access to education increased and levels of literacy were gradually raised, public libraries played a great role in the access of lower classes to knowledge resources.

Throughout modernity, the central role of cultural sharing in modes of artistic production, distribution and consumption was evident in the spatial concentration of artistic activity and the formation of cultural centres. Nineteenth-century urbanisation led to the reproduction of a public space open to aesthetic and intellectual sharing, association and cooperation on common cultural projects and artistic expression. In this urban public space, informal and formal structures of sharing and collaboration accumulated, converged and produced cultural centres and capitals (O'Connor 2011, 42). Through this social process, London and, of course, Paris gradually became the major poles of attraction for the social forces of cultural production and their mediating structures, thus rising as the incontestable cultural capitals of modernity (Newman 2009), whereas New York emerged as the definite cultural metropolis after the first half of the twentieth century (Kaufmann 2004, 161). Hence, the modernistic mode of artistic production, distribution and consumption was geographically expressed in a division between cultural centres and peripheries and the interrelation between them strongly determined the cartography and the orientation of artistic activity, at least until the emergence of post-industrial information and communication networks (Castelnuovo 1989).

Artistic activity in the modern era was determined by the gradual abatement of artists' dependence on patronage and by the loosening of the overt control from political/religious powers over the creative practice (Bourdieu 1993, 112). Artists were freed from the various constraints existing under feudalism, communal bonds and guild artisanship, yet they became also free to sell nothing other than their creative work as labour in commodity markets at prices imposed by capital. By being engulfed in the structural power of commodity markets, artists were increasingly influenced in the practice of their creativity by capital's inherent tendency for profit maximisation (Bourdieu 1995, 49). Whether as wage labourers in the creative industries or as independent professionals within art commodity markets, creators were forced to adhere to the limitations posed by capital on their creativity, so as to be able to sell their power of creativity and access the resources necessary for their physical and artistic reproduction (Vazquez 1973, 84). Nation states with developed art commodity markets enacted copyright laws in order to regulate the relevant industrial sectors and outcompete other states in the regional and, later, global division of labour. In this way, states became motors for the facilitation of processes of commodification in the field of art. Conversely, during the twentieth century, states acquired a more active role as collective patrons of the arts within their boundaries. Hence, ministries of culture were established and public funding was used as an instrument to encourage artistic production. After the eighteenth century, technological developments along with social and political transformations resulted in the domination of commodity markets over all other social institutions for the social diffusion of art. The capitalist industries of art distribution pushed forward for the development of iron-frame printing presses, which further accelerated the mass production of fixated works of literature (James 1976, 17). In the twilight of the twentieth century, novel inventions, such as photograph and film, facilitated mass fixation and reproduction of visual and performing art, thus making the latter susceptible to extensive commodification (Nesbit 1987, 235–237). In parallel, the nineteenth century signified the emergence of the new wealthy middle classes, which boosted the consumption of art via commodity markets (White and White 1965, 78–82). Finally, legal institutions in the form of copyright laws reflected and reinforced the forces of commodification in art. At the same time, law had a counter-influencing constitutive effect on societies, by forging the art commodity as the dominant form of the modern work of art and by projecting the Promethean individual artist as the prevalent subject in artistic production (Coombe 2011, 81). All these developments jointly transformed both the creative practice and the power relations in artistic production and distribution in a non-linear manner.

On the one hand, the industrialisation of artistic production and, on the other hand, the increasing commodification of the distribution of art were also reflected on legal institutions. Processes of industrialisation and commodification brought the privilege regime of the Renaissance to an end and pushed for its replacement by copyright law. The rupture with the old trade regulation of privileges and the birth of copyright was first marked by the 1710 Statute of Anne in England.[22] At that time, the Stationers' monopoly over book printing and its adverse effects on the freedom of expression came increasingly under fire both by artists and statesmen (Goldstein 2003, 33). Simultaneously, authors started openly defending their interests by asserting natural rights of ownership over their works.[23] Under such pressure, the 1662 Licensing Act,[24] which expired in 1694, was never renewed by the House of Commons. When their petition for the extension of the privilege system of censorship failed, the powerful Stationers' Company called for a legal recognition of their incumbent interests on the grounds of a natural right of authors' ownership over their works (Deazley 2004, 31–50). Similar arguments related to Lockean justifications of ownership over intellectual works based on authors' labour were invoked by the Paris Publishers' Guild during the eighteenth century, so as to bring their trade monopolies under state protection (Hesse 1990, 112, 122–123). Hence, forces of commodification significantly contributed to the birth of the modern individualistic conceptualisation of the creative process. In England, this conflictual and contradictory process led to the enaction of the Statute of Anne. The new legislation signified a tectonic shift in the regulation of artistic creativity. Before 1710, authors' interests were invoked in order to legitimise publishers' monopolies (Peifer 2010, 351). After 1710, the author was established as a legally empowered figure and the modern conception of authorship was engraved in the law (Rose 1993, 4). The statute also freed artistic expression and the flow of art commodities from the restraints of state censorship, which was exerted through the prior system of privileges (Lessig 2004, 85–94). Yet, the fundamental transformation in the new system of regulation was the subjection of private monopolies over intellectual works to the rule of law and its explicit orientation towards serving the public interest (Lunney 2001, 813–818). Whereas prior Licensing Acts grounded the justification of privileges on the private welfare of national publishers' guilds, the nascent copyright legislation granted private monopolies for 'the encouragement of learning'.[25] Furthermore, whereas the prior regime was exploited for the assignment of printing privileges of unlimited scope, in its vote to enact the Statute of Anne Parliament refused to recognise a natural right of ownership upon ideas.[26] Instead, the statute established private monopolies over intellectual works, which were subject to limitations imprinted in statutory provisions.

The advent and evolution of copyright laws has been a process of rationalisation in the regulation of cultural production, distribution and consumption through formality, codification and the acquisition of an abstract, impartial and impersonal form (Weber 1978). Through this process of rationalisation, case-specific and discretionary privileges were transformed into general standardised legal rights according to predefined statutory criteria and subject to purposes of public interest. The clearly delineated scope of protection and the powerful ideological justification of copyright law set robust preconditions for the diffusion of functional commodity markets in the commons of the intellect. Hence, the transition from the privilege regime to copyright law signifies a process of rationalisation and consolidation of the private enclosures of the social intellect. Before the end of the eighteenth century, pieces of copyright legislation were passed in key industrialised countries. In the 1790s, the United States Constitution was amended, so as to incorporate the recognition of a fundamental right of private monopoly over intellectual works, and the first US copyright act was enacted.[27] The French equivalent of droits d'auteur was enacted in 1793 by the revolution (Nesbit 1987, 230–233; Hesse 1990, 127–130). Simultaneously, a series of copyright laws were passed in various German states (Woodmansee 1984, 445). Overall, the emerging modern copyright law employed an individualistic notion of authorship, which constituted the figure of the ingenious Promethean artist as the archetype of creativity and ideologically reconstructed artistic production as a solitary non-collaborative engagement disconnected from its dependence on the intellectual commons (Jaszi 1991). The juridical notion of the Promethean artist as a legal subject having the right to own her work and being free to transfer her property through contract in the market reflected the social relations in the art commodity market and facilitated the circulation of art commodities (Fisher 1999, 12–13). The legal form was, however, not only reflective of the relations in the commodity art market. The recognition of the Promethean artist in law also defined the nature of the creative practice, by classifying artists as individual property owners of their creative skills and as sellers of their works of art in the form of commodities within the unequal power relations of the art commodity market (Pashukanis 1978). Still, the statutory recognition of private monopolies over cultural works was counter-balanced by explicit limitations grounded on public interest objectives, an outcome that reflected in itself the correlations of power between forces of commodification/commonification at the time. Such correlations were, though, ultimately framed by copyright law, which disabled practices of commoning and empowered the capitalist mode of cultural production, distribution and consumption through sanctioning and legitimisation.

The history of copyright law is an expression of the dialectics between the enclosing power of industrial capital over the products of the social intellect and the opposite need for the ideological justification of such enclosures in the name of the public interest. Yet, in the course of the nineteenth and, especially, twentieth centuries, and as the commercialisation of culture shifted correlations of power in favour of the forces of commodification and against the social practices of commoning (Bollier 2008, 44–50), the balance, which guaranteed the prevalence of the public interest in policy choices related to copyright, gradually ceased to be sustainable. The theoretical dichotomy between ideas and their expressive fixations tended to liquify, as copyright protection was evoked to protect the market value of increasingly abstract and elusive intellectual assets (Bracha 2008, 238). By being influenced from moral justifications related to the labour theory of copyright and 'sweat of the brow' arguments, the threshold of originality was interpreted, more often than not, to reflect evaluations related to the significance of the private investment for the production of intellectual works as eligibility criterion for enclosure (Bracha 2008, 201). The scope of copyright protection followed a trend of consistent expansion, approximating a status of Blackstonian property-ness (Fisher 1999, 1–4; Lessig 2002a, 108–110, 250). And, in the twentieth century, the increase in the extension of the term of copyright protection accelerated at an unprecedented pace (Patry 2009, 67–68). Finally, the 'work-for-hire' doctrine, which spread in countries with powerful creative industries during the first half of the twentieth century, ensured the alienability and, thus, the unencumbered flow of art commodities within markets. In this case, the ideological function of law, as expressed in the copyright theory of authorship, was bypassed and absorbed by the prevalent social function of commodification, as exhibited in the recognition of the transfer of copyright ownership from creative workers to their employers (Bracha 2008, 189–190). In conclusion, notwithstanding significant instances of resistance, the general tendency of modern copyright law was to expand its subject matter and scope to any usage of information, knowledge and culture worth appropriating for its exchange value in commodity markets and to facilitate the commodification of art and culture. Hence, despite its various forms and internal contradictions, with the rise and consolidation of market-based societies modern copyright evolved to finally become a unified family of monopoly theories of the social intellect. Since then, monopoly theories set the political and institutional landscape in these issues, having internalised both the orthodoxy of enclosure and its inherent contradictions in a unified theory of property over intellectual works.

In conclusion, the forces, structures and ideologies conditioning creativity in modernity took the forms set out in the following table:

Unit of collaboration	Structures of sharing	Forces controlling access to resources	Structures controlling distribution	Perception of the author	Normative framework
Art movement/ creative factory	Academies, libraries, exhibitions, museums, cultural capitals	State, capital	Commodity markets	Promethean artist	Copyright

Table 4.2: The framework of creativity in modernity.
Source: Author

Overall, modernity was marked by a fundamental contradiction between the actual practices of artistic production and the regulation of creativity. The more art and culture became dependent on collective practices of sharing and collaboration, the more social institutions intervened to regulate the creative process according to the individualistic perception of the Promethean artist and, thus, reinforce cycles of private appropriation and commodification.[28] Yet, no matter how contradictory the modern epoch proved to be, this tendency did not reach its apogee before the coming of the postmodern historical condition.

4.4. Cultural Commons and the Law in Postmodernity

The postmodern era signifies the centrality of informational capital in production and the generalised penetration of the cultural commons by processes of commodification in distribution and consumption of intangible resources, i.e. the expansion of commodities, market exchange and monetary values to most facets of cultural reproduction. Hence, postmodernity marks the 'extension of the power of the market over the whole range of cultural production' (Harvey 1989, 62). Furthermore, the generalisation of commodification and the rise of consumer culture have resulted in the 'prodigious expansion of culture throughout the social realm, to the point at which everything in our social life [...] can be said to have become "cultural"' (Jameson 1991, 48). In postmodern times, intangible goods have acquired principal importance in capitalist production, the cultural industries have global reach and everyday life is permeated by cultural commodities. In this social context, culture has acquired materiality to such an extent that it has rendered the dichotomy between the base and the superstructure redundant (Lash and Lury 2007). In this sense, postmodernity deepens and multiplies the tendencies and contradictions of modernity. It thus constitutes the master narrative of modernity, rather than marking a socio-historical discontinuity with the latter (De Angelis 2007, 214). Yet, postmodernity also marks extensive transformations in co-relations of power between capital and the commons. The decentralisation of the creative practice and the construction of multiple cultural identities across society is claimed to open possibilities for cultural declassification, democratisation and de-Westernisation (Featherstone 2007, 16–20, 139–140). In the latter sense, there arises the potential for alternative commons-based practices of social reproduction, including the potential for the expansion of the cultural commons.

The turn of the twenty-first century finds the dominant mode of cultural production consolidated in the form of concentrated and internationalised cultural industries, as a sector of the increasingly dominant informational capital. Human creativity in the postmodern cultural industry is hierarchically organised in the form of creative labour and aggregated in the creative factory. The latter is the main unit of informationalised cultural production and the locus where creative labour is pooled together, organised through sophisticated techniques for the division of labour, conjoined with digital communications machinofacture and valorised by informational capital to produce cultural artefacts on a massive scale. The organisation of work under informational capital is based on 'the polyvalent complementarity of different lots of knowledge collectively mobilised by workers in order to achieve a productive goal' (Fumagalli et al. 2019, 46). Hence, creative labour is a social relation reproduced within the assemblage of the creative factory, the frame, organisation and everyday actuality of which are preceded, established and determined by the social power of capital. Far from pertaining to the ideological abstraction of the solitary Promethean artist, the figure of the postmodern creative labourer constitutes the subjective element immersed in the wider social relations that synthesise the capitalist mode of cultural production (Lazzarato 2014, 25–29). The relations of production in the creative factory are inherently machinic, i.e. composed of humans and machines, and socialised, i.e. based on sharing and collaboration among multiple artists. In the cultural industries, work acquires forms of horizontal coordination and creative expression becomes a collective and collaborative process taking place within the organisational framework of capital. It could thus be claimed that artistic production has never before been a process of collective endeavour to such an extent. And, yet, the socialisation of artistic production in the cultural industries is distorted by the inherent contradictions of the capitalist mode of production. Access to, sharing and use of prior art are severely limited by contemporary intellectual property laws. Collaboration among artists both within and between industrial units of cultural production is mired in competition. Corporate hierarchies fail to provide the social climate of unrestrained inspiration, in which human creativity may thrive and achieve its full potential.

In this contradictory context arises the postmodern figure of the celebrity artist. It is in itself a social relation, which constitutes at the same time a factory and a commodity. Its archetype, Andy Warhol, vividly depicts its characteristics. Andy Warhol's studio from 1962 to 1968 was purportedly named the 'Factory', in order to associate its artistic production with industrial manufacture. The Factory brought together multiple artists, who worked on Warhol's projects under his supervision and mass-produced handmade copies of cultural artefacts. Even though artistic production in the Factory was a collective and communal process (Watson 2003), its output was solely attributed to the celebrity artist himself. In addition, Andy Warhol became a pop icon, marketising and valorising on his eccentric personality, artistic style, social life and image. In line with its archetype, the postmodern figure of the artist is a hypercommodified simulation of the modern Promethean artist. It is a commercial enterprise, which has the 'person' celebrity artist as its point of reference in order to valorise on both the latter's artistic innovations and popular image in industrial mode. The simulacrum of the celebrity artist exploits and, at the same time, reinforces the social and legal infrastructures which still reproduce the ideology of the Promethean artist, so as to capture value and extract profit.

Contradictions in the dominant mode of postmodern cultural production produce centrifugal tendencies in cultural expression. The digitisation of prior art and the social diffusion of the means for artistic production and mass self-communication have created the material and social conditions for the rise of commons-based peer production in art and culture (Benkler 2006, 285–296). In this alternative mode of production, networks of peers physically or electronically join their creative forces in order to share information, knowledge and culture, collaborate and practise their collective cultural expression. Hence, commons-based peer-produced art and culture is the outcome of a communal process, in which peers collectively construct common meanings, aesthetics, techniques and practices through repetitive patterns of sharing and collaboration. The unit of commons-based peer production is the productive community, which takes its particular form in the horizontal and decentralised peer-to-peer collectivity. Peer-to-peer collectivities connect together, share information, knowledge and culture and collaborate through techno-social peer-to-peer networks. Peer-to-peer collectivities are claimed to generate an alternative participatory culture, which has relatively lower barriers to artistic expression and higher degrees of civic engagement than those encountered in the dominant forms of commodified culture (Jenkins et al. 2009, 5–6). The appropriation of real objects and pre-existing works of art and their mix through techniques of reworking, collation and derivation are core characteristics of the creative practices of peer-to-peer collectivities (Lessig 2008, 51–83). Commoners within these collective entities also use techniques of bricolage by utilising common materials available in their environment and by combining them in original aesthetic uses and meanings in order to create new cultural identities (Hebdige 2003, 102–106). Often, peer-to-peer collectivities employ techniques of détournement in order to convey their cultural and political messages to wider audiences.[29] These techniques involve the reuse of mainstream cultural artefacts, such as corporate logos, in variations laden with meanings that are antagonistic to their original cultural and social use (Dery 2010).

The canvas of the emerging peer-to-peer collectivities is the public space. Either in cyberspace or on the urban terrain, or even with the use of both these domains, peer-to-peer collectivities engage in the production of a participatory folk art and culture, which circulates and is pooled as a commons. Do-it-yourself culture, mix culture, mashup art, culture jamming, graffiti art, ephemeral art, openly accessible user-generated cultural content, works of art licensed under copyleft licences, internet and urban cultures and memes and, generally, all contemporary non-commodified and openly accessible forms of cultural expression constitute a kaleidoscope of sharing, collective creativity and collaborative artistic innovation, which reshapes our common conceptions of art and aesthetics (Jenkins 2006; Lessig 2004, 2008). Such practices of commoning produce malleable, unfixed and fluid forms of culture (Poster 2006, 138). In this sense, they reconstruct our urban and digitised environments not as private enclosures but as shared public space, a social sphere divergent from the one (re)produced by the market and the state: the sphere of a renewed postmodern cultural commons. The centrifugal cultural tendencies of postmodernity generate an alternative insurgent artistic figure, which is best personified by the work and activity of Banksy. The street art of Banksy is ripe with techniques of appropriation, bricolage and détournement. Its mode of distribution and consumption is also commons-based, since it freely circulates as an open access commons. While its canvas is the public urban space, Banksy purportedly breaks the barriers between the ephemeral physical embodiment of his art and its digitisation. His pieces of art comfortably penetrate the digital public space and become viral in contemporary social media so as to reach wider audiences and become eternally reproduced and conserved. Both the content and form of his art directly challenge dominant social perceptions about the role and use of art in society, i.e. art as commodity and as a means for capital accumulation. At the same time, it becomes an effective means of circulating alternative aesthetic and political messages which also challenge dominant social, economic and political institutions and their adjacent ways of life. Banksy's art is always pseudonymously published and the artist himself has diligently protected his pseudonymity during all the years of his practice. The value of Banksy's street art lies in the characteristics that constitute it as a commons. In other words, it is valued for its free circulation and for the use values, i.e. alternative aesthetic, social and political values and meanings, that it freely circulates.

The deep transformations in the forces and relations of power in postmodern cultural production have stamped their mark on postmodern art and aesthetics. In the 1960s, the generalisation of rationalised, semi-automated industrial production gave birth to the pop art, minimalist and post-minimalist movements, which conjugated art with industrial production and emphasised repetition and iteration (Kealy 1979). Accordingly, the increasing similarity of art works with industrially mass-produced goods has undermined dominant social perceptions over the importance of individual style in artistic expression (Daskalothanasis 2004, 200–201). Furthermore, the appropriation of everyday objects or prior works of art and their reworking and mixing into new genres of art has become the prevalent mode of postmodern creative expression, as expressed by pop artists, Fluxus, minimalist, neo-geo movements and contemporary art (Evans 2009). In this context, technologies and tools of digitisation and mass self-communication have intensified appropriation by unleashing the creative potential of artistic techniques, such as intertextuality, digital sampling, mixing, collage and pastiche. The exploitation of these technologies along with concurrent processes of cultural globalisation have boosted patterns of sharing both between different genres of art and among civilisations.[30] The increased dependence of postmodern cultural production on sharing and collaboration is evident in the leveraged role of cultural capitals, such as New York and Berlin, within the globalised cultural context and in the divide between these cultural centres and their periphery. As a result, the fusion of prior artistic and cultural styles, techniques and contents into new aesthetic contexts has come to be the fundamental characteristic of postmodern art since the 1980s (Buskirk 2003, 10–12).

The shifts taking place in the field of artistic production and the postmodern restructuring of channels and modes of distribution have disenchanted the aesthetic experience. In postmodernity, the work of art is iteratively experienced as copy and the artist as copier of symbols. Whereas the modernist artefact 'is the commodity as fetish resisting the commodity as exchange', its post-modernist counterpart collapses into such a conflict, 'becoming aesthetically what it is economically', i.e. '[t]he commodity as mechanically reproducible exchange ousts the commodity as magical aura' (Eagleton 1986, 132–133). Inevitably, the ideology of the originality of the work of art is constantly being undermined by generalised appropriation, mass culture and the distribution of the commodity artwork as copy. Yet, at the same time, the commodification of culture has promoted and reinforced the same ideology it has undermined. Since exchange value is the primal metric in a commodified culture, certain generally accepted criteria are needed for the evaluation of the quality of art. In an ocean of art commodities, massively produced through patterns of sharing and appropriation, 'authenticity' and innovation have been promoted as the primal criterion for the evaluation of the quality of art. The postmodern capitalist mode of cultural production and consumption has thus become increasingly reliant on the construction of difference as a means to simulate the heterogeneity of the artwork within the homogeneity of the cultural commodity (Lash and Lury 2007, 187–188). 'The search for and the praise of innovation for the sake of innovation'

(Greenfeld 1989, 101) in the world of art and culture have thus become the mirror image of accumulation for the sake of accumulation, of capital's valorisation process in the cultural industries and the art commodity markets (Marx 1990, 742).

In postmodernity, forces of commodification dominate the cultural domain by controlling access to the means, raw materials and value cycles of cultural reproduction. In recent decades the cultural industries have experienced an enormous growth and expansion in most terrains of cultural activity (Power and Scott 2004) and cultural economic activity has become an integral feature in capitalist production, the circulation of finance, the allocation of commodities, the exploitation of affect, mass consumption and, hence, capital accumulation (Amin and Thrift 2004). In the capitalist mode of cultural reproduction, capital controls the definite means of cultural production and distribution and also has the corresponding capacity to determine the form and content of cultural consumption. Such power upon consumption is evident in the increasingly important role of brands and commodity branding. Brands are cultural forms mediating commodity market relations, through which consumer demand for commodities is organised, controlled and governed (Lury 2004). In postmodern cultures dominated by capital, the art commodity is the cell-form of circulation and the market becomes the dominant value system, i.e. the system that determines which form of social value is valued the most and how such value is distributed and accumulated. As a corollary, the dominance of commodity markets has consolidated the social prevalence of the exchange over the use value of art. This means that art is primarily valued not for the social needs it addresses. Rather, what attributes value to works of art is their socio-economic function in market exchange. In this context, the resurging cultural commons spawning from digital networks become entangled with the commodity in multiple ways, giving birth to a hybrid gift-commodity internet economy of art and culture (Fuchs 2008, 171–189).

Instead of being the outcome of the supposedly invisible hand of the market, the processes of commodification described above are forcefully imposed by state enforcement. State intervention takes place through the systematic enactment of intellectual property laws at the (trans-)national and international levels, which protect, enforce, expand and prolong private monopolies over cultural works. By analogy to the historical enclosure movement that took place in the advent of capitalism, the expansion of intellectual property protections by state enforcement constitutes a second enclosure movement for the submission of the 'intangible commons of the intellect' to the capitalist mode of production (Boyle 2003). In this process of dispossession of the commons, the institution of the state crucially functions as the collective commodifying agent of our common culture.

From the Renaissance to postmodernity, the enclosure of art and culture through regulation has evolved towards its consolidation into intellectual property, albeit with serious contradictions, setbacks and resistance. In postmodernity, regulatory enclosures of information, knowledge and culture have expanded and multiplied to the detriment of the intellectual commons (Lemley 1997, 886-887; Hunter 2003, 501; May and Sell 2006, 145-153, 181-185). The transition of dominance from industrial to informational capital has led to shifts in intellectual property law and jurisprudence towards an ever-expanding enclosure over increasingly valuable intangible goods, as marked by the adoption of the 1994 WTO TRIPS Agreement and the 1996 WIPO internet treaties;[31] the enactment of the 1976 Copyright Act and the 1998 Digital Millennium Copyright Act in the US; the enactment of the copyright directives in the EU;[32] and the US Supreme Court landmark case of *Diamond v. Chakrabarty*.[33] On the other hand, copyright laws have ceased to function solely at the level of industrial activity and their scope, application and enforcement have acquired a horizontal social effect, as the technological means for electronic access, copying and reworking diffused in societies (De Sola Pool 1983, 214; Doctorow 2014, 103, 131). Finally, intellectual property over cultural works has acquired a truly global reach by the enactment of the WTO TRIPS Agreement and the WIPO internet treaties[34] (Drahos and Braithwaite 2002, 108-149; May 2010, 71-97). These developments in the field of law are symmetrical to the augmentation of the cultural industries and the dissemination of the commodity to most facets of socio-cultural activity.

Postmodern intellectual property is a mutation of modern industrial copyright and, as with all mutations, an inherently contradictory and unstable one. Being simultaneously a legal institution for the regulation of sharing and collaboration in cultural production and an ideology of appropriation, postmodern intellectual property rises replete with systemic contradictions and negative externalities. The possessive individualist conception of authorship in postmodern intellectual property disregards the collaboration taking place in cultural production and is, therefore, effectively configured in conjunction with dominant relations of social power to favour the exploitative appropriation of cultural works by singular entities more than its outspoken incentivisation of actual creators (Lemley 1996, 882-884). Under postmodern intellectual property, private monopolies over cultural works tend to approximate the absolute exclusivity of Blackstonian property (Netanel 1996, 311-313; Lemley 1997, 895-904; Boyle 2008, 54-55; Patry 2009, 112-114).[35] Such approximation intensely dilutes the categories and undermines the ideology of industrial copyright. The expansion of its scope to subject matter, from weather forecasts and all other types of factual data to photos, objects of craftsmanship, databases, motion picture plots, trade secrets and computer programs, dilutes the idea/expression dichotomy. This radical relocation of the boundary between the private and the public in favour of commodification tends to have stifling effects on artistic and cultural innovation (Rose 1993, 141). The expansion of both the types and scope of private rights of exclusion, from the right to make creative works available to the public to new generation neighbouring rights, multiplies the chances of anti-commons market failures (Heller 2008, 10–16) and increases the transaction costs of copyright clearance (Aufderheide and Jaszi 2004). The ever-expanding duration of intellectual property to quasi-indefinite levels encloses unprecedented quantities of cultural content, thus significantly weakening the public domain, which forms the raw material of creativity (Lessig 2002a, 110; 2004, 133–135). The foundation of private monopolies over cultural works on the doctrine of originality ignores patterns of sharing over prior culture and, hence, overvalues the creative contribution of existing authors, who in essence 'recombin[e] the resources of the [intellectual] commons' accumulated by their predecessors (Boyle 1996, 74). The expansion of the scope of intellectual property rights through contemporary law and practice, such as the three-step test of the Berne Convention,[36] and its narrow juridical interpretation,[37] concedes increased power to right-holders, has a corresponding diminishing effect on copyright limitations and, as a result, stifles public policies to adjust social access to prior art and culture to the potential of the digital era. The legal conception of limitations as exceptions and exclusivity as the rule in postmodern intellectual property law establishes a hierarchy between the two and construes any limitations to private monopolies over intellectual works as 'islands of freedom within an ocean of exclusivity' (Geiger 2004, 273). In conclusion, regarding the intellectual commons, the postmodern tendency of copyright law towards propertisation has been considered to be 'a wholesale attack on the public domain' (Lemley 1996, 902).

In a nutshell, the main characteristics of the postmodern framework of creativity are manifested as follows:

Unit of collaboration	Creative factory/P2P collectivity
Structures of sharing	Internet, public space, cultural capitals
Forces controlling access to resources	Capital, state
Structures controlling distribution	P2P networks/commodity markets
Perception of the author	Celebrity artist
Normative framework	Intellectual property

Table 4.3: The framework of creativity in postmodernity.
Source: Author

To sum up, postmodernity deepens and intensifies the modern contradiction between the actual practices of cultural production and the regulation of creativity. On the one hand, resurging practices of cultural sharing and collaboration at the social base are increasingly impeded by reinforced cycles of enclosure and their regulatory entrenchment. On the other hand, the expansion of commodification undermines the vitality of the intellectual commons and in many ways acts as a fetter upon processes of cultural production, distribution and consumption by obstructing the generation of cultural wealth. Postmodern intellectual property regulation of culture both internalises and exacerbates these contradictions.

4.5. Conclusion

Set out in historical sequence and from a comparative perspective, the findings of the current analysis help to elucidate the evolution of creative practice from the Renaissance to postmodernity (see below).

	Renaissance	Modernity	Postmodernity
Unit of collaboration	Workshop, individual artist as contributor to the creative process	Art movement/ creative factory	Creative factory/ P2P collectivity
Structures of sharing	Guilds, academies	Academies, libraries, exhibitions, museums, cultural capitals	Internet, public space, cultural capitals
Forces controlling access to resources	Patron, publisher (after the sixteenth century)	State, capital	Capital, state
Structures controlling distribution	Exchange markets/ commodity markets	Commodity markets	P2P networks/ commodity markets
Perception of the author	Artisan, master	Promethean artist	Celebrity artist
Normative framework	Honorarium, privilege	Copyright	Intellectual property

Table 4.4: The evolution of the creative practice from the Renaissance to postmodernity.
Source: Author

From the workshop of the Renaissance to the creative factory and the P2P network of postmodernity, creative collectivities have been the main factors of cultural production, their specific forms only varying over time. Furthermore, practices of sharing among creators have always constituted an integral element of cultural production, distribution and consumption, gradually shifting from more structured organisations in the Renaissance and modernity to the widely diffused networks of cultural sharing in postmodernity. Accordingly, forces controlling access to material and financial resources gradually consolidated from the castes of patrons and printer/publisher guilds into full-fledged industries controlling the distribution and consumption of cultural resources under the protection and promotion of the state. These forces have been shaped and determined by the transformations in production, distribution and consumption taking place owing to the transition from the dominance of mercantile and industrial to the postmodern dominance of informational capital. In the same historical period, the social status of the author shifted from the periphery to the core of the creative practice, commencing from the perception of the medieval craftsman and reaching its climax with the simulacrum of the celebrity artist. Finally, the regulation of art and culture was characterised by a general tendency of formalisation and standardisation from the assignment of ad hoc and ad personam privileges towards alienable property rights over cultural works.

Such conclusions help us to ground more general assumptions in relation to the essence of the creative practice. Along these lines, it can be claimed that the evolution of art and culture is an inherently collective and communal process. Any culture in history is a common pool of cultural resources aggregated through the creative contribution of multiple creators, past and present, connected together by common meanings and world views. The resources of the cultural commons are thus the primal means of artistic production, the raw material upon which artists draw to collate their own creations. In the words of James Boyle, the 'public domain is the place we quarry the building blocks of our culture. It is, in fact, the majority of our culture' (Boyle 2008, 51). In addition, artistic production takes place on the basis of patterns of sharing and collaboration. Creativity and its supportive knowledge are cognitive resources widely dispersed in society. Their aggregation and transformation through sharing and collaboration are the cornerstone of the productive process. Creativity is a sui generis human trait. Even though its elements are allocated in single brains, it is unlocked and ignited through social exchange and constructed incrementally into art through a collective endeavour of multiple minds. This is the reason why it may only thrive in social contexts that facilitate the open exchange of ideas and individual/collective autonomy in collaboration and experimentation (Amabile 1996, 115–120).

An alternative history of art from the perspective of the cultural commons approaches artistic change on the basis of the transformation of the relations between the artistic collectivity and the world around it, considering the artistic collectivity as an active agent in the process. The work of art is the generative moment of creativity, in which all powers active in the social context are exerted and reflected. It should thus be viewed as the product of a particular time and place, deeply influenced by its social context, as much as the product of an artistic collectivity. As a corollary, the production of art and culture is neither a productive process in which individual agency plays no role at all nor a process that can be solely attributed to singular entities. Beyond these two opposing conceptions lies the notion of cultural production as a process, wherein the creative individual is dialectically related to the multitudinous productive collectivity, being constantly constructed by the forces/relations of cultural production and, at the same time, contributing to their dynamism. It is only through a dialectical perspective that we are able to grasp that, in fact, cultural works 'are the product of the collective mind as much as of individual mind' (Mauss 1990, 85–86). Through this dialectic we are able to grasp the subjective productive force of our cultural commons, the social intellect.

Law regulates creativity, by framing the creative practice, formulating its processes and constructing social perceptions over its subjects and objects. In this sense, law has a material transformative effect upon art and culture. Copyright law and practice consolidates and entrenches the dominance of the capitalist mode of cultural production, distribution and consumption by means of both violence and ideology. Its negative definition, fragmentary regulation and exception-based recognition of the intellectual commons guarantee the subordination of commons-based peer production and the ceaseless capture of its wealth by capital. At the same time, the interrelation of copyright law with the intellectual commons reveals the dependence of capital accumulation in the cultural industries upon practices of commoning in art and culture. Nowadays, transformations in the relations of cultural production, distribution and consumption unveil new forms of commoning and bring about a resurgence of the intellectual commons.

Along these lines, this chapter has aimed to provide the historical arguments in favour of an intellectual commons law, which will, on the one hand, calibrate the aggravating contradictions of the dominant capitalist mode and, on the other hand, exploit in full the potential of the alternative mode of commons-based cultural production, distribution and consumption. The next chapters contain the social research of the book, which examines the circulation of value within and beyond the intellectual commons. The research renders visible the existence of alternative forms and flows of commons-based value in our societies, which circulate in parallel to the flow of commodities and money. The aim of the research is to unveil the inherent moral value and the social benefit of the intellectual commons, by providing solid evidence on the immense amounts of value generated, pooled together and redistributed to wider society by these institutions.

CHAPTER 5

Researching the Social Value of the Intellectual Commons: Methodology and Design

5.1. Introduction

The previous chapter described the historical significance of the commons for art and culture. The current chapter is the methodological part of a social research endeavour on the political economy of the intellectual commons, focusing on the circulation of commons-based values. The aim of this research is to identify the contemporary revelations of the relations of commonification in the circulation of social value and, thus, grasp the actual formations of the intellectual commons, both offline and online, in the current socio-historical context. The research decrypts the generation, circulation, pooling together and redistribution of social value observed in the intellectual commons communities of the sample, with the aim of showing the importance of the intellectual commons for social reproduction. By providing solid empirical evidence that the communities of the intellectual commons generate and redistribute social values to society, the social research part of the book thus supports its overall normative argumentation that the intellectual commons have significant moral value, which justifies their independent protection and promotion by the law.

This chapter sets out the methodological bases and the design of the research in the next three sections. The first of these spells out the methodological orientation of the research. The second unveils the design of the research. The third describes the coding process followed in relation to data collected from the eight Greek intellectual commons communities, which constitute the sample of the current research. The current chapter is then followed by chapters on the findings and conclusions of the research.

How to cite this book chapter:
Broumas, A. 2020. *Intellectual Commons and the Law: A Normative Theory for Commons-Based Peer Production*. Pp. 89–101. London: University of Westminster Press. DOI: https://doi.org/10.16997/book49.e. License: CC-BY-NC-ND

5.2. Research Theory

The current research project adheres to a critical realist epistemology. Through the critical realist prism, the mission of scientific research with regard to the intellectual commons is the examination of the causal mechanisms framing the events, activities and social phenomena within their context (Archer et al. 1998, xi–xii; Fletcher 2017, 183). Such causal mechanisms are not conceived as natural phenomena disconnected for their socio-historical context but rather as contingent social products, being in themselves dependent on social activity for the manifestation of their outcomes (Bhaskar 1979, 48). The underlying purpose is thus to ascertain the tendencies of the intellectual commons, unveil the general causal mechanisms of commonification and explore the specific formations of the intellectual commons in their dialectical relation with capital.

In addition, this research project follows a critical realist, processual and dialectical ontology. The intellectual commons and intellectual property-enabled commodity markets are viewed as instituted sets of practices with inherent capacities, tendencies and potentialities (Psillos 2007; Bhaskar 2008, 51). The tendencies of these practices are correspondingly determined by contending forces of commonification and commodification.[38] In other words, the intellectual commons are analysed as manifestations of the clash between commonification and commodification. Furthermore, social structures are conceived not as external but rather as dialectically interrelated to social agency (Bhaskar 2008, 248). On the one hand, these structures are constantly reproduced and transformed in daily life from the bottom up through the iterative practices of active agents in their social context. On the other hand, the structural properties of intellectual commons and commodity markets are perceived to feature mechanisms that frame social activity in a top-down manner, by enabling or restricting practices of commoning and processes of commodification (Sayer 2010, 70–79).

Accordingly, the intellectual commons are investigated as sets of iterative social practices with specific tendencies towards commonification, which are, though in constant flux, penetrating and penetrated by commodity market exchange and in dialectical relation with the dominant power of capital. On these grounds, it is claimed that the causal powers of commonification constitute tendencies, not laws (Danemark et al. 2002, 70). Such tendencies unveil themselves within open social formations. This means that tendencies of commonification can be prevented from or facilitated in manifesting themselves by the conditions set out in each specific social context, in which intellectual commons communities are placed. Hence, the intellectual commons are not searched out in pure form as clear-cut and fixed entities but, rather, as partial or dispersed manifestations of commonification enmeshed within societies primarily reproduced according to the capitalist mode of intellectual production, distribution and consumption. In this sense, the commons-based mode of intellectual production, distribution and consumption is conceptualised as a proto-mode of social reproduction, i.e. not yet integrated as a mode proper in contemporary societies.

As far as its research paradigm is concerned, this research applies a critical political economic analysis to the alternative mode of social reproduction, based on the commons. Such an intellectual endeavour holds power as central to social relations and structured in the institutions of society, understood as both a resource to achieve goals and an instrument of control within social hierarchies (Mosco 2009, 24). The present research on the critical political economy of the intellectual commons unfolds in two dimensions. On the one hand, it studies the power relations that mutually constitute the production, distribution and consumption of intangible resources. And, on the other hand, it deals with the circulation and pooling of social values within and beyond the spheres of the intellectual commons.

In normative terms, the present research project approaches facts as necessarily theory-dependent, in terms of both semantics and perceptions (Popper 1963; Kuhn 1970). Therefore, such an approach rejects the view of scientific objectivism as ideologically laden, i.e. in reality concealing a specific subjective normative stance concerning the interrelation between social research and its objects of analysis (Habermas 1966). Instead, it openly adopts an alternative subjective approach to science in terms of the categorical imperative of critical theory, the content of which is, in Karl Marx's words, 'to overthrow all conditions in which man is a degraded, enslaved, neglected, contemptible being' (Marx 1997, 257–258). In the context of the intellectual commons, the aim of the research is to highlight their potential for social emancipation and the abolishment of all forms of domination.

5.3. Research Method

5.3.1. Constructing the Research Methodology

In terms of methodology, a twofold iterative method of analysis is employed regarding the dialectical pairs of both theory/research and society/agency. Theory and research are viewed as interpenetrating and, therefore, the research follows a spiralling back-and-forth movement between theory and data to arrive at findings and conclusions. Such an approach ensures that the normative perspective mentioned above is thoroughly observed throughout the research project. Accordingly, the mutual conditioning and interrelation between agency and structure necessitate a combined bottom-up and top-down analysis of forces of commonification and their social context, so as to understand the social causes behind the specific manifestations of the intellectual commons.

In this context, it is claimed that both the capacities and the mechanisms generated within the intellectual commons can be identified and become known through a dialectical combination of empirical observation and abstract theorisation (Lawson 1998, 156; Danemark et al. 2002, 22). Such a dialectical movement from the empirical to the real follows a specific sequence of scientific understanding. According to this sequence, the processing of empirical data first reveals the existence of social phenomena within the intellectual commons, which are then resolved into their components and redescribed through abduction, so that any contingent regularities are revealed. Next, any plausible understandings on the causal powers behind these regularities are hypothesised by means of retroduction. Furthermore, the reality of the inferred causal mechanisms is subsequently subjected to empirical scrutiny. In addition, the empirical adequacy of the hypotheses under examination is checked in comparison to that of competing explanations. Finally, the relevant social mechanism is unearthed and analysed (Archer et al. 1998, xvi; Bhaskar 2008, 135; Bhaskar 2014, vii–viii). In this context, abduction is the cognitive exercise of redescribing social phenomena in an abstracted way, so as to give account to the existence of demi-regularities and potential causal powers behind them (O'Mahoney and Vincent 2014, 17). Accordingly, retroduction refers to the cognitive exercise of constructing 'a theory of a mechanism that, if it were to work in the postulated way, could account for the phenomenon in question' (Bhaskar and Lawson 1998, 5).

5.3.2. Building a Research Strategy

Value in the commons and the practices of value circulation and pooling are socially determined phenomena related to dominant and alternative perceptions regarding the attribution or not of importance to productive activity, which are therefore not equated to the intransitive natural characteristics of correlated resources (Marx 1990, 138–140). Furthermore, value circulation in the intellectual commons is strongly determined by the ways in which commoners and the society in general interpret productive practices taking place within intellectual commons communities. Finally, commons-based forms of value are relatively incommensurable, at least compared to the exchange value of intangible commodities in monetised intellectual property-enabled markets. For all these reasons, a primarily qualitative strategy has been opted for the empirical examination of value circulation in the intellectual commons.

5.3.3. Designing the Research

The research is designed in a comparative style of analysis. Along these lines, the deviations in the circulation of commons-based value are comparatively analysed on the basis of two meaningful distinctions between intellectual commons communities (see Table 5.1 below).

	Types	Spheres
Value circulation	Offline	Contested
	Online	Co-opted

Table 5.1: Commons-based value circulation in comparison.
Source: Author

Depending on the medium of circulation, intellectual commons communities are examined as circulating their produced values either mainly offline or chiefly online. As most communities both have a presence on the internet and their production also involves tangible resources, this distinction is not taken in absolute terms but rather on the basis of whether the internet constitutes the primary medium of value circulation.

Depending on the dialectical relation with intellectual property-enabled commodity markets, intellectual commons communities are examined as circulating their produced values either in a contentious or in a co-opted mode of interrelation with the commodity-form of value circulation. The contentious or co-opted nature of such an interrelation is evaluated depending on the extent that commons-based values are transformed into exchange value and put into circulation in the sphere of commodity markets. Since the dialectical relation mentioned above is in constant flux and subject to their subordination to commodity markets and the state, this distinction between intellectual commons communities is also fragile and should be viewed as changing over time.

5.3.4. Research Sampling

In the relevant research sampling, the Greek society is chosen as the wider field of analysis. There are two reasons for such a choice in the design of the project. For the past eight years, Greece has been facing a severe economic and social crisis, which has destabilised incumbent state and market institutions. As a result, the Greek society is undergoing a period of rapid change and reorientation, in which existing social structures enter a stage of reform and readjustment to the new environment and new structures emerge. In addition, the economic crisis has brought about a corresponding crisis of social reproduction, during which large social groups have been forced to find new ways of meeting their collective needs and desires through sharing, mutual aid and collaboration. This social tendency has resulted in the emergence of various commons in the fields of sustenance, housing, health, education, art, technology, mass media, communications and social innovation. In this light, the Greek crisis is not only a story of pain, poverty and misery. It can also be reconstructed into a

	Contested	Co-opted
Offline	Embros Theatre Athens Hackerspace	Athens Impact Hub CommonsLab
Online	Libre Space Foundation Self-managed ERT	Sarantaporo.gr P2P Lab

Table 5.2: Intellectual commons communities in times of crisis: The case of Greece.
Source: Author

narrative of courage, hope, social struggle and progressive change: a narrative of the commons.

On the basis of the factors of distinction designed above, eight communities of the intellectual commons that are active in the crisis-stricken Greek society are selected as objects of empirical analysis and comparison.

The Case of Greece

The 'Embros' Free Self-Managed Theatre is an artistic urban commons at the heart of Athens, Greece. It is housed in an ex-theatre abandoned by the Ministry of Culture that has been occupied since 2011 by artistic and political collectives. In its six years of operation, the artistic community of the Embros Theatre has managed to organise hundreds of minor and major cultural events, from theatrical plays and cultural festivals to political events and social mobilisations.[39] The social space is self-managed by the assembly of the members of the community, which meets every Sunday. Participation in this assembly is open to artistic collectives and whoever is interested in contributing to the community. Proposals to host events are freely submitted and accepted by the assembly after evaluation. The Embros Theatre community is explicitly against the commodification of art and culture. Entrance to the events of the social space has never had any entrance fee. Voluntary contributions of any type, however, have always been welcome. The social impact of the Embros Theatre in the urban culture of Athens is significant and its events and festivals are as a rule heavily attended. The theatre is accommodated in a de facto occupation of a building that is planned to be sold by the state as part of the privatisation programme imposed on Greece by external debtors. Furthermore, the occupied theatre is located in a neighbourhood near the city centre, which is undergoing processes of gentrification under pressure from strong private real estate interests. Therefore, this intellectual commons community is in constant confrontation with law enforcement authorities, with a number of acts of sabotage, evacuation and activists' persecutions on the part of the state. Its contention with art commodity markets and the state classifies this important intellectual commons community at the contested offline pole of the research sample.

The Athens Hackerspace.gr is a community of producers inspired by the practices of the free software movement, which has established a collectively managed and shared makerspace since May 2011 in the city of Athens.[40] According to the constituent rules of the makerspace, the various projects hosted within the Hackerspace.gr community enjoy relative autonomy but are still obliged to comply with its values of behavioural excellence, collaborative sharing, consensus-based decision-making and hacker-inspired do-ocracy. The shared makerspace as a whole is managed by an open assembly, meeting periodically to decide and administer its operations. Over the years Hackerspace.gr has become the main meeting-place of the Athens hacking community and has spawned a number of projects in the fields of open hardware, free software and, in general, open science and technology. The community is intentionally non-commercial, self-funded and self-sustained by the contributions of its members. These characteristics clearly place Hackerspace.gr as an intellectual commons community at the contested offline category of the research sample.

The Libre Space Foundation is a trailblazing community that designs, develops and delivers space-related projects the libre (open source) way. Its common pool resource features, among others, UPSat and SatNOGS. UPSat is the first open source hardware and software satellite, which has been already released in orbit since 18 May 2017. SatNOGS is an open source hardware and software satellite ground station and a network that enables the remote management of multiple ground station operations. Both of these projects have been built from readily available and affordable tools and resources. As stated on the website of the community,[41] the Libre Space Foundation has the vision of an open and accessible outer space for all, by offering the relevant infrastructure to commoners around the world to build satellite and ground station infrastructure and networks. The whole project spawned from the Athens Hackerspace and still holds its productive activities there, the latter being in itself another vibrant intellectual commons community of Greece. Until now the project has been financed by a grant from winning the first prize in the 2014 Hackaday competition and by collaborating with the University of Patras in a relevant EU-funded programme. The community consists of almost twenty core team commoners but has been gradually building an emerging community of contributors around the world through the online dissemination, reuse and improvement of its openly accessible work. Its founding values of openness, sharing and collaboration make this intellectual commons community an innovative for-benefit open source project and, as such, appropriate as a contested online sample community for the present research.

The self-managed ERT is a historically unique example of an ex-state broadcaster transformed into a media commons. It was born on 11 June 2013 amid the social turmoil ignited by the decision of the right-wing-leaning coalition government of the years 2012–15 to switch off the signal of ERT, the Greek national radio and television broadcaster, overnight. The day after the disconnection, the headquarters of ERT in Athens was occupied by citizens and employees during a massive social mobilisation of 100,000 people. Through this social process the website ertopen.com was established within a few days, the production of the radio and television programme started again as a media commons and its transmission through the internet began reaching millions of viewers. From January 2014 the self-managed ERT was able to retransmit and broadcast one television and 17 radio channels over the airwaves across the country, by occupying the necessary infrastructure and by mobilising a mixed workforce of ex-employees and citizens on a daily basis. Up to June 2015, when the newly elected left-leaning coalition government led by SYRIZA re-established the national broadcaster as a state form of media, the self-managed ERT had already produced hundreds of thousands of hours of television and radio programme as a media commons. Even though almost all its former employees joined the state broadcaster, ERTOpen still produces and transmits its radio programme both online and over the radio spectrum.[42] Its history and its political and social significance thus make the self-managed ERT an ideal media commons for the online contested category of the research sample. The two focus group interviews of self-managed ERT interviewees were conducted in 2017. These interviews cover the history and evolution of the community both before and after the re-establishment of ERT as a state-run public medium.

The Athens Impact Hub is a business incubator for social enterprises and entrepreneurships oriented towards creating a positive social impact. In its statement of purpose, the hub presents itself as promoting an economy of co-creation under the motto '[i]mpact cannot happen in isolation'.[43] Having been incorporated as a non-profit company under the laws of Greece, the hub is part of a wider association of similar hubs across 81 cities around the world. It offers resources for work and knowledge sharing among its members. It is structured as a community of sharing and collaboration, featuring community-oriented events from common lunches and business clinics to skill-sharing sessions, and it employs hub hosts who have the task of facilitating connectivity and interaction among participants in the community. The Athens Impact Hub partners and collaborates with both non-profit and for-profit entities to ensure sources of income. In its four years of operation, the hub has been capable of becoming the undisputable meeting point of the city for civil society and other non-profit initiatives, social economy entrepreneurs and private sector companies with a commitment to corporate responsibility. Even though it operates as an intellectual commons community at the level of incubating projects, the hub spawns and accommodates for-profit start-ups, attracts sponsorships from for-profit market players and, thus, leaves open its productive output to private appropriation and commodification. As a corollary, the Athens Impact Hub has introduced a fresh model of operation into the Greek incubators' industry, which hybridises the intellectual commons with the commodity market in novel ways. As such, it provides an ideal testbed for empirical analysis as the offline co-opted sample of the present research project.

CommonsLab is a social cooperative running a makerspace at the city of Herakleion, Crete. Its members were the core organisers of CommonsFest, an innovative festival for commons communities, which greatly contributed to the launch of informed public discourse about the commons in Greece.[44] The makerspace is equipped with ordinary construction tools, 3D printers, FabLab infrastructure and free software programmes. The makerspace and its infrastructure are open to the public subject to a fee. The CommonsLab team also offers knowledge sharing courses under remuneration for a diversity of activities spanning from free software programming and 3D printing to biological farming and permaculture. Furthermore, CommonsLab has developed certain commons-oriented products, such as DonationBox, a network of interconnected end-devices that have the capacity to remotely run donation campaigns and are purported to be installed in cooperatives and social centres across the country. CommonsLab operates in many ways as an intellectual commons community, yielding valuable knowledge to local societies and actively produces commons-oriented projects. Nevertheless, its dependence on the commodity market forecloses its clients from decision-making and necessitates a fee-based access to its services. As such, CommonsLab has been classified as a co-opted offline community for the needs of the current research project.

The Sarantaporo.gr project is a community that has been building wireless mesh electronic communication networks as a commons since 2010 in a series of remotely located villages inhabiting the slopes of Mount Olympus. The community network of the project consists of 21 backbone nodes, 27 point-to-point links and more than 180 OpenMesh devices, interconnecting approximately fifteen villages, including agricultural farms, schools and public medical centres. In addition, since March 2014 the network has been interconnected through the public internet with the Athens Wireless Metropolitan Network and a dozen other community networks throughout Europe. The community network has been collectively built and is today sustained through the joint efforts, on the one hand, of a core team of ten commoners and, on the other hand, of fourteen local support groups of villagers, who have been offering work hours, financial contributions and the space and electricity from their houses necessary to host and operate the network infrastructure. Furthermore, the community has organised twelve info-points and several major events in the area, including an international battlemesh summit and a social economy conference. The community network is sustained as a common pool resource by the contributions of the core commoners, who hold the necessary know-how and provide the support services needed, and with the help and contribution of villagers. Apart from the network itself, the community offers high-speed wireless internet access services via the network infrastructure on an unrestricted basis and without remuneration. Internet access is provided in both private and public spaces, reaching a consumer base of up to 5,000 end users. The dissemination of internet access on a free basis has been rendered possible though an agreement between the community and the University of Thessaly for the provision of the latter's excess bandwidth to the community network for the execution of joint research projects. In addition, the core infrastructure of the project was financed through the participation of the community in a European Union research project on community Wi-Fi networks. The sustenance of the project is endangered because of its incompatibilities with the legal framework, which is solely structured for the regulation of the electronic communications commodity market and, as such, disregards communications as a commons. Furthermore, the projects face difficulties of sustenance, since a number of user groups and communities in the villages that participate in the network have equated the access to the commons for free and gratis, thus becoming reluctant to share the workload and the economic burden for sustaining the network. As a result, the Sarantaporo.gr project is heavily pressurised by the dominant value system and legal framework, thus lingering between contestation and cooptation. For these reasons, this project was chosen for the online co-opted category of the current research.

P2P Lab is an independent research hub focusing on peer-to-peer practices and the commons, which has its offices at Ioannina city in the north-western part of Greece. The hub is affiliated with the University of Tallinn and the P2P Foundation. It consists of a core team of six researchers, a council of mentors, a number of external collaborators and a network of activists interested in its theoretical work. P2P Lab's projects involve cutting-edge social research related to issues as diverse as free software, open design and manufacturing, blockchain technologies, open cooperativism, smart cities, P2P energy production, P2P value and, in general, commons-oriented policies. Since its activation in December 2012, the lab has produced a vast intellectual wealth of research projects, journal articles, conference papers, book chapters and book-length endeavours. The intellectual production of P2P Lab is freely available in its entirety to the public under a creative commons attribution non-commercial licence though its website.[45] The research hub is fully dependent on state and intergovernmental research programmes either directly or indirectly through other organisations in order to finance the work of its researchers. This dependence makes P2P Lab vulnerable to external pressures on the orientation of its work and puts it in a precarious position as to its long-term sustenance. Therefore, P2P is examined as an intellectual commons community listed at the online co-opted category of the research sample.

All eight of the foregoing intellectual commons communities have been selected as objects of empirical analysis for the qualitative research of the current project on the grounds of the importance of social values they produce and the social impact they have within and beyond the crisis-ridden Greek society. Furthermore, the different socio-political visions, value practices, objects of production, means of value circulation and governing institutions of these communities have rendered them ideal for comparative analysis and the induction of valuable findings.

5.3.5. Carving Out the Method of Data Collection

Data collection regarding the circulation of commons-based value in intellectual commons communities has been conducted according to mixed-methods research, featuring a mutually illuminating combination of qualitative and quantitative methods. During the stage of data collection, the qualitative temporally preceded the quantitative method. Next, quantitative and qualitative data were analysed in parallel. Finally, the two strands of data were merged at the interpretation stage. In this convergent parallel design, the qualitative data were given priority over the quantitative method, with the qualitative being the principal data-gathering tool and the quantitative acting as data coding tool (Creswell and Plano Clark 2011, 66–67).

As a starting point, a series of ten interviews were executed in the form of focus group interviews with members of the communities that constituted the object of the social research. The focus group method of interviewing was chosen for several substantive reasons. First, each focus group consisted of individuals sharing the experience of being involved in the same intellectual commons community (Merton, Lowenthal and Kendal 1956, 3). Secondly, the interviews focused on the ways through which interviewees construed social value in their community (Puchta and Potter 2004, 6; Bryman 2012, 502–503). Thirdly, since values are essentially based on common meanings and mind-frames, interviews aimed to trigger lively discussion, argumentation and, even, disagreement between interviewees on what is valuable or not in their community, thus generating a synergistic group effect between interviewees, which would not be possible to unravel from individual interviews (Stewart and Shamdasani 2015, 45–46). All of these characteristics made focus group interviewing more appropriate as a research method in order to achieve inclusive data collection, collect qualitative information on the subject matter under examination and arrive at valid findings.

Along these lines, the focus group interviews took place in an environment that was familiar to the interviewees, i.e. the social spaces of their communities. An interview guide was applied and flexibly adopted according to the course of each focus group discussion. The guide was deemed necessary to ensure that all research areas were adequately covered. Nevertheless, since their subject matter referred to cultural values and social value, in general, the interviews adhered to a flexible pattern, allowing the participants to take the lead, offer their own interpretations and narratives about matters asked, discuss together and, even, argue with one another (Arthur and Nazroo 2003, 110–112).

The structure of the interview guide comprised proposed main questions, as well as probing and follow-up questions, wherever needed, as a means to enrich collected data from interviewees. Main questions were structured as elaborate questions, which were, then, unpacked by probing and follow-up questions, the latter often including ranges of candidate answers to help participants in the conduct of their response (Puchta and Potter 2004, 64). Focusing on what is directly observable, questions sought to unravel concrete experiences, observations and feelings, instead of just the impressions and opinions, of the interviewees. In certain cases, alternatives between potential questions were devised to take into account the diversity of interviewees' responses. The questions were formulated in a way so as to elicit the interviewees' subjective descriptions about their communal life-words and reveal any possible intersubjective meanings and shared pre-reflections and pre-theorisations (Brinkman 2014, 286–289).

After the conclusion of the interviews, the members of the focus groups were given a self-completion questionnaire with structured multiple choices. In the general context of the current project, the self-completion questionnaire was utilised as an appropriate tool for the application of the iterative research method in action. With this intention, the interviewees were first called upon to digest the discussion which had taken place during the focus group interviews and, after self-reflecting, asked to complete the questionnaire according to their informed assumptions. In this sequence of qualitative and quantitative research, the purpose of the questionnaire was to act as a data coding tool with the participation of the researched subjects themselves.

To cover the needs of data analysis, the main parts of the audio-taped interviews encompassing the core arguments of the interviewees were transcribed and qualitatively coded in the form of a coding guide for each of the eight communities of the research sample. Next, with the help of the guide, the qualitatively coded data were scrutinised and compared with the quantitative data collected through the self-completion questionnaire. Finally, points of convergence and discrepancy between the two streams of data were identified and interpreted.

Having the coded data from the two data collection methods and the points of discrepancy in mind, the stage of data analysis was drawn to a close. Henceforth, with the step-by-step process analysed above, a solid empirical basis was established for the comparison of the eight communities under examination. In the next chapters of the book, the available data are interpreted in order to arrive at safe theoretical findings and conclusions regarding aspects of the circulation of commons-based value in the communities of the research sample.

5.4. Data Coding

As already mentioned in the previous methodological sections, the current research on commons-based value combined both qualitative and quantitative elements. Its qualitative element consisted of ten focus group interviews, each varying in participation between five and seven interviewees. The coding of the qualitative element was executed through the development of themes and their corresponding codes from raw data. This thematic coding evolved as a step-by-step process, spiralling towards higher levels of complexity through a back-and-forth movement between data-driven induction and theory-driven deduction. First, implicit and explicit ideas were identified and described from patterns of repetition in collected data (Guest, MacQueen and Namey 2012, 10–11). Next, codes were generated by collapsing of data into labels. Following that, generated codes were grouped and combined into overarching themes. In this process, initial themes were reviewed and confirmed or amended, wherever appropriate (Braun and Clarke 2006, 86–93). Afterwards, themes were structured according to relevant research questions in order to present a coherent narrative of the sequences of value circulation and value pooling. Produced themes and codes were then used to write down a general coding guide. Finally, the coding guide was applied to the eight communities of the sample, generating a coding report for each of them. In conclusion, the coding guide is the outcome of an iterative process, combining processes of both coding up from transcribed empirical data and coding down from the theoretical variables, questions and hypotheses of the research (Miles and Huberman 1994, 58–65).

In order to formulate an all-inclusive coding of available data, i.e. both qualitative and quantitative, the coding guide was designed with a threefold structure. In particular, the coding process took place in three separate parts. The first coding part featured the codification of qualitative data from focus group interviews. The second coding part featured the codification of quantitative data from the self-completion questionnaire. The third part codified the comparison between the other two columns and located discrepancies. Overall, though, the outcomes of both the qualitative and quantitative codification were found to generally correspond and complement each other, hence consolidating the findings and conclusions of the research.

5.5. Conclusion

The current methodological chapter has set out the framework of the research project on the social value of the intellectual commons. In terms of theory, it has described the critical realist and political economic approach followed throughout the research. In terms of method, it has determined the aim and demonstrates the strategy, design and sampling of the research project. The last section described the thematic method of coding the collected data. Overall, this chapter has laid down in systematic form the methodological foundations of the research and developed an appropriate framework to elicit the research findings and conclusions exhibited in the following chapters.

CHAPTER 6

Social Value of the Intellectual Commons: Dimensions of Commons-Based Value

6.1. Introduction

This chapter is an extensive elaboration of the research findings on the sequences and circuits of commons-based value within and beyond the communities under examination. Its key finding is that commons-based value circulates in the form of economic, social, cultural and political values. The next four sections of the chapter offer an analysis of collected research data as a basis to ground findings in relation to each of these four dimensions of commons-based values. The concluding section elicits general findings on the circulation of commons-based value, arising from common characteristics found in all four dimensions. Overall, the findings of the research show that social value within and beyond intellectual commons communities is circulated in specific forms, which can be revealed through social research and depicted in general formulae.

6.2. The Economic Dimension of Commons-Based Value

According to the findings of the research, the economic value circuits in the communities of the sample are exhibited in the table below:

How to cite this book chapter:
Broumas, A. 2020. *Intellectual Commons and the Law: A Normative Theory for Commons-Based Peer Production.* Pp. 103–112. London: University of Westminster Press. DOI: https://doi.org/10.16997/book49.f. License: CC-BY-NC-ND

	Offline contested		Online contested		Offline co-opted		Online co-opted	
Communities	Embros Theatre	Athens Hackerspace	Libre Space Foundation	Self-managed ERT	Athens Impact Hub	Commons Lab	Sarantaporo.gr	P2P Lab
Value-producing practices	Collaboration/ collective appropriation	Collaboration	Collaboration	Collaboration/ collective appropriation	Collaboration	Collaboration/ competition	Collaboration	Collaboration
Values	Use value/ exchange value	Use value	Use value	Use value	Use value/ exchange value	Use value/ exchange value	Use value	Use value/ exchange value
Flows	Gifts	Gifts	Gifts	Gifts	Gifts/ commodities	Gifts/ commodities	Gifts	Gifts
Accumulation	Common pool resource	Common pool resource	Common pool resource	Common pool resource	Common pool resource/ private appropriation	Common pool resource/ private appropriation	Common pool resource/ private appropriation	Common pool resource/ private appropriation
Redistribution	Gifts/ generalised reciprocity	Gifts/ generalised reciprocity	Generalised reciprocity	Gifts/ generalised reciprocity	Gifts/ commodities	Gifts/ commodities	Gifts/ use values/ economic development	Gifts

Table 6.1: The circuit of commons-based economic value circulation.
Source: Author

Practices of commons-based value circulation and value pooling in the economic dimension of social activity examined in the study take certain forms, which can be depicted as a general formula. Along these lines, data analysis shows that the generation, formulation, circulation, pooling and redistribution of commons-based economic values take the general form of collaboration, use value, gifts, common pool resources and, again, gifts. Hence, the main commons-based economic value circuit in the intellectual commons communities under examination can be represented by the following formula:

Collaboration → Use value → Gift → Common pool resource → Gift (CL→UV→G→CPR→G).

Nevertheless, in the process of data analysis, explicit and implicit differentiations emerged between the economic value circuits of contested and co-opted communities. Apart from the general circuit of commons-based economic value mentioned above, research findings show the presence of an alternative value circuit in the economic dimension of social activity, which is more distinct in the co-opted communities of the sample. The alternative economic value circuit develops in the following form in parallel to the main economic value circuit in most of the co-opted communities under examination:

Competition → Exchange value → Commodity → Private appropriation → Commodity (CP→EV→C→PA→C).

6.3. The Social Dimension of Commons-Based Value

With regard to the commons-based social value circuit, the findings of the research reveal a great variety of value-producing practices. The codification of this value circuit is presented in Table 6.2.

In its generality, the commons-based social value circuit takes the form of productive contribution, merit, trust, communal cohesion and social cohesion, which can be represented by the following formula:

Productive contribution → Merit → Trust → Communal cohesion → Social cohesion (PP→MR→T→CC→SC).

As in the case of the commons-based economic value circuit, the differences between the social value circuits of contested and co-opted communities reveal an alternative social value circuit, which operates in parallel to the main social value circuit in both the co-opted and contested communities of the study:

Financial contribution → Control of infrastructure → Monetary exchange → Social capital → No redistribution (F→MR→M→SCa→SC/N).

	Offline contested		Online contested		Offline co-opted		Online co-opted	
Communities	Embros Theatre	Athens Hackerspace	Libre Space Foundation	Self-managed ERT	Athens Impact Hub	CommonsLab	Sarantaporo.gr	P2P Lab
Value-producing practices	Contribution in productive activity/ contribution in kind	Contribution in productive activity/financial contribution	Contribution in productive activity/ contribution in kind	Contribution in productive activity/ contribution in kind	Contribution in productive activity/ financial contribution	Contribution in productive activity/ financial contribution	Contribution in productive activity/ financial contribution/ contribution in kind	Contribution in productive activity
Values	Quantity of contribution/ merit/personal capabilities/ control of infrastructure	Quantity of contribution/ merit/personal capabilities	Quantity of contribution/ merit	Quantity of contribution/ merit/personal capabilities	Merit/control of infrastructure/ quantity of contribution/ personal capabilities	Merit/control of infrastructure/ quantity of contribution/ personal capabilities	Merit/control of infrastructure/ quantity of contribution/ personal capabilities	Merit
Flows	Trust/power conflicts	Trust	Trust	Trust/power conflicts	Trust/monetary exchange	Trust	Trust	Trust
Redistribution	Social cohesion/ network	Social cohesion/ network	Social cohesion/ network	Social cohesion	Social cohesion/ network	Social cohesion/ network	Social cohesion/ network	Social cohesion

Table 6.2: The circuit of commons-based social value circulation.
Source: Author

6.4. The Cultural Dimension of Commons-Based Value

The data analysis revealed that the cultural dimension of commons-based values shows the least diversity of value forms, with the interviewees of the sample extensively converging in their assessments of what is valued in their communities in terms of culture. As displayed in the following Table 6.3, the research has shown that the cultural value circuit generally consists of sharing as its value-producing practice, mutual aid as its cultural value form, the formulation of a shared ethos as its type of value flow, the construction of common communal identity as value pooling and the diffusion of mutual aid ethics in society as the form of redistributing its value to society. Only at the sequence of redistribution did communities display more diverse forms of value, stating the limited presence of two other forms of cultural value redistribution, in particular the dissemination of symbols and art, in the case of the Embros Theatre, and the diffusion of an ethos of political resistance, in the case of the self-managed ERT.

Based on the foregoing, the general formula of the commons-based cultural value circuit is consolidated in the form of sharing, mutual aid, shared ethics, communal identity and mutuality ethics, which can be summarised as follows:

Sharing → Mutual aid → Shared ethos → Communal identity → Mutuality ethics (S→MA→SE→CI→ME).

6.5. The Political Dimension of Commons-Based Value

The commons-based political value circuits of the communities of the sample were found to exhibit wide diversity. In particular, the codification of commons-based political value circulation has taken the following form, as presented in Table 6.4.

The commons-based political value circuit thus unfolds in the form of participation in decision-making, self-empowerment, collective empowerment, community self-governance and, again, collective empowerment, which can be formulated as follows:

Participation → Self-empowerment → Collective empowerment → Community self-governance → Collective empowerment (P→SE→CE→CSG→CE).

Apart from the general circuit of political value, an alternative political value circuit develops in certain co-opted communities in the form shown below:

Deliberation → Self-empowerment → Collective empowerment → No accumulation → No redistribution (D→SE→CE).

	Communities	Value-producing practices	Values	Flows	Accumulation	Redistribution
Offline contested	Embros Theatre	Sharing	Mutual aid	Relative shared ethos	Relative common identity	Mutuality ethics/ symbol and art
	Athens Hackerspace	Sharing	Mutual aid	Strong shared ethos	Strong common identity	Mutuality ethics
Online contested	Libre Space Foundation	Sharing	Mutual aid	Strong shared ethos	Relative common identity	Mutuality ethics
	Self-managed ERT	Sharing	Mutual aid	Strong shared ethos	Relative common identity	Mutuality ethics/ ethos of political resistance
Offline co-opted	Athens Impact Hub	Sharing	Mutual aid	Relative shared ethos	Relative common identity	Mutuality ethics
	CommonsLab	Sharing	Mutual aid	Strong shared ethos	Relative common identity	Mutuality ethics
Online co-opted	Sarantaporo.gr	Sharing	Mutual aid	Relative shared ethos	Weak common identity	Mutuality ethics
	P2P Lab	Sharing	Mutual aid	Strong shared ethos	Strong common identity	Mutuality ethics

Table 6.3: The circuit of cultural commons-based value circulation.
Source: Author

	Offline contested		Online contested		Offline co-opted		Online co-opted	
Communities	Embros Theatre	Athens Hackerspace	Libre Space Foundation	Self-managed ERT	Athens Impact Hub	CommonsLab	Sarantaporo.gr	P2P Lab
Value-producing practices	Participation	Participation	Deliberation	Participation	Deliberation	Deliberation	Deliberation	Participation
Values	Self-empowerment	Self-empowerment	Self-empowerment	Self-empowerment	Self-empowerment	Self-empowerment	Self-empowerment	Self-empowerment
Flows	Collective empowerment	Collective empowerment	Collective empowerment	Collective empowerment	Collective empowerment	Collective empowerment	Collective empowerment	Collective empowerment
Redistribution	Collective empowerment/ melting pot of political values	Collective empowerment	Collective empowerment/ vision for social transformation	Collective empowerment/ freedom of information/ media pluralism	No	Collective empowerment/ vision for social transformation	Collective empowerment	Collective empowerment

Table 6.4: The circuit of commons-based political value circulation.
Source: *Author*

6.6. General Dimensions of Commons-Based Value

Based on the foregoing analysis, the first general finding of the study is related to the value sequences and circuits of commons-based value. Elaboration on coded data has confirmed that commons-based value does not remain static but rather undergoes various phases of transformation in its form. Repetition in data patterns shows that value transformation generally follows specific sequences. As a rule, interviewees have confirmed the transformation of value throughout the sequences of generation, circulation and pooling. Correspondingly, almost all interviewees responded with a definite yes to the question of whether their community redistributed values to society. Furthermore, the data analysis showed that commons-based values and their circulation spread across all dimensions of social activity, i.e. economic, stricto sensu social, cultural and political, forming specific circuits of value transformation in each of these dimensions. Thus, practices of commons-based value circulation and value pooling in all four of the dimensions of social activity examined in the study take certain forms, which can be depicted as general formulae.[46]

Nevertheless, an unexpected finding emerged in the conduct of the research. Commons-based value circuits appear to be interconnected. Furthermore, they seem to be constituted in two stages. At the first stage, commoners build interpersonal circuits of reciprocity, by circulating commons-based values among themselves. Dense value kettles at this stage strengthen the second stage of value circulation, in which interpersonal gives its place to circular reciprocity. Multiple kettles of commons-based values form common pools of value, which then feed back and reinforce the interpersonal circulation of value. Finally, the establishment of robust common pools of value within intellectual commons makes them capable of redistributing commons-based values to society. By contrast, weak value practices at the phases of generation and circulation generally result in weak or no value pooling and redistribution, and vice versa. The two stages of value circulation are thus dialectically interrelated, with constant sequences of influence and counter-influence between each other. This key finding concurs with the phenomenon observed in all communities, in which the quality of value circulation at the first stage is reflected in the quality of value pooling and redistribution.

The second general finding of the study is related to the comparison between the contested and co-opted communities of the sample. In the process of data analysis, explicit and implicit differentiations emerged between the value circuits of contested and co-opted communities. Apart from the general circuits of commons-based value mentioned above, research findings show the presence of alternative value circuits in three dimensions of social activity, which were more distinct in the co-opted communities of the sample. These alternative circuits are constituted by value forms, which can be widely found in commodity markets and the capitalist mode of intellectual production, distribution and consumption.

Hence, the intellectual commons communities of the sample are reproduced by two types of value circuits in each of the four social dimensions of the study.

The first value circuit is constituted by commons-based values. The second value circuit is constituted by forms of value, which dominate commodity markets and the capitalist mode of intellectual production, distribution and consumption. These two distinct circuits of value co-exist within communities and reproduce them in a contentious and contradictory relationship between each other. The prevalence of commons-based value circulation and value pooling over capitalist-based forms of value constructs contested communities of the intellectual commons. The dominance of capitalist-based value circulation and accumulation over commons-based values co-opts communities of the intellectual commons to forces of commodification.

To sum up, the contested and co-opted circuits of value in the communities of the study take the general forms described in the two tables below:

	Economic	Social	Cultural	Political
Value-producing practices	Collaboration	Contribution to productive activity	Sharing	Participation
Values	Use value	Merit	Mutual aid	Self-empowerment
Flows	Gift	Trust	Shared ethos	Collective empowerment
Accumulation	CPR	Communal cohesion	Communal identity	Community self-governance
Redistribution	Gift	Social cohesion	Mutuality ethics	Collective empowerment

Table 6.5: Contested circuit of value in the communities of the intellectual commons.
Source: Author

	Economic	Social	Cultural	Political
Value-producing practices	Competition	Financial contribution	x	Deliberation
Values	Exchange value	Control of infrastructure	x	Self-empowerment
Flows	Commodity	Monetary exchange	x	Collective empowerment
Accumulation	Private appropriation	Social capital	x	No accumulation
Redistribution	Commodity	No redistribution	x	No redistribution

Table 6.6: Co-opted circuit of value in the communities of the intellectual commons.
Source: Author

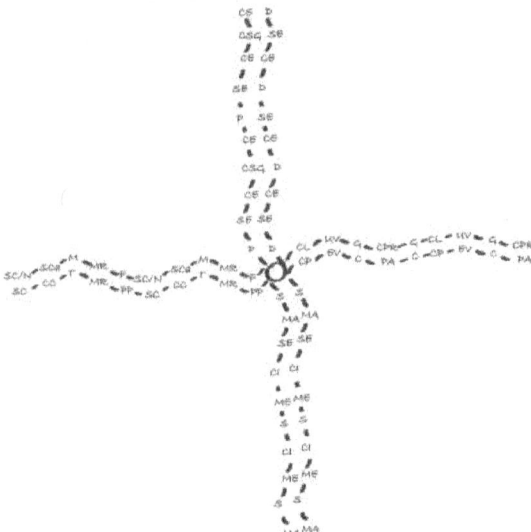

Figure 6.1: Value circulation and value pooling in intellectual commons communities.

In conclusion, each of the intellectual commons communities of the research sample is in terms of social value the outcome of the interrelation between contested and co-opted circuits of value circulation and value pooling and their variations. Value circulation and value pooling in the intellectual commons can be depicted according to the above graphic representation.

The exact formulations of value flows in each community depend on the resolutions of commons-based and monetary value dialectics attained by communal institutions, which in themselves are subject to internal and external influence by forces of commonification and commodification. Hence, communities of the intellectual commons should be conceptualised as entities in constant flux, in which contestation is always constant and co-optation imminent.

This chapter has laid down the formulae through which commons-based value is circulated, pooled together and redistributed within and beyond the communities of the intellectual commons. The ethical argument of this chapter is that these alternative circuits of value have both inherent moral value and are beneficial for society. Therefore, they ought to be protected and promoted by the law. The next chapter investigates the dialectics between commons-based and monetary values, in an effort to specify the mutual influences between them and the overall consequences for the characteristics and manifestations of the intellectual commons.

CHAPTER 7

The Social Value of the Intellectual Commons: Commons-Based and Monetary Value Dialectics

7.1. Introduction

Having already examined the circuits of commons-based value in the previous chapter, the current chapter further proceeds with an analysis of the dialectics between commons-based and monetary values, as recorded in the study. It also deals with the comparison of value circulation between the offline and online communities of the sample. Its key finding is that commons-based value circuits are in constant contestation with monetary values both in offline and online communities of the intellectual commons. Furthermore, it gives a view of the actual forms that such contestation takes and their impact on the evolution of the intellectual commons. As a corollary, the current chapter on commons-based and monetary value dialectics reveals that communities of the intellectual commons formulate their own specific modes of value circulation and value pooling, which come into contentious interrelation with the corresponding mode of commodity and capital circulation and accumulation.

7.2. Commons-Based and Monetary Value Dialectics

Coding and analysis of collected data in relation to the dialectics between commons-based and monetary values revealed the following general picture of sampled communities, as set out in the Table 7.1.

How to cite this book chapter:
Broumas, A. 2020. *Intellectual Commons and the Law: A Normative Theory for Commons-Based Peer Production.* Pp. 113–118. London: University of Westminster Press. DOI: https://doi.org/10.16997/book49.g. License: CC-BY-NC-ND

	Communities	Reliance on monetary exchange	Impact of monetary scarcity	Influence of monetary scarcity on commoning	Conflicts related to monetary exchange
Offline contested	Embros Theatre	Limited	Sharing among members/financial donations/unremunerated work/expropriation	Relative	Relative
	Athens Hackerspace	Limited	Sharing among members/donations/unremunerated work	Limited	Relative
Online contested	Libre Space Foundation	Relative	Unremunerated work/external funding	Relative	Limited
	Self-managed ERT	Limited	Sharing among members/financial donations/unremunerated work/resource expropriation	Extensive	Limited
Offline co-opted	Athens Impact Hub	Extensive	External funding/commodity market exchange	Relative	Limited
	CommonsLab	Extensive	Sharing among members/unremunerated work/external funding/commodity market exchange	Extensive	Extensive
Online co-opted	Sarantaporo.gr	Relative	Sharing among members/financial donations/external funding/unremunerated work	Extensive	Extensive
	P2P Lab	Relative	Sharing among members/external funding/unremunerated work	Relative	Limited

Table 7.1: The dialectic between commons-based and monetary value circulation.
Source: Author

Data analysis showed that, as a rule, co-opted communities are more dependent than contested communities on monetary value circulation for their reproduction. In particular, monetary flows penetrate co-opted deeper than contested communities, taking the form of commodity market exchange, external funding and financial donations. On the other hand, and in order to work around the mediation of money, contested communities depend more heavily on practices of sharing and are far more inventive in terms of other commons-based practices, such as the unremunerated productive activity of their members and resource expropriation, than co-opted communities. Workarounds again vary. All contested communities depend heavily on the productive activity of their members. Most communities also rely on voluntary contributions in kind, such as resources or member donations. Additionally, two of the sampled communities (the self-managed ERT and the Embros Theatre) expropriated and recuperated resources, such as water, electricity, communications and radio spectrum, in order to be able to redistribute common goods to society.

The foregoing analysis shows that both the contested and the co-opted communities of the sample receive pressure from monetary scarcity to varying degrees. To resolve monetary scarcity and achieve sustainability, co-opted communities resort in part to modes of external funding, commodity market exchange and, generally, monetary alongside commons-based value circulation. The pursuit of monetary remuneration as a means to ensure sustainability both within and beyond the limits of the community creates pressing dilemmas to these communities over the preservation of commons-based value practices or their partial transformation into exchange value. The degree of co-optation in each community depends both on the success of its model of sustainability and on its level of democratic consolidation. Co-opted communities that have been successful in becoming, even temporarily, financially sustainable through their chosen mode of interrelation with commodity markets, correspondingly ameliorate the extent of the pressure by monetary scarcity. In addition, when such communities have robust self-governing mechanisms in place that help them to hold on to underlying founding values and orientations, financial sustainability gives them space to expand commons-based value circuits and increase commons-based value redistribution to society. By contrast, co-opted communities that struggle hard to sustain themselves for periods longer than their capacities to endure gradually delimit commons-based value circuits and decrease commons-based value redistribution to society, as they fight for survival in commodity markets. Prolonged unsustainability increases value-laden tensions among members and has a negative impact on social, cultural and political value circulation and value pooling within the community. At this stage, communities either disband or enter a process of full co-optation within commodity markets, whereby their commons-based value circuits are displaced by monetary and commodity market exchange.

By contrast, contested communities employ different means to resolve issues of resource scarcity. Such communities delimit their reliance on monetary exchange as a way of both reducing the extent of its influence on their reproduction and becoming more independent from commodity markets. Workarounds to monetary and resource scarcity in contested communities mainly refer to commons-based practices of sharing and pooling together resources among members, accepting micro-donations by members or third-party natural persons or other commons-oriented groups and collectivities in solidarity, resorting to resource expropriation and, last but not least, mobilising members' unremunerated productive activity. Nevertheless, their relative independence from commodity markets makes contested communities more dependent on the unremunerated productive activity of their members. Pressure from monetary scarcity thus shifts to the level of the individual. Both contested and co-opted communities have entered conflicts related to the role of monetary exchange to varying degrees and extents. The nature of such conflicts, however, differs among communities. Whereas conflicts in co-opted communities mainly rotate around the success or failure of their model of sustainability, conflicts in contested communities explicitly surface in reference to the degree of monetary penetration and intermediation in everyday community practices. In contested communities with shortcomings of self-governance, conflicts may again be implicitly connected with monetary scarcity. Such conflicts intensify after financially successful events and revolve around the collective management of the treasury. In many respects, the disregard of individual remuneration in contested communities has an implied connection with phenomena of non-transparent management and informal hierarchies on the part of members who contribute more to the community in terms of productive activity and free time.

In conclusion, the contested and co-opted communities in the sample resolved the dialectics between commons-based and monetary value in different manners. Co-opted communities are relatively more dependent on monetary circulation and more prone to displacement of their commons-based value circuits than contested communities. Contested communities are relatively more dependent on non-remunerated productive activity from their members and more prone to power conflicts in relation to monetary resources held in common, when such resources increase. Co-opted communities exit the value sphere of the intellectual commons when their value circuits become predominated by monetary values and commodity market exchange or when they collapse under the weight of irreconcilable contradictions between their principles and everyday practices. Contested communities become redundant when they lose the capacity to motivate their members to offer their productive activity in large quantities on a non-remunerated basis. Hence, it is not by chance that the more resilient and commons-oriented communities, either co-opted or contested, have proven to be those with robust and participatory political institutions of self-governance. In contemporary societies, dominated by capital and commodity markets, the political circuit of commons-based values appears to determine contestation from co-optation.

7.3. The Comparison between Offline and Online Communities

Elaboration of data in terms of the offline/online distinction has yielded interesting key findings regarding the mediation of practices of commoning by contemporary information and communication technologies. In a nutshell, research has revealed that such technologies have the potential to strengthen and multiply elements of commons-based peer production, distribution and consumption in the communities of the sample, when utilised by commoners for such purposes.

In particular, the data coding of the economic circuit showed that the mediation of value circulation by money and commodity exchange appears to be significantly wider in the offline compared to the online communities of the sample. Accordingly, the data analysis of the dialectics between commons-based and monetary values revealed that the dependence of offline co-opted communities on monetary exchange and their reliance on commodity market exchange appears more extensive than in online co-opted communities. The augmented role of co-opted monetary and commodity exchange value circuits in offline communities has the side effect that these communities institute more fragile circuits of commons-based value, which tend to be suppressed and displaced by the former. Hence, this key finding supports the assumption that the use of contemporary information and communication technologies is connected with the influence of money and commodity exchange in intellectual commons communities in contextual causality. When such technologies do not directly promote practices of commoning, they at least delimit the influence of money and commodities in the value circuits of communities. Furthermore, coded data in the other three researched dimensions of social activity, i.e. stricto sensu social, cultural and political, show a lack of significant differences between the value circuits of offline/online communities. Indicatively, practices of sharing and mutual aid or networked forms of social value redistribution appear in both types of communities. This lack of difference runs counter to the commonsensical view that information and communication technologies weaken social bonds.

Taking into account these research outcomes in combination, the overall comparison between offline/online communities shows that the technological factor plays a significant role in the circulation of value within the intellectual commons. Information and communication technologies have certain capacities, which can be exploited by communities to amplify the circulation and pooling together of commons-based vis-à-vis monetary and commodified values. Nevertheless, as further examined below, such capacities can and will remain unfulfilled as long as forces of commonification do not circulate and pool together additional social and political values, which establish strong shared ethics, communal identities and, most important, self-governing mechanisms, which will give them the level of politicisation to become a social power 'for themselves'.

7.4. Conclusion

The data analysis in the current chapter has revealed the dialectics between opposing forms of social value within value circuits, which dynamically determine the physiognomy of each sampled community. The core of this dialectic is the confrontation between commons-based values and the universal equivalent of value in our societies, i.e. monetary value. Such a confrontation permeates and frames the communities of the intellectual commons. According to this dialectic, the intellectual commons are suppressed by the dominant value system of commodity markets and its universal equivalent of value in the form of money upon the intellectual commons. Such pressure, which may even lead to the extinction of intellectual commons communities, comes into contradiction with the overall conclusion regarding their social value and potential. Even though such communities may as a rule not be as productive as corporations in terms of money circulation, profits, jobs and taxes, this does not make them unproductive in terms of social value. On the contrary, the communities of the intellectual commons contain and emanate a wealth of social values, which ought to be protected through legal means. The next chapter of the research offers relevant arguments and conclusions.

CHAPTER 8

The Social Value of the Intellectual Commons: Conclusions on Commons-Based Value

8.1. Introduction

This chapter of the research elaborates on key findings of previous chapters in order to come up with more abstract statements on commons-based value, its sources, forms and mode of circulation and, finally, the value crisis challenging the interrelation between intellectual commons and capital. It is structured into the five following sections. The first offers a working definition of commons-based value in accordance with the findings of the research. The second determines productive communal activity as the source of commons-based value. The third analyses the forms of commons-based value. The fourth sketches out the basic characteristics of the mode of commons-based value circulation. The fifth and final substantive section examines the crises of value encountered in the sphere of the intellectual commons. Overall, this chapter offers a social theory of commons-based value circulation with normative dimensions in respect of the morality of the intellectual commons.

8.2. Social Value in the Intellectual Commons

Throughout the conduct of the research, participants have defined social value as what is important in their specific social context. This importance has been attributed to various practices of commoning, such as collaboration and utility, voluntary contribution and trust, openness and solidarity, participation and consensual decision-making. Taking into account these findings, commons-based values can be defined as collectively constructed representations in the particular context of intellectual commons communities of what constitutes meaningful social activity. This concurs with the anthropological conception

---

How to cite this book chapter:
Broumas, A. 2020. *Intellectual Commons and the Law: A Normative Theory for Commons-Based Peer Production*. Pp. 119–127. London: University of Westminster Press. DOI: https://doi.org/10.16997/book49.h. License: CC-BY-NC-ND

of social value as 'the meaning or importance society ascribes to an object' (Graeber 2001, 15, 39, 46–47).

The specificities of commons-based value in the communities of the sample have been found to be inherently related to their communal context. What is valuable for commoners depends on collective judgements about value constructed within their community (Simmel 2001, 65). This supports the assumption that the evaluation of what is important is preceded by the collective attribution of meaning to action, which in itself presupposes a total system of meaning (Saussure 1966). As Castoriadis writes, 'society cannot institute itself without instituting itself as "something" and this "something" is necessarily already an imaginary signification' (Castoriadis 1997, 269). The collective attribution of importance to a specific activity of commoning thus presupposes the existence of a commons community with a collective conception about social value and its own place in society. Commons-based value thus appears to be preceded by a communal plexus of imaginary significations regarding the commons and their value for society. It is only by being integrated into this larger action-guiding mechanism that each practice of commoning acquires meaning and becomes worth pursuing.

8.3. Productive Communal Activity as the Source of Commons-Based Value

Social value in the intellectual commons occurs through the movement and transformation of matter. The movement of matter is both an objective/non-transitive phenomenon and a social phenomenon that acquires meaning and value within and through its social context (Fuchs 2016, 35). The movement of matter within the spheres of the intellectual commons therefore circulates and pools together social values.

It follows that social value necessarily comes into being through human action consolidated in social practices. Rather than being an individual activity, any practice of commoning is a communal process – many commoners act together in the community as a combined worker. Value production in the commons is, therefore, inherently socialised. In addition, to produce value, practices of commoning are necessarily intentional and productive in the sense of contributing to social reproduction (Graeber 2001, 58–59, 76). Along these lines, research findings reveal the following value-producing practices in each of the four social dimensions under examination:

	Economic	Social	Cultural	Political
Value-producing practices	Collaboration	Contribution in productive activity/ unalienated work	Sharing	Participation

Table 8.1: Forms of productive communal activity in the communities of the intellectual commons.
Source: Author

Commons-based values are objectified in the movement and transformation of matter caused by the foregoing practices. The common denominator of all these practices is that they constitute forms of productive communal activity, i.e. unalienated work defined in the widest possible way (De Angelis 2007, 24; Fuchs 2014, 37; Graeber 2001, 68). As a corollary, productive communal activity – intermingled with matter – should be considered the source of commons-based values.

8.4. The Forms of Commons-Based Value

What is valued in each social formation is greatly dependent on the interrelation between dominant and alternative social forces in each socio-historical context. Contests over value lie at the heart of politics. For conventional economics, value is considered to be solely produced at the point of exchange and, therefore, the only form of social value that supposedly exists is exchange value. Hence, all other forms of social value are either concealed or at best described as positive externalities or spillovers to the commodity market value system.

By monitoring the circulation of commons-based value in its multitudinous manifestations, the current research follows a non-economistic approach to the phenomenon of social value, examining its formulations in all facets of social activity on an equal footing. According to the outcomes of the current research, commons-based values unfold in economic, stricto sensu social, cultural and political manifestations. The following table exhibits the main forms that commons-based value takes in the communities under examination:

	Economic	Social	Cultural	Political
Values	Use value	Merit	Mutual aid	Self-empowerment

Table 8.2: Main forms of commons-based value in the communities of the intellectual commons.
Source: Author

By no means do such manifestations imply the existence of separate domains of social activity. Rather, they refer to aspects and characteristics of the same communal practices of production, distribution and consumption of intellectual resources pooled together in common. In other words, they constitute dimensions of the same value practices and value spheres, which emerge in undifferentiated continuity, as they constitute integrated sets of social relations.

In contemporary capital-dominated societies, commodity markets are the dominant system of value circulation. In the framework of commodity markets, actors interrelate through impersonal transactions mediated by the exchange of monetary values. Monetary value prevails as the universal equivalent of value and, as a result, frames and conditions the attribution, production, circulation and ranking of all other social values. Yet, the primary social function of money is its accumulation as capital. In this function, money operates less as a means of exchange and more as an end in itself, i.e. as the final outcome of the tendency to accumulate. The function of accumulation thus transforms money into the dominant social power of our age. Apart from operating as the universal equivalent of all other values, this makes money in our societies the ultimate form of the accumulation of social power. By contrast, commons-based values in all their forms are generated and are, thus, dependent upon face-to-face interpersonal and communal relationships (Bollier 2008, 251). Owing to this characteristic they become both means of value circulation and ends in themselves. Their strong connection with face-to-face human relations also renders the qualities of their formulations difficult to quantify and essentially different from each other. As a result, commons-based values, especially their non-economic forms, are relatively incommensurable and commons-based value spheres lack general forms of value equivalence.

Despite the finding that commons-based value circulation and value pooling lack a universal equivalent of value, research has shown that a certain value form has central importance in commons-based value spheres due to their dependence on the flourishing of communal bonds. This value form is communal trust. Interviewees from both the contested and co-opted communities under examination have repeatedly stressed the crucial role that trust plays in the sustenance of practices of commoning. Indicatively, Hackerspace members characterised trust as very important for the community, since it is the reason for the smooth operation of community affairs. Overall, research coding and analysis on trust have yielded data in greater quality and quantity than other codes of the research. For this reason, it can be safely claimed that trust appears to constitute the cornerstone of commons-based value circulation and value pooling.

8.5. The Mode of Commons-Based Value Circulation

In the current research, the circulation of commons-based values is analysed as a totality. In this context, the research outcomes reveal a rich diversity of forms and circuits of commons-based value. This inherent attribute of the intellectual commons makes them inappropriate to be conceptualised, described, analysed and governed as systems. The inertness of the systemic approach entails the risk of disregarding the diversity and of ignoring the fluid interrelation of the intellectual commons with their environment. Instead of approaching the intellectual commons as systems, analysis should rather focus on modes of value circulation and value pooling. Such modes evolve through time in a dialectical manner, both framing practices of commoning and being reproduced and reformulated by them in reflexivity to internal and external factors of change.

As a starting point, it can be claimed that social value and its circulation/ allocation take specific historical forms depending on each social context and modes of social reproduction. In relation to the intellectual commons, the repetition of practices of commoning converges into a specific mode of commons-based value circulation and value pooling. Such a mode is constituted by sequences of value transformation and circuits of value flow. In terms of value sequences, research has revealed that the transformation of value is structured around practices of value generation, value flow/circulation, value pooling and, finally, value redistribution. In the intellectual commons, value allocation is achieved by practices of pooling intangible resources together in pools of information, communication, knowledge and culture held in common. Pooling, instead of reciprocity, is the foundation of the mode of circulation/allocation of commons-based values. Instead of being privately appropriated as in commodity markets, value allocation within the spheres of the intellectual commons is socialised.

Pooling is a superior mode of value allocation. When productive communities of the intellectual commons possess institutions that guarantee that the value output of their production remains within the virtuous circle of commons-based peer production, then practices of pooling resources in common acquire network effects. This gives rise to an expansion of both the quantity/quality of production and the size of productive communities, which has been characterised as the 'cornucopia of the commons' (Bollier 2007, 34). The communities of the study have deliberately constructed specific mechanisms to pool together their value output and avoid its capture by commodity market forces. First of all, contested communities have reduced their exposure to monetary exchange and have invented alternative practices to garner resources and work. Secondly, commoners have managed to construct practices of exchange based on generalised reciprocity as means to avoid the quantification of commons-based value and its subsequent co-optation by the commodity market value system.[47] Accordingly, communities have developed non-commodified social practices of transvestment in order to transfer value flows from the commodity market to the sphere of the commons, such as peer-to-peer donations and funding.[48] Furthermore, certain communities, especially contested ones, employ more aggressive strategies of social appropriation vis-à-vis commodity markets in order to pool together social values, such as the expropriation of privately owned commodities. Finally, all the contested and most of the co-opted communities in the sample instituted informal communal rules and/or adopted legal norms, such as copyleft licences, to prohibit the private appropriation and commodification of common pool resources. This phenomenon of deliberately expanding the pooling of resources in common can be termed commonification. Contrary to the opposite transformations of commodification, commonification transforms social relations, which generate marketable commodities valued for what they can bring in exchange, into social relations, which generate resources produced by multiple creators in communal collaboration, openly accessible to communities or the wider society and valued for their use. For this reason, pooling should be considered the most important practice of commoning in the quest of the intellectual commons for value sovereignty.

Society is reproduced through the circulation and allocation of multiple forms of social value and according to diverse value spheres (Appadurai 1988, 14–15). Any time social forces of commonification reveal themselves by producing forms of value alternative to the dominant value system of commodity markets, these sets of communal value practices articulate themselves in commons-based value spheres. The transformation from one form of value to another renders possible the transition of value between different value spheres. As Gregory describes it, 'things are valued in many different ways over the course of their "life" [...] people can switch from one value regime to another as, for example, when gold is purchased as a commodity, given as a gift to a daughter and passed on to descendants as a family heirloom' (Gregory 2000, 110). The boundaries between intellectual commons and commodity markets are thus porous and susceptible to permeability and interchange. Nevertheless, capital holds a strategic position in the general circulation of values in society owing to the imposition of commodity market institutions from the state as the dominant value system of society. Such a position gives capital the structural power to control the switch between diverse and heterogeneous social values and money.

Along these lines, the mode of commons-based value circulation is dialectically interrelated with the dominant mode of capitalist value circulation and the dominant value system of commodity markets. This dialectical relation takes various forms. Alternative conceptions of the importance people attribute to action, which are generated within the intellectual commons, are heavily influenced by the social prevalence of economic exchange value and commodity markets. When coping with resource scarcity in societies inundated with commodities, intellectual commons communities face severe pressure to transform part or the entirety of their value output into economic exchange values and money. This influence upon the circulation and pooling of commons-based values by exchanging value and money is manifested in hybrid forms of co-opted value circuits within the intellectual commons. Co-opted value forms, as described in the previous section, act as switches of value transformation from the commons-based value spheres to the commodity market value system. At the point when co-opted circuits predominate contested circuits of commons-based value, intellectual commons communities either break down or are gradually transformed into for-profit enterprises and their social aims are subsumed under the prevailing logic of capital accumulation. From this follows that intellectual commons are nowhere to be found as full-fledged realisations of the potential of commonification but rather appear as sets of practices fulfilled to the extent possible by the co-relations between forces of commonification and commodification.

By contrast, commons-based values constitute conceptions of what is socially important activity not just within communities of the intellectual commons but also in society as a whole (De Angelis 2007, 179). Communities of the intellectual commons are not isolated but, rather, lie at the core of socially reproductive activity. Commons-based values are constantly redistributed to society, thus contributing to its reproduction. Through its widespread social circulation, commons-based value redistribution challenges dominant perceptions about social value. In particular, it challenges the dominant perception of economic exchange value as the primary, or even exclusive, form of social value and of commodity markets as the primary, or even exclusive, societal value system. Practices of commoning that generate commons-based values reveal in practice the fallacy that social activities are not productive if they do not create economic exchange value and are, therefore, not monetarily quantifiable. In this way, the flow of commons-based values to society calls into question hegemonic ideologies regarding what should be rewarded or not by social institutions. It is the moment when the intellectual commons loom out of invisibility that social reorientation on a mass scale gradually becomes possible.

8.6. Crises of Value

Key findings of the research show that both the contested and the co-opted communities of the sample receive pressure from monetary scarcity to varying degrees. This breakdown of value circulation is due to the fact that the flow of commons-based values to society, as explicitly confirmed to be taking place by all participants in the study, is basically not remunerated by a counter-flow of social values towards the communities of the intellectual commons.

The unsustainable value flows recorded in the study give a hint of a more general contradiction in the current sublation between intellectual commons and capital. By controlling the dominant system (commodity market) and the universal equivalent (money) of social value, capital is in a position to dominate the circuits of commons-based value circulation and value pooling. This structural superiority gives the power to capital to capture the values of the commons and switch them into money. Value capture is a more appropriate term than wage labour to describe such strategies of capital accumulation. Wage labour is a specific co-relation of social power between labour and capital. Yet, even in orthodox Marxist political economy, wage labour was never considered to be the sole means through which capital accumulates its socio-economic power. Marxists always acknowledged other ways of value capture by capital, which involve co-relations of social power other than wage labour. Marx talked of the primitive accumulation of capital (Marx 1990, 896). Luxemburg observed that primitive accumulation is a continuous phenomenon throughout colonialist and imperialist epochs (Luxemburg 2003, 447). Harvey conjoined various contemporary phenomena of value capture under the term 'accumulation by dispossession' (Harvey 2003, 137). All such phenomena have in common the capturing of value through power mechanisms other than wage labour. Along the same lines, Hardt and Negri write, 'exploitation under the hegemony of immaterial labor is no longer primarily the expropriation of value measured by individual or collective labor time but rather the capture of value that is produced by cooperative labor and that becomes increasingly common through its circulation in social networks' (Hardt and Negri 2004, 113). For them, commons-based values are produced in relative autonomy to the power of capital: 'In contrast to industry, extraction relies on forms of wealth that to a large extent preexist the engagement of capital [...] Whereas in the factory workers cooperate according to schemes and discipline dictated by the capitalist, here value is produced through social cooperation not directly organized by capital—social cooperation that is, in that sense, relatively autonomous' (Hardt and Negri 2017, 120). Accordingly, apart from non-remunerated labour, a variety of value capture mechanisms takes place in the dialectics between commons-based and commodity market value spheres, which can be generally described under the umbrella term 'value capture'. Through value capture, commons-based value spheres are to varying degrees ravaged by the hijacking of commons-based values by capital without opposite value flows to counter-balance the loss (Kostakis and Bauwens 2014, 26). Accordingly, communal relations of value circulation/allocation, which sustain the intellectual commons, are eroded by the penetration of the commodity and the logic of capital accumulation (De Angelis 2007, 215; Hyde 2007, 96–99). The result is a crisis of value circulation, wherein the producers of value (commoners) are deprived of the means to reproduce the social relations (intellectual commons), which make such value generation and circulation possible (Bauwens and Niaros 2017).

This value crisis appears to be confined within the boundaries of the intellectual commons. Nevertheless, such a hypothesis remains on the surface of things. Deeper analysis reveals that the capitalist mode of intellectual production, distribution and consumption is dependent on the intellectual commons. The fundamental 'law of motion' of capital is its tendency to expand by subsuming terrains of commoning previously left relatively outside the reproduction of capital. With regard to the intellectual commons, such subsumption is accomplished by valorising the output of commons-based peer production in multiple ways. Yet, capital is incapable of reproducing the relations of commons-based peer production, upon which its mechanisms of value capture are dependent, since such mechanisms are external to the organisation of commons-based value generation. Even in the co-opted spheres of the commons their subsumption by capital remains formal and does not penetrate the organisation of commons-based peer production. Secondly, value capture is a transformative process of valorisation. Through this process, relations of commonification are dissolved, i.e. commons-based values are displaced by economic exchange and monetary forms of value. By dissolving the commons, capital destroys the very productive base upon which it stands. Hence, capitalist reproduction at the level of intellectual social activity becomes unsustainable and destroys its own conditions of existence. In this context, dysfunctions of intellectual property-enabled commodity markets and capital accumulation in the networked information economy should be viewed as repercussions of the unsustainable commodification of our commonwealth.

In conclusion, the unsustainable value flows monitored in the current study indicate the existence of wider crises of value in the interrelation between intellectual commons and capital. This unsustainability reveals the pressing need for the institution of counter-flows of value from commodity markets to the intellectual commons, in order to restore the balance in the circulation of social value between these two spheres. As Bauwens and Niaros have spelled out, value sovereignty for the communities of the intellectual commons necessitates the constitution of practices of commoning for the 'reverse co-optation' of capitalist values and their transformation into commons-based values (Bauwens and Niaros 2017, 4–6).

8.7. Conclusion

The current research backs with empirical data the presence of an alternative proto-mode of value circulation based on the intellectual commons, which supports the reproduction of the intellectual bases of our societies in dialectical interrelation to the dominant capitalist mode. It is, therefore, a straightforward dispute of the ideological perspective that money is the sole form of social value and that commodity markets subsume the totality of value circulation in our societies. By contrast, this research generally supports the hypothesis that commons-based circuits of value circulation and value pooling are at work in all dimensions of social activity, thus significantly contributing to social reproduction. Finally, by exploiting the power of critical political economy as a methodological tool for sociological research on the commons, this study has the aim of rendering commons-based value visible to activists, researchers and policymakers and fuelling practices, policies and laws that unleash their potential.

The next chapter of the book recapitulates the arguments of both the current social research project on commons-based value and all other previous chapters regarding the moral significance of the intellectual commons with the aim of offering a unified normative theory of the intellectual commons in support of an intellectual commons law.

CHAPTER 9

Towards a Normative Theory of the Intellectual Commons

9.1. Introduction

This chapter builds upon the ontological, epistemological, historical and social research outcomes of the book. The second chapter of the book exhibited the elements of the intellectual commons, i.e. commoners, communities and common pool resources, and highlighted their strong ontological connection with personal autonomy and practices of sharing and collaboration. The third chapter was an analysis of the main characteristics of commons-based peer production from the perspective of contemporary theories of the intellectual commons. The fourth chapter demonstrated the inherent sociality of cultural production across history. Chapters 5–8 provided solid research findings on the social value of the intellectual commons. This chapter is purported to constitute the normative denouement of the book, by laying down the foundations for the critical normative theory of the intellectual commons and the moral justification of an intellectual commons law. The chapter is structured into six interlinked sections. The next section sets out the basic tenets of a critical normative theory of the intellectual commons. The subsequent four sections examine the normative dimensions of the intellectual commons, i.e. personhood, work, value and community. The concluding sections briefly list the contours of an intellectual commons law in alignment with the normative evaluations of the chapter.

9.2. Foundations of the Critical Normative Theory of the Intellectual Commons

The critical normative theory of the intellectual commons is founded on (i) an explicit orientation towards progressive social transformation, (ii) the dialectics

---

How to cite this book chapter:
Broumas, A. 2020. *Intellectual Commons and the Law: A Normative Theory for Commons-Based Peer Production*. Pp. 129–153. London: University of Westminster Press. DOI: https://doi.org/10.16997/book49.i. License: CC-BY-NC-ND

between potentiality and actuality, (iii) the interrelation between structure and agency, and (iv) the moral significance of the dimensions of the intellectual commons.

In terms of its orientation, critical normative theory is guided by the 'categoric imperative to overthrow all conditions in which man is a degraded, enslaved, neglected, contemptible being' (Marx 1997, 257–258). The critical normative perspective asserts that policy choices in relation to the organisation of intellectual production, distribution and consumption are fundamentally political. These choices not only frame our freedom of creativity and innovation but also determine the evolution of our science, technology and culture and influence the quality of our public sphere, channels of political participation and networked information economy. Therefore, the question of how we govern our creative practice relates in a sense to the broader question in which society we want to live in. According to the critical normative perspective, the rules governing our creative practice ought to be designed according to what is morally right for society. It is, hence, mainly founded either on deontological moral arguments in favour of the inherent social value of the intellectual commons or on a rule-based consequentialism oriented towards countering social domination and promoting freedom, equality and democracy. Within this framework, the intellectual commons are held to embrace social relations, which are inherently moral because of their value for collective empowerment, social justice and democracy. Productive communities of commoners are considered to contribute to the welfare of both their members and the wider public and to cultivate sets of commons-based communal relations with inherent moral value. In this light, commons-based creative practices are morally justified in respect of their value for collective empowerment, social justice, freedom from domination, cultural diversity and democratic participation. Based on this normative perspective, the critical normative theory of the intellectual commons accommodates, on the one hand, a thorough critique of contemporary intellectual property laws and, on the other hand, an adequate moral evaluation of the social potential of the intellectual commons for social welfare, freedom and democracy.

The critical normative perspective of the intellectual commons is further determined by the dialectics between the actuality and the potentiality of contemporary intellectual production, distribution and consumption, with a definite orientation towards the realisation of the positive social potential of commons-based practices. Such an approach recognises the social value of the intellectual commons as the cornerstone of our culture, science and technology and as a major part of contemporary intellectual production, distribution and consumption. In addition, the critical normative approach acknowledges the phenomenon of social creativity and innovation at the cutting edge of contemporary economic and social transformations and its immense social value. It is also receptive of the capacities of contemporary information and communication technologies to unleash the powers of the social intellect. Hence, it is argued that an institutional ecology for commons-based peer production ought to be designed in such a way as to decouple the current conjoinment of intellectual commons and commodity markets under the rule of capital and provide the institutional infrastructure for the exploitation in full of the potential of the intellectual commons for self-development, collective empowerment, social justice and democracy.

The 'philosophical anthropology' of critical normative theory is determined by its approach to the dialectics between structure and agency. Contrary to one-dimensional approaches that view creators either as pre-social agents or as entirely socially determined, the critical normative approach takes the stance that the intellectual commons emerge from a dialectical interrelation between the individual agency of commoners and the communal structures in which they participate. In the context of commons-based peer production, individual creators interrelate to produce in community as a collective subjective force, while production takes place as a collective and socialised practice essentially based on sharing and collaboration. Within this framework, individual creative activity is immersed in cooperative production. As such, individual contributions are inextricably fused and entangled in an inseparable whole, the value of which is superior to the sum of its parts. Individual well-being is therefore unattainable without collective well-being. In this context, the essence of the link between the commoner and her intellectual work is understood by virtue of the links between the commoner, her community and society in general. Hence, in all cases that private interests justify the award to commoners of individual rights upon common pool resources, such rights are granted on the condition and to the extent that they operate to the virtue of the relevant community and the wider society.

Last but not least, critical normative theory commences its moral argumentation from the ontological elements of the intellectual commons. As already exhibited in the second chapter of the book, the intellectual commons are held to be the outcome of the interrelation between, on the one hand, their subjective elements, i.e. producers and communities, and, on the other hand, their objective element, i.e. commonly pooled intangible resources. Yet, at the point of production such elements are transformed and sublated to a higher level of ontological complexity into commons-based forms of personhood, work, value and community. Producers are interpenetrated by communal relations and transformed into commoners, exhibiting novel characteristics of personhood in community with their kind. Intellectual work in the form of individual contributions is transformed into a commons-based peer proto-mode of production. The dialectical interrelation between the subjective and objective elements of the intellectual commons produces commons-based forms of value, which circulate within and beyond the communities of the intellectual commons. Finally, through the productive practice, communities are also in themselves constantly reproduced, while communal relations are diffused in society. This practice of transformation is depicted in Figure 9.1.

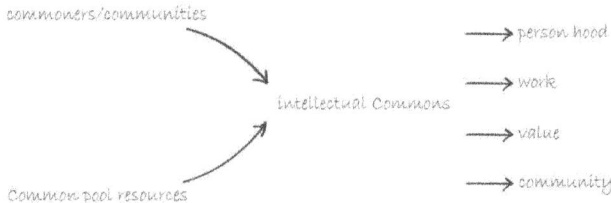

Figure 9.1: The normative dimensions of the intellectual commons.
Source: Author

From a critical normative perspective, personhood, work, value and community are thus considered dimensions of the intellectual commons with moral significance. Each of the following sections gives an analysis of the ethical considerations with regard to these four dimensions with the aim of constructing a coherent and integrated normative theory for the intellectual commons.

9.3. Personhood

Starting from the premise that human beings are social beings, the critical normative theory of the intellectual commons takes the position that human agency is dialectically interrelated with social structure. Contrary to opposing common understandings of intellectual production as a strictly either solitary or collective endeavour, the critical normative perspective approaches the creative practice as a constant dialectical exchange between the poles of agency and structure, through which both the creative individual and the intellectual commons community are being constantly reconstructed by their mutual influences.[49] The task of the philosopher is to unearth each time the particularities of such an exchange and determine the impact exerted by each dialectical pole.

Personhood in the context of the intellectual commons arises in the form of the commoner. The characteristics of the commoner are two-dimensional. On the one hand, individual contribution to intellectual production takes the communal form of sharing and collaboration among peers.[50] On the other hand, participation in the productive community influences the commoner's personal world view, incentives, values and identity.[51] Within this framework, personhood acquires characteristics, which have moral significance. The contribution of the commoner to the community is strongly connected with the freedom of science and culture and with human dignity. The influence of the community on the commoner is evaluated from the perspective of the capacity of communal relations to accommodate personal autonomy and cultivate self-development.

Perspective	Moral significance
Commoner → Community	Freedom of science and culture
	Human dignity
Community → Commoner	Personal autonomy
	Self-development

Table 9.1: The moral significance of the commoner.
Source: Author

The critical normative theory of the intellectual commons holds the unrestricted freedom to contribute to the intellectual commons to be fundamental for the well-being of commoners, communities and society in general. Concomitantly, it gives moral priority to the right to participate in scientific progress and cultural life in the form of a general freedom of scientific research and creative activity within the intellectual commons, both individually and in association with others. Embracing this normative premise has important repercussions in terms of positive law. At the level of human rights law, the participatory aspect of the human right to science and culture is given equal weight vis-à-vis the aspect of authors' exclusive rights established on international human rights law treaties. Secondly, the human right to science and culture is given primacy over international or national intellectual property law, on the legal grounds that the promotion and protection of human rights takes precedence over any other objectives and obligations of signatory states of international human rights treaties. Following the above, it is held that states are morally committed to respecting, protecting and fulfilling the freedom to contribute to the intellectual commons, thereby abstaining from its restriction through intellectual property laws, which are not compatible with international human rights treaties. In addition, the critical normative theory of the intellectual commons holds that the freedom to contribute to the intellectual commons ought to acquire statutory content substantive enough to give commoners the ability for its meaningful practice. Such a substantive normative content to the human right to participate in scientific progress and cultural life within the intellectual commons shall include (i) the right of everyone to access the public domain without discrimination; (ii) the freedom of all to contribute to the scientific and cultural commons, especially the freedoms to create, share, collectively transform prior or newly produced resources and pool them in common; (iii) the right of communities to defend the intellectual commons from enclosure or commodification and receive compensation from any type of commercial use of common pooled resources; and (iv) an enabling social environment fostering the foregoing rights and freedoms through commons-oriented state policies.

The critical normative theory of the intellectual commons further asserts that participation in the intellectual commons is inextricably connected with human dignity. Access to the fundamentals of information, knowledge and culture is a prerequisite of one's capacity to exercise all other human rights and freedoms. Furthermore, the freedom to contribute to the intellectual commons is essential for commoners' autonomy and self-development. Therefore, the deprivation of one's access or freedom to take part in the scientific and cultural commons disregards her dignity as a person. The extensive enclosure of the intellectual commons disables individual autonomy to the extent that it may constitute an offence to the human dignity of impoverished individuals without the social and economic means to restore access to our intellectual commonwealth. As a result, it is claimed that the freedom of participation in the intellectual commons lies at the core of human dignity and ought not to be restricted, should commoners be paid due respect as dignified individuals. Along the same lines, commons-oriented rules and institutions are ethically necessary either on the ground that the latter shield from private appropriation artefacts essential for authors and inventors to express their creative 'wills' or on the ground that they create social conditions conducive to creative intellectual activity, which is in turn important to the flourishing of individuals as autonomous moral agents.

Apart from the foregoing, the peer relations of the intellectual commons are deontologically justified on individual autonomy and personal self-development. First of all, any form of artistic expression and scientific discovery is an elemental exercise of personal autonomy and self-determination. Creativity and innovativeness are generated through the activation of superior intellectual human capacities and qualities, such as enquiry, critical reflection, inspiration and imagination. The self-emancipatory aspect of these qualities is what constitutes autonomous human beings. Therefore, the freedom to contribute to science and culture can be claimed as the upmost expression of individual autonomy, an upfront act of changing the world for the better. Secondly, creativity and innovativeness are fundamental to personal self-development. The active participation in one's scientific and cultural environment is important to personal well-being. Accordingly, creative capacities are closely bound up with the way we constitute ourselves, posit ourselves in the world and draw up our short- and long-term life plans. In addition, the practice of creativity and innovativeness are strongly connected to human flourishing. Becoming creative is the medium to proper self-development and the fulfilment of one's own potential. Hence, the self-constituting aspect of the creative practice render it an essential element of personhood. Nevertheless, self-development presupposes one's ability to access and transform resources in his or her social environment (Radin 1982, 957). Communal relations and commons-based practices are thus held to be moral and worthy of protection and institutional promotion, because they embrace the capacity of individuals to express autonomously, self-develop and realise their creative capacities to the full.

In general, the critical normative theory provides moral justifications of the intellectual commons from the perspective of the creative individual as an end in herself and the concomitant imperative for her empowerment through appropriate social institutions. From this theoretical prism, intellectual property laws are subsumed under the framework of international human rights treaties, which then become the primal legal institutions for the regulation of contemporary intellectual production, distribution and consumption. Furthermore, the deontological and positive law foundations of the right to participate in the intellectual commons are held to justify an extensive legal status of the public domain in terms of both the freedom of access and transformative use and the obligation of states to respect and empower such freedom. As a result, such an ethical theory strikes an equitable balance between the right to participate in science and culture and individual authors' rights within the system of human rights law and, therefore, morally justifies the reform and reorientation of intellectual property laws in such a direction.

9.4. Work

The critical normative theory of the intellectual commons commences from a conception of the creator as a socio-historical and yet autonomous person in the conduct of her creative practice. Creators are socio-historical selves in the sense that they are embedded in their social and historical context. Their creative cognitive practices, such as their use of language, attribution of meaning and construction of aesthetic values, are defined interpersonally vis-à-vis their co-creators, audience and wider society. The experiences fuelling their imagination are related to their social context. Their emotions and affects have interpersonal causes. Their motivations and overall self-narrative are heavily determined by reference to the groups they participate and the society they live in. Yet, creators are autonomous in their creative practice in the sense that they are capable of self-reflecting on their socio-historical context in the conduct of producing intellectual works.

Socio-historically framed creativity only partly accounts for the advancement of arts and science. Additional traits inherent to intellectual production depict a view of authors and inventors that is far away from the dominant conception of the Promethean or solitary creator. In practice, creators quarry the form and content of their intellectual achievements from the vast deposits of information, knowledge and culture accumulated through time by the collective endeavours of prior generations.[52] Across history, authors and inventors have worked on their creations directly or indirectly through practices of sharing and collaboration.[53] Creativity and innovativeness are practices in which the singular is interrelated with the plural, with the mediation of relations of production, social norms and positive law. Hence, from a wider perspective, intellectual work is not strictly attributed to the individual creator but rather refers to a social relation in which the latter's contribution operates as input to social modes of intellectual production, distribution and consumption.

Work in the context of intellectual production has moral significance. The link between the creator and the outcome of her work gives rise to ethical considerations about the protection and promotion of certain interests of the creator vis-à-vis the collectivity. The link between the community and the collective productive output of its members calls for the respect of the interests of the community by society in general. And the common interest of current and future creators to access and work upon the public domain requires its protection and promotion from generalised enclosure and commodification. Whether individual or collective, rights upon the use of intellectual works presuppose moral demands and corresponding duties to respect the foregoing interests. In accordance, the ethical considerations brought about by intellectual work are analysed in the table below from the perspectives of the creator, the productive community and society in general:

Perspective	Moral significance
The interests of the creator	Work/commons mix
	Joint authorship
The interests of the community	Collective work
	Inherent sociality of intellectual work
The common interest	No harm to others
	No spoilage of the commons

Table 9.2: The moral significance of intellectual work.
Source: Author

Within the framework of the critical normative theory of the intellectual commons, the rights of creators upon the products of their labour are determined by the morally significant elements of the social relation of work. These are located in the link of the creator's individual contribution with the public domain and the work of others. The work/commons mixing argument asserts that intellectual works ought to be managed as commons rather than property, because such works are built upon intangible resources that already embody the work of prior generations. In contrast to natural resources, the public domain is thus constituted by objects that do not lie in a primordial state of nature. Instead, it is a social domain of information, knowledge and culture commonly pooled by the accumulated efforts of prior generations. Since the raw materials of intellectual production already incorporate the work of others, their interests ought to be taken equally into account as those of contemporary creators. Hence, in the absence of contractual means with prior authors and inventors, the mixture of resources in the public domain with one's own work cannot morally justify the establishment of private property, at least in its Blackstonian form.[54] Rather, the moral imperative to treat the interests of prior and contemporary creators alike necessitates the harmonisation of rights to individual contributions within a management regime oriented towards the commons.

Accordingly, the critical normative theory of the intellectual commons raises concerns with regard to the treatment of joint intellectual creations under contemporary intellectual property laws. Such concerns are especially relevant today since the production of contemporary artistic works, scientific discoveries or technological breakthroughs revolves more and more around collaborative creativity and innovation by multitudes of workers joined together in industrial or commons-based modes of production.[55] In contrast to contemporary relations of production, today's doctrines of authorship act as social constructs, which obfuscate the collective character of contemporary intellectual production and tend to promote the concentration of exclusive intellectual property rights to single natural persons or legal entities as means to centralise control over the latter and facilitate their exchange in commodity markets.[56] Within the framework of the critical normative theory of the intellectual commons, disregard of the actual expenditure of individual efforts in joint intellectual works is considered morally wrong. In this context, collaborating creators ought to be able to invoke rights that appropriately pay tribute to the actuality of joint authorship in contemporary relations of intellectual production.

In reference to the interests of the community of producers, critical normative theory focuses on the moral evaluation of the collective and socialised character of the social relation of work. From a moral standpoint, the transformation of a commonly held resource through one's work justifies the entitlement of rights over the outcome of the mixture of the commons with work, on the condition that the worker's expedited effort makes the major part of the value of the novel object.[57] As already exhibited in previous chapters, any intellectual creation is inherently derivative and referential upon pre-existing knowledge. Furthermore, intellectual production is by its nature a practice of incremental, sequential and complementary advancement upon prior achievements, which in themselves are founded on the collective endeavour of science and the arts as a whole. For these reasons, individual contributions to intellectual production do not have sufficient moral standing compared to the immense wealth of the intellectual commons to qualify for the establishment of individual rights of absolute private enclosure upon intellectual works.

More importantly, intellectual production is an essentially socialised practice, in which individual contributions are, on the one hand, heavily influenced by prior and present knowledge and, on the other hand, intertwined through collaboration among multiple creators in an inseparable whole. Science, technology and culture develop in a process of sharing and collaboration between creative collectivities of both the past and the present, wherein the individual author/inventor dialectically receives influence from her social environment, from co-creators and from prior intellectual achievements and, at the same time, contributes to the dynamism of collective creativity and innovativeness. The advancement of arts and science as a whole can in itself be conceived of as a collective and collaborative social enterprise for the search of truth, beauty and social flourishment.[58] Any intellectual work is thus an amalgam of individual and collective achievement, always reflecting the creative and innovative contribution of an individual author/inventor upon prior intellectual advancements. In addition, most contemporary intellectual works embody in one way or another the joint collaborative effort of multiple workers and derive their social value from the fact that they contribute to a wider knowledge field or cultural current. From this standpoint, the attribution of an intellectual expression or application in its entirety to single individuals or legal entities does not correspond to the actuality of the form of postmodern intellectual production and cannot be held to be morally acceptable. On the contrary, the allocation of rights and duties between the commoner and the collectivity needs to take seriously into account the ethical implications arising from the fundamentally social character of human creativity and innovation.

From the perspective of the common interest, the critical normative theory of the intellectual commons asserts that everyone ought to have equal privilege to access and use the public domain. Inspired by the Lockean 'no harm' proviso, it then argues that creators ought to be morally entitled to individual rights upon their work so long as there is 'enough and as good' left in common for others to practise their freedom of science and culture. Therefore, intangible resources belonging in the public domain, which are fundamental for the practice of creativity and inventiveness, need to remain absolutely open to access, use and transformation in common. Given that it favours an expanded notion of the right to participate in scientific progress and cultural life, critical normative theory also claims that the same regime ought to be enforced to any type of intellectual resource on the condition that its access and use are conducted for transformative non-commercial purposes.

Finally, the critical normative theory of the intellectual commons requires that intellectual resources be protected from under-use caused by acts of enclosure. Exclusive rights, which result in under-use, run counter to the common interest, because they injure others' privilege over the intellectual commons and breach the general moral requirement for their noble stewardship. According to John Locke, any loss of value due to under-use is incompatible with morality, since nothing has been created by God to be spoiled (Locke 1988, 291).[59] Despite their inherent characteristics of non-rivalry and non-subtractability, intangible resources can also be wasted. As pointed out in previous chapters, information, knowledge and culture acquire their social value through sharing and transformative use. Spoliation of intellectual works thus occurs each time that enclosure either prevents their wide dissemination or results in their under-use. In addition, spoliation also takes place whenever the social potential of intangible resources for the flourishing of arts and the progress of science is wasted. In contemporary context, the over-expansive scope and duration of intellectual property laws leads to significant wastage of the social value and potential of our intellectual commonwealth. Hence, there arises the need for an independent body of intellectual commons law to guarantee individual privileges of enjoyment over intangible resources and avert value spoliation.

From the perspective of the critical normative theory of the intellectual commons, work-related arguments follow an agent-centred line of thought to justify the protection of the public domain and the recognition of commons-oriented management regimes for intellectual resources. In this context, individual creators are held to bear rights upon intellectual works, which ought to be balanced with the interests of productive communities and society in general.

9.5. Value

The critical normative theory of the intellectual commons commences from a plural conception of social value in the context of the intellectual commons. In particular, social value is held to circulate within and beyond the communities of the intellectual commons in multiple forms of economic, social, cultural and political values.[60]

Commons-based value has moral significance. From generation to pooling and redistribution, intellectual commons communities produce and diffuse to society immense amounts of value, which supersede the economic form and have positive social outcomes in the aggregate. On the one hand, the institution of the public domain has overall positive social effects, by maximising net social benefits through open access to intellectual resources, especially those that constitute the infrastructure for scientific, technological and cultural progress. On the other hand, commons-based peer production exhibits impressive results in the contemporary framework of intellectual production. Overall, the intellectual commons produce social outcomes that promote 'the greatest good of the greatest number', by maximising the aggregate sum of individual benefits versus individual losses in the pursuit towards freedom, equality and democracy. From the perspective of rule consequentialism, the moral arguments in favour of the intellectual commons can be categorised according to their reference to access ('consumption'), production and distribution, as displayed in the following table:

Perspective	Moral significance
Access ('consumption')	Static efficiency
	Dynamic efficiency
	Infrastructure as a commons
Production	Efficiency in production
	Quality in production
	Superiority of the mode of production
	Accommodation of multiple incentives
Distribution	Efficient allocation

Table 9.3: The moral significance of commons-based value.
Source: Author

Open access to intellectual resources is as a rule the most efficient mode of maximising the positive social impact of information, knowledge and culture from the perspectives of both static and dynamic efficiency. From the perspective of static efficiency, intellectual resources are public goods in the economic sense. This means that their social value is realised upon consumption. Owing to their public good character, the more widely information, knowledge and culture are shared the more people benefit and the more the social potential of intellectual goods is realised. As a result, from the standpoint of social utility, sharing ought to be the rule and exclusive rights the exception to the management of intangible resources. In addition, open access is the most efficient mode of maximising the social value of intellectual resources from the perspective of dynamic efficiency. Should intellectual resources be treated as a commons, i.e. open to access and subject to rules of pooling in common, the social potential of our intellectual commonwealth will be fully realised and the benefit derived therefrom will be maximised. Furthermore, wider rights of access and transformative use over intellectual resources tend to have positive effects on intellectual production. On the one hand, a wider interpretation of the fair use doctrine has the potential to promote technological innovation by permitting a greater spectrum of innovative uses over existing technologies. On the other hand, greater rights of access and transformative use have the potential to boost creativity and increase the quantity and quality of produced intellectual works. In this respect, the enactment of substantive copyright exceptions and limitations are expected to result in the production of more creative works. In general, the expansion of open access and transformative use tends to produce positive social externalities and spillover effects, which, though not recorded in the commodity market system, significantly contribute to technoscientific progress and the thriving of arts and culture.

In addition to the above, the social utility of the intellectual commons is supported by the 'infrastructure as a commons' argument. According to this argument, certain categories of intellectual resources are so central for the overall process of intellectual production that they ought to be subject to commons management. Due to the fact that these resources constitute the infrastructure for any type of creative or innovative activity, the social costs of their enclosure on the evolution of science, technology and culture outweigh the benefits of incentivising creators through the bestowal of exclusive rights upon them.[61] According to Frischmann, intellectual resources can be claimed to attain an 'infrastructural' character when they are primarily used as core input into downstream activities of intellectual production, especially non-market intellectual resources (Frischmann 2012, 61). Commons-based management of the intellectual infrastructure maximises net social benefit, since any fetters of enclosure at this level tend to have amplifying cascade effects on lower levels of production. The scope of the intellectual infrastructure essentially applies to all categories of intangible resources, which constitute core raw materials for creativity and innovation, such as data, information, discoveries, scientific theories, ideas, procedures, standards, methods of operation, mathematical concepts, schemes and rules. Yet, infrastructure is a socially constructed institution that only partly relies on the inherent characteristics of resources. From the perspective of consequentialist ethics, infrastructure ought to be considered all those categories of resources and types of access and use that, when commonified, generate positive externalities of social value greater than their market exchange value when they remain enclosed. This includes strategic resources in each economic sector, the ownership of which creates high barriers to entry for newcomers and tends to lead to market oligopolies or monopolies. Infrastructure is today regulated as a commons in a number of network industries worldwide, such as the energy and electronic communications sectors. From a consequentialist perspective, this ought to be expanded to the intellectual infrastructure of knowledge-based industries.

Apart from the net social benefit of access and transformative use, the critical normative theory of the intellectual commons takes seriously into account the social utility of commons-based peer production on the grounds of its efficiency in the most advanced sectors of the networked information economy. Nowadays, the social diffusion and prominence of commons-based practices in our societies is related to contemporary relations of intellectual production. The economics of improvement in the highly complex environment of today's science and technology reveal that innovation is more than ever based on building upon preceding achievements, by complementing technology already available with novel breakthroughs. Contemporary relations of intellectual production also leverage the aspects of sharing and collaboration to centre stage. Decentralised peer-to-peer modes of work management emerge on the basis of collective empowerment and participation in task allocation and decision-making. Technological advancements and the decentralisation of the means of production further provide the basis for interactive asynchronous many-to-many sharing and collaboration among peers. The foregoing techno-social changes construct intellectual commons that create 'large-scale, effective systems for the provisioning of goods, services and resources' (Benkler 2004, 276). In this context, the mode of commons-based peer production dynamically penetrates and transforms the value-producing processes of the dominant capitalist mode of intellectual production. The critical normative theory of the intellectual commons thus claims that commons-based peer production is ideally equipped with the capacity to unleash the potential of the social intellect in the digital era. It therefore calls for the enactment of the appropriate institutional framework for the promotion of commons-based peer production in all cases that its application has positive social outcomes.

From the perspective of intellectual production, commons-based practices are also held to enhance the quality of the productive output and, thus, benefit society. The open mode of intellectual production has the capacity to pool together individual skills, capabilities and effort in a collective worker, who produces in unity. In contrast to closed models, the collaborative combination of multiple minds is thus capable of generating intellectual works of higher complexity with fewer flaws and better properties. Twenty years after Eric Raymond's statement that, 'given enough eyeballs, all bugs are shallow' (Raymond 1999, 30), the superior quality of free and open source over enclosed software programs has led to the former dominating the critical infrastructure of our information society. Since then, similar modes of production open to voluntary contribution have spread in most fields of creative activity, with impressive results, such as in open modes of design, hardware, systems, standards, data, digital content, publishing, journals, science, engineering and medicine.

In comparison to capital and commodity markets, commons-based peer production also arises in its unity as a superior social mode of production of intellectual resources. Commodity market allocation presupposes the transformation of intellectual resources into well-delineated units with strictly determined boundaries capable of being circulated through private contracts among market players. The social construct of parcelling intellectual resources into commodities disregards their essentially relational and referential character. Obstructing the establishment of potential links between intellectual resources by means of private enclosure inevitably hinders the production of new information, knowledge and culture and functions as a fetter to collaboration among multiple intellectual workers. As a result, commodity market allocation has a negative impact on the overall process of intellectual production. Instead, creativity and inventiveness are inherently socialised practices ignited by the common work of multiple minds and pollinated by prior intellectual achievements. Commons-based peer production is compatible with the incremental, sequential, relational and referential nature of the creative practice. The freedom of access and transformative use dominating the intellectual commons removes the fetters over production and, thus, unleashes the creative potential of commoners. Taking the latter into account, the critical theory of the intellectual commons holds that commons-based peer production is superior to the capitalist mode of intellectual production, regardless of whether the latter is driven by the state or commodity markets, since it has the capacity to make faster and more important breakthroughs at the cutting edge of contemporary science and technology.

The beneficial effect of commons-based peer production is evident not only in production but also at the stage of the allocation of intangible resources. Creativity and inventiveness are resources widely dispersed across members of society. In the wider social context, in which commodity markets function as the primal institutions defining the distribution of resources, allocation is determined by monetary capacity. From the perspective of efficiency, more often than not the capability to create does not correspond to monetary capacity. In societies with unequal opportunities, such as ours, those with the capacity to innovate will in most cases lack the monetary resources to realise their ideas. By contrast, in the intellectual commons prior information, knowledge and culture are openly accessible and free for transformative use by all. Hence, allocated resources inevitably reach individual creators or teams of creators who are most capable of achieving the greatest breakthroughs for the common good.

In addition to the foregoing arguments, the critical normative theory of the intellectual commons generally questions the utilitarian presupposition underlying intellectual property law, according to which the stimulation of creativity and inventiveness is solely dependent on monetary incentives. Instead, it counter-proposes a multiple-incentive approach to creative practice, in which non-monetary incentives ought to be equally embraced and promoted by legal institutions owing to their contribution to the common good. In practice, artists and inventors are usually spurred by a multiplicity of non-monetary social rewards, which in certain contexts may also prevail over money and profit. As demonstrated in Chapters 5–8 of this book, the intellectual commons are based on alternative value practices that are dominated by non-market values and incentivise individuals alternatively and in parallel to the value system of the commodity market in most, if not all, formations of intellectual production, distribution and consumption. In this context, critical normative theory takes seriously into account the existence of these values in its felicific calculus and emphasises their beneficial effect for the flourishing of arts, science and technology. On the grounds of their net social benefit, such an ethical approach calls for the institutionalisation of alternative reward systems through law, which will accommodate and promote such value practices for the greater good.

In conclusion, from the perspective of social utility, the critical normative theory of the intellectual commons raises consequentialist arguments on the grounds of the net social benefit of the intellectual commons to justify their promotion for the common good. In this context, it provides the philosophical basis for the proactive institutionalisation of a vibrant non-commercial zone of creativity and innovation as a means to achieve the flourishing of art, science and technology and spur economic growth at a faster pace than proprietary models of intellectual production, distribution and consumption.

9.6. Community

According to critical normative theory, the commons of the information age lift the traditional form of the human community to a superior level. In contrast to the closed and hierarchical communities of the past, contemporary communities within the framework of the intellectual commons are open, participatory and cosmolocalist, combining in a dialectical way the element of face-to-face relations of intimacy with the element of decentralisation across space and time through the use of information and communication technologies.

Through the productive process intellectual commons communities both produce intangible resources and, at the same time, reproduce themselves and evolve through time into novel forms of community through their dialectic with capital and commodity markets. In its wider sense, communal reproduction also involves the multiplication of intellectual commons communities and the diffusion of commons-oriented social relations in society. In this context, the community of the intellectual commons tends to display elements and characteristics that have moral substance from the standpoint of deontological ethics. Such elements can be approached from the perspectives exhibited in the table below:

Perspective	Moral significance
Resilience	Counter-enclosure
	Counter-domination
Freedom	Collective empowerment
Equality	Social justice
	Fairness
Democracy	Freedom of expression
	Democratisation of intellectual production

Table 9.4: The moral significance of the intellectual commons community. *Source: Author*

The intellectual commons community is founded on the principle of knowledge sharing among its members. Consequently, the communities of the intellectual commons put any regimes of enclosure into question by virtue of both their constitutional rules and everyday practice. In the context of the intellectual commons, the enclosure of intangible resources is disputed on moral grounds. According to this moral stance, some things ought not to be absolute property and knowledge is one of them.[62] Throughout most of human history, the products of the intellect were treated as common to all and any assertion of private property upon them was considered absurd and morally condemnable.[63] In contemporary societies, which are fraught with the ever-expansive commodification of intangible resources, intellectual commons communities represent the social movement against enclosure, by practising the non-commodifiability of certain categories of resources.[64] Borrowing the words of Karl Marx, commoners act not as owners but as possessors and usufructuaries of intellectual resources, 'and like boni patres familias, they must hand [them] down to succeeding generations in an improved condition' (Marx 1992, 776). Furthermore, commonly pooled resources are subject to regimes of communal proprietorship or ownership and based on contractually enacted rights of use. In contrast to absolute property, they take the form of bundles of legal rights upon intellectual resources, which embody rules of open access, non-excludability, protection from state or private ownership, governance in a decentralised or communal manner and limited sovereignty.[65] Commons-based practices are generally motivated by the moral argument that freedom to access and use intellectual resources should be the general principle for the governance of creativity and innovation. Accordingly, legal regimes of qualified property in the form of intellectual property rights ought to be the exception and only in morally justified cases.[66] Communal relations within the intellectual commons, therefore, constitute a fundamental shift in the institution of property from exclusive ownership to inclusive stewardship and trusteeship of intangible resources.

Furthermore, the critical normative theory of the intellectual commons asserts that property over intellectual resources is immoral owing to its deep impact on power relations in society. According to this perspective, the institution of intellectual property constructs an asymmetric power relation between owners and non-owners of intangible resources. In particular, intellectual property rights are conceived as privileges designated by the state to private entities, which bestow exclusive decision-making power over the use of a wide spectrum of intellectual resources. The enclosure of the commons of the intellect is not without social repercussions. Exclusive rights not only grant control but also demarcate the framework and the opportunities of others to exercise the freedom of science and culture and the freedom to receive and impart information. In particular, property on intellectual resources confers control over the limits of creativity and innovation of other persons. Furthermore, private enclosures imposed on the raw materials of expression frame the public sphere on the basis of criteria extrinsic or even hostile to the common interest. Hence, from being an institution for the control over intangible resources, intellectual property is transformed into an idiosyncratic tool of control over persons and communities in terrains of activity crucial for social autonomy.[67] In line with the foregoing, the critical normative theory of the intellectual commons critiques the aspect of domination inherent in intellectual property from the standpoint of collective empowerment and democracy. As an alternative, it holds the enactment of commons-oriented rights of access, sharing, transformative use and pooling in common over intellectual resources as morally justified means to reduce private powers of exclusion and to unleash the freedom of creativity and innovation for all in the digital age.

Notwithstanding the critique of domination, critical normative theory also supports the moral viewpoint that the intellectual commons constitute an integral element of collective empowerment in contemporary societies and should, therefore, be institutionally promoted. First of all, the intellectual commons and their supportive social institutions, such as schools and libraries, provide the essential infrastructure for the education of the general population. In a democratic society, the social dissemination of knowledge for educational purposes is morally justified on the grounds that it constitutes the main prerequisite for individual and collective empowerment. On the other hand, robust and thriving intellectual commons also broaden the spectrum of resources and types of uses available for the intellectual advancement of the population as a whole.[68] Apart from provisioning the raw materials for education, the freedom embodied in the intellectual commons is also crucial for human flourishing. The advanced level of sharing and collaboration encountered in communities renders creativity and innovativeness in the intellectual commons an exercise of inherently collective development and self-determination. In particular, the increased degree of participation in the creative environment of the intellectual commons provides the organisational basis for the production of a more self-reflective and critical science and culture. Hence, the decentralised organisation of commons-based peer production contributes to the pursuit of 'a more genuinely participatory political system, a critical culture, and social justice' (Benkler 2006, 8). In addition, practices of commoning in the fields of science, technology, art and culture constitute as such an important political expression of collective empowerment in contemporary societies, which ought to be promoted as an end in itself.[69] Practices of commoning, therefore, fully embrace the freedom of collectivities 'to develop and express their humanity, their world view and the meanings they give to their existence and their development through, inter alia, values, beliefs, languages, knowledge and the arts, and ways of life'.[70] Taking the above into account, the critical normative theory of the intellectual commons justifies the morality of commons-oriented legal institutions on the grounds of the inherent value of communal relations of sharing and collaboration thriving in the intellectual commons and the essential role that such relations play in the collective empowerment of social groups and communities.

Of equal importance to collective empowerment is the relation of the intellectual commons with social justice and the inclusiveness of vulnerable social groups. According to the egalitarian justification of the intellectual commons, by empowering the right of everyone to science and culture on an equal footing, the open access commons of the human intellect play a crucial role in the elimination of all forms of social discrimination based on wealth, social status, position in social reproduction, gender, race, colour, cultural identity, belief or sexual orientation. In a democratic society, intellectual goods are considered to be properly distributed in a moral sense when they are disseminated on the basis of equality or according to one's needs, rather than on the basis of commodity market allocation. Equal opportunities for all to access the intellectual commonwealth of humanity is fundamental for critical thinking, individual empowerment, social justice, civic engagement and democracy. For this reason, democratic societies are generally prone to sustaining public institutions, which guarantee minimal levels of education and access to knowledge for the general population. In parallel, the open access institutions of the intellectual commons tend to remove socially constructed restrictions to access intangible resources and to facilitate the exercise of the fundamental right of everyone to take part in scientific development and cultural life through communal practices of participatory co-creation. In the spheres of the commons, the term 'everyone' acquires its true meaning by including 'women as well as men, children as well as adults, popular classes as well as elites, rural dwellers as well as urbanites, the poor as well as the wealthy, and amateurs as well as professionals' (Shaver and Sganga 2009, 646–647). As in every other regime of generalised reciprocity, production and allocation in the intellectual commons takes place from each according to his abilities, to each according to his needs (Marx 1970). As a result, the intellectual commons create the conditions that allow all people to access, participate in and contribute to science and culture without discrimination and on an equal footing.

On the other hand, the critical normative theory of the intellectual commons disqualifies the morality of commodity markets as primal mechanisms for the allocation of intangible resources on the grounds of their incompatibility with the principle of fairness. In this context, Yochai Benkler comments that '[i]n the presence of extreme distribution differences like those that characterize the global economy, the market is a poor measure of comparative welfare. A system that signals what innovations are most desirable and rations access to these innovations based on ability, as well as willingness, to pay, over-represents welfare gains of the wealthy and under-represents welfare gains of the poor' (Benkler 2006, 303). Along these lines, the three moral principles of the Rawlsian conception of justice as fairness are helpful in evaluating the relation of intellectual property-enabled commodity markets with social justice. First of all, the Rawlsian moral construct raises the imperative that 'each person has an equal claim to a fully adequate scheme of equal basic rights and liberties' (Rawls 2005, 5). Furthermore, social and economic inequalities are according to John Rawls morally acceptable, when 'they are both a) reasonably expected to be to everyone's advantage, and b) attached to positions and offices open to all' (Rawls 2009, 53). Interpreted in the context of creativity and inventiveness, the first basic liberties principle of Rawlsian moral theory dictates the universal equal access to infrastructural intangible resources. The second difference principle prescribes that inequalities in the treatment of the right of all to science and culture are permitted only when they benefit the worst off. Finally, the third equality of opportunity principle requires that individuals ought to enjoy an effective equality of opportunities in exercising the right to science and culture. Contrary to the regimes of the intellectual commons, commodity markets are by definition not appropriately modelled to grant access to all to those intangible resources, which are of an infrastructural nature and are, thus, essential for the meaningful exercise of the right of everyone to science and culture.[71] In addition, the commodification of information, knowledge and culture brought about by over-expansive intellectual property laws has given rise to significant barriers to participatory modes of creativity and innovation, thus encroaching upon the fundamental freedom to take part in scientific progress and cultural life. Overall, in our hierarchical and stratified societies, commodity markets inevitably fail to allocate access and use rights to intangible resources according to the moral imperatives of fairness. Hence, the critical normative theory grounds the morality of commons-oriented legal regimes on the basis that the intellectual commons construct more fair and inclusive environments for creativity and innovation than intellectual property-enabled commodity markets.

Collective empowerment, social justice and democracy are interdependent and mutually reinforcing.[72] The empowering and egalitarian characteristics of the intellectual commons have a positive effect on freedom of expression, the development of critical perspectives to science and culture, cultural diversity, meaningful citizenship and, as a corollary, the quality of democratic institutions. First of all, freedom of speech presupposes a public sphere with an extensive public domain of informational, communicational, scientific and cultural resources.[73] The public domain is a legal institution representing the scope of uses of intellectual works that do not necessitate the prior acquisition of the permission of right-holders. Hence, resources in the public domain are openly available to the public without restriction and everyone is equally privileged to use them in expressing him- or herself. In juxtaposition to the public domain, intellectual property law establishes exclusive rights on speech. Since they correspondingly decrease the scope of the public domain, the extensive reach of contemporary private enclosures upon intangible resources may have a chilling effect on free speech. In democratic societies, copyright has been structured as a semi-commons institution in order to internally resolve the tension between exclusive rights and the freedom of expression. In this context, the doctrine of the idea/expression dichotomy is dedicated to preserving a common pool of ideas, which remain free to access, and the generation of creative expressions. Furthermore, exceptions of fair use grant immunity to unlicensed forms of expression, which involve socially desirable uses of protected works related to the freedom of speech. Resolving the tension within the system of intellectual property law, however, tilts the balance in favour of exclusion rather than freedom. First of all, freedom-enabling copyright doctrines lie within the system of copyright law and are not co-extensive with the protection of the fundamental right to free speech granted in international human rights treaties. Secondly, within the framework of intellectual property, such doctrines are structured as exceptions to the basic principle of exclusion and are only invoked under very restrictive conditions, which end up subsuming the freedom of expression of all to the private economic interests of the right-holder. As a result, in the majority of real-life cases in which they collide, the exclusive control that intellectual property confers over intangible resources trumps the fundamental right to free speech. On the other hand, there is a fundamental connection of the intellectual commons with freedom of expression and the construction of a vibrant democratic public sphere. By giving substance to the right to take part in science and culture under conditions of equipotency, the communities of the intellectual commons are in themselves an important collective form of free speech that ought to be accommodated and promoted by the law. In addition, these communities tend to revitalise the public domain by expanding its contours and leveraging its quality with newly produced and virally growing constellations of information, knowledge and culture. Viewed from the prism of the intellectual commons, the traditional negative definition of the public domain as a 'wasteland of undeserving detritus' (Samuelson 2003, 147–161) is superseded by the reconception of the commonwealth of the human intellect as the rule to the exception of private enclosures over intangible resources (De Rosnay and De Martin 2012, xv).[74] From such a perspective, the critical normative theory of the intellectual commons ethically requires a user-rights approach to the governance of the tension between intellectual property and freedom of speech. According to this approach, permissible uses of free speech under copyright law ought to be articulated and treated as rights. Accordingly, any tensions between intellectual property rights and the fundamental right to free speech ought to be resolved in dubio pro libertate, i.e. in favour of freedom, on the moral grounds that intellectual property rights are the exceptions to the major principle of the freedom of use (Geiger 2017). As a corollary, the reversal and replacement of the rule of exclusivity by the rule of freedom, which characterises the critical normative theory of the intellectual commons, purports to guarantee and safeguard the institution of the public domain as a common space of free speech within a participatory and democratic public sphere.

Taking into account their connection with free speech, intellectual commons can also be claimed to cultivate critical and diverse scientific, technological and cultural environments. According to article 2 § 1 of the UNESCO Convention on the Protection and Promotion of the Diversity of Cultural Expressions, '[c]ultural diversity can be protected and promoted only if human rights and fundamental freedoms, such as freedom of expression, information and communication, as well as the ability of individuals to choose cultural expressions, are guaranteed'.[75] The wide diffusion of the means of intellectual production in societies constitutes an environment of open and equipotential opportunities of participation to science and culture for individuals and communities and, eventually, makes possible decentralised forms of scientific discourse and the growth of cultural diversity. The objective conditions for the rise of the intellectual commons are enjoined with the creative force of the social intellect, which is manifested in the mass intellectuality of commoners both within and beyond the workplace. The participatory and communal aspects of the intellectual commons encourage individuals and social groups to create, innovate, collaborate, share and disseminate their own intellectual achievements and facilitate access to the intellectual achievements of others. These characteristics of commons-based peer production give rise to collaborative innovation and a novel folk culture in the networked information economy and render science, technology and art more transparent, critical and self-reflective. Commons-based peer production thus has a democratising effect on the organisation of intellectual production and the content of science, technology and culture. Through increased participation in the process of contributing to scientific progress and making cultural meaning in the communities of the intellectual commons, citizens are transformed from passive receivers of centrally manufactured intangible commodities into co-shapers of the social world they inhabit. Furthermore, to the extent that such communities take control of aspects of intellectual production, there is a power shift from the state and corporations to modes of decentralised decision-making regarding the evolution of our scientific and cultural environments. Even though they are not tautological with democracy nor do they automatically lead to more democratic polities, the intellectual commons constitute spaces and vehicles for the democratisation of science, technology and culture in contemporary societies. The critical normative theory of the intellectual commons justifies the morality of commons-oriented institutions and policies on the grounds of the link between the intellectual commons and democracy. From such a standpoint, the aspects of participation, creative pluralism, critical discourse and self-governance, which generally characterise commons-based peer production, are held to democratise facets of economic and political power in our societies. For all these reasons and drawing from the inherent moral value of the democratic ideal, the critical normative theory of the intellectual commons advocates the institution of an independent body of intellectual commons law with the purpose of unleashing the democratising potential of the intellectual commons.

9.7. Basic Elements of an Intellectual Commons Law

The ethical and political considerations exhibited in this chapter justify the enactment of an independent body of law for the protection and promotion of the intellectual commons. The cornerstone for the legislation of an intellectual commons law is the human right of everyone to take part in science and culture. Its full realisation requires detailed statutory provisions for the interrelation of the freedom of science and culture with individual authors' rights on an equal footing.

A law for the intellectual commons needs to be based on independent legal principles, as a means to acquire independence from the system of intellectual property law. The formulation of its principles should benefit from existing proposals for the reform of intellectual property law. Such proposals mainly focus on copyright exceptions and limitations. In the quest for a more equitable balance between the freedom of science and culture and private enclosures, scholars and policymakers have often called for their flexibility (indicatively Hugenholtz and Senftleben 2011; Samuelson 2017) or for the expansion of their scope and subject matter (indicatively Von Lohmann 2008; Hargreaves 2011). In this respect, an independent body of law for the intellectual commons should embody principles of law that will effectively delineate its contours from the system of intellectual property law and create a new pro-commons system of statutory rules. In this new system of law, the freedom of non-commercial creativity and innovation shall be the rule, thus trumping any types of enclosure upon intangible resources, and its encroachment by exclusive rights shall be the exception, applicable only in cases justified by ethical considerations and empirical evidence.

In addition, intellectual property reform proponents stress the need of protecting the public domain (Lange 1981; Litman 1990; Benkler 1999; Boyle 2003). In this context, access to the public domain is viewed as crucial for the independent creation of intellectual works by members of the public. Yet, several scholars point out the lack of an explicit recognition and protection of the public domain under the law (Cahir 2007; Dusollier 2011; De Rosnay and De Martin 2012). In the context of an intellectual commons law, the public domain will need to acquire a positive legal status through its affirmative recognition by statute. Furthermore, public domain material will have to be converted by law from its current state of res nullius imposed by intellectual property law into the legal status of res communis omnium, i.e. used by all but appropriated by none. Finally, the scope of the public domain will need to be expanded, in order to accommodate and protect all categories of intangible resources, which have an infrastructural role in intellectual production.

Furthermore, certain scholars and interest groups propose a user-rights approach to intellectual property law reform. In particular, it has been asserted that access to knowledge needs to be protected and promoted by the law, because it leverages economic development and social cohesion (International Federation of Library Associations and Institutions and Technology and Social Change Group 2017, 2019). Accordingly, a number of scholars have called for the recognition of rights of non-commercial access and use of protected works within the system of copyright law (Cotter 2010; Voorhoof 2015; Koren 2017; Geiger 2018). According to the normative perspective taken in this study, legal rules for the regulation of commercial and non-commercial use of intangible resources should differ for ethical and political reasons. In relation to commercial use, it should be noted that property interests emerge as a result of resource scarcity. Given that intangible resources are essentially abundant, exclusive rights are mainly granted to forbid free-riders from economically exploiting protected intellectual works. Yet, this justification holds no water in relation to the non-commercial use of intellectual works, the economic value of which takes the form of use value, not exchange value. Within the framework of an intellectual commons law, affirmative rights of non-commercial access and transformative use of pre-existing intangible goods will need to be recognised for the exercise of everyone's creativity and innovation. Hence, the interrelation between intellectual property and intellectual commons law will be clearly demarcated, with the former regulating commodity markets of intangible goods and the latter establishing a non-commercial sphere of unleashed social creativity and innovation, which will also have beneficial spillover effects to commodity markets.

Given the foregoing, an independent body of law for the intellectual commons can be based on the following principles of law:

- The principle of the freedom of non-commercial creativity and innovation, according to which any types of transformative use of intangible resources ought not to be restricted on the condition that they remain non-commodifiable.
- The principle of the exceptional nature of exclusivity, according to which exclusive rights upon intangible resources ought to be granted by the state only when and up to the extent that such rights are justified, backed up by empirically sound evidence produced through independent and impartial impact assessments. In compliance with this principle, intellectual works considered fundamental for creativity and innovation will have to be placed by default in the public domain.
- The principle of the lawfulness of exclusivity, according to which exclusive rights upon intellectual works ought to be conferred only for the purpose of providing sufficient remuneration to creators and producers, so as to promote the progress of science and the wide circulation of information and ideas. Protection that goes further and is incompatible with this purpose should be deemed illegitimate and should not be granted.
- The principle of the proportionality of exclusivity, according to which exclusive rights upon intellectual works ought to be protected only insofar as this protection is adequate, relevant and necessary in relation to the purpose for which they are protected.
- The principle of the temporality of exclusivity, according to which the duration of exclusive rights ought to be determined in accordance with the type of the relevant intellectual work and the purposes of their protection. Thus, works should not be protected longer than is necessary for the purpose for which they are protected.

Furthermore, such a body of law ought to have the following core elements:

- The reconstitution of the freedom to take part in science and culture as the rule to the exception of private rights of exclusivity upon intellectual works.
- The introduction of sets of extensive rights to access, work upon and transform information, knowledge and culture for non-commercial purposes.
- The reconstitution of the public domain as a positive common space of sharing, collaboration, innovation, and freedom of expression through proactive laws and policies for its protection and promotion.
- The expansion of the public domain to cover all types of infrastructural intangible resources and social uses that are important for intellectual production, social justice and democracy.

9.8. Conclusion

Dominant normative perspectives of intellectual production, distribution and consumption are generally oriented towards the justification of property. As a result, such perspectives remain confined within the framework of intellectual property law and, thus, fail to provide adequate ethical grounds for legal institutions enabling commons-based practices of knowledge sharing and collaborative creativity and innovation. This failure necessitates the establishment of an alternative normative approach oriented towards the intellectual commons.

By benefiting from the arguments of the previous chapters of the study, the current chapter has aimed to provide a normative model for the moral justification of the intellectual commons as a social totality. This model has unfolded at three levels. At the first level, it has focused on the fundamental ontological elements of the intellectual commons, i.e. the elements of personhood, work, value and community. At the second level, it has examined the morally significant characteristics of each of the foregoing elements. At the third level, the ethical arguments of the model have provided the moral grounds for a distinct and independent body of law for the protection and promotion of the intellectual commons beyond the inherent limitations of intellectual property law. A summary of this model is displayed in the below figure.

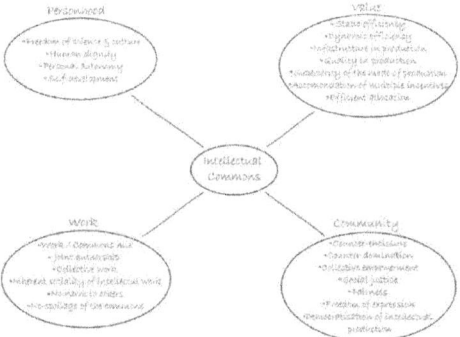

Figure 9.2: A normative model for the intellectual commons.
Source: Author

As a corollary, the ethical considerations exhibited in this chapter outline the contours of a law for the intellectual commons.

CHAPTER 10

Conclusion

10.1. The Moral Dimension of the Intellectual Commons

This book asserts that the intellectual commons are of academic and, generally, social interest, because they have the potential to (i) increase access to information, knowledge and culture, (ii) empower individual creators and productive communities, (iii) enhance the quantity and quality of intellectual production, and (iv) democratise creativity and innovation. Therefore, it is argued that the intellectual commons ought to be regulated in ways that accommodate the potential mentioned above. The inherent values and net social benefit of aspects related to personhood, work, value and community within the sphere of the intellectual commons morally justify the enactment of a distinct body of law with the purpose of protecting and promoting commons-based peer production.

Throughout the book, the intellectual commons have been conceived as productive self-governed communities that generate and pool together intangible resources in conditions of relative equipotency. They consist of three main elements, which more or less refer to the social practice of pooling a resource, the social cooperation of productive activity among peers and, finally, a community with a collective process governing the production and management of the resource (Hess and Ostrom 2007a, 6; Caffentzis 2008; De Angelis 2009; Bollier and Helfrich 2015). Their main difference from the institutions of the state and the commodity market is that social power in the commons is not separated but, rather, remains immanent within the body of the community and is guarded and sustained as such.

Owing to their determining elements stated above, the intellectual commons exhibit propensities with a positive potential for society, which therefore bear ethical substance and are in need of protection and advancement under the

---

How to cite this book chapter:
Broumas, A. 2020. *Intellectual Commons and the Law: A Normative Theory for Commons-Based Peer Production.* Pp. 155–168. London: University of Westminster Press. DOI: https://doi.org/10.16997/book49.j. License: CC-BY-NC-ND

auspices of law. The relation of such tendencies and manifestations with morality is exhibited in the table below.

Tendencies	Manifestations	Moral dimensions
Sharing	Sharing as cultural value-producing practice	No spoilage of the commons Counter-enclosure
Collaboration	Collaboration as economic value-producing practice	Joint authorship Collective work Inherent sociality of intellectual work Efficiency in production Quality in production Superiority of the mode of production
Open access	Use value as form of economic value	Work/commons mix Static efficiency Dynamic efficiency
Circular reciprocity	Mutual aid as form of cultural value	Infrastructure as a commons Efficient allocation
Self-empowerment	Self-empowerment as form of political value	No harm to others Freedom of science and culture Human dignity Personal autonomy Self-development Accommodation of multiple incentives
Self-governance	Self-governance as form of political value flow	Social justice Fairness Democratisation of intellectual production
Collective empowerment	Collective empowerment as form of political value redistribution	Counter-domination Collective empowerment Freedom of expression

Table 10.1: The tendencies, manifestations and moral dimensions of the intellectual commons.
Source: Author

The theories of the intellectual commons provide substantial justifications for the promotion of commons-oriented institutions in contemporary societies. Nevertheless, their perspectives as to the potential of the intellectual commons and capacity to generate progressive social change diverge. Rational choice theories provide consequentialist justifications of the intellectual commons criteria, by evaluating the efficiency of commons-oriented institutions for social utility. According to such theories, where the institutions of the state and the commodity market are incapable of producing positive outcomes, commons-based practices ought to be established, protected and promoted by legislators and policymakers. As such, rational choice theories provide a theoretical framework for the evaluation of the intellectual commons in relation to their potential for social change, which limits the latter in a complementary position to intellectual property-enabled markets. Given the dominance of the capitalist mode of intellectual production, distribution and consumption, the vast asymmetries of power this dominance entails and its contentious relationship with the intellectual commons, this supposed complementarity is inevitably translated in reality as a patch to capital.

On the other hand, neoliberal theories justify the morality of commons-based peer production from a utilitarian perspective. Such theories consider the intellectual commons to be valuable owing to their potential for capital accumulation. Neoliberal theorists claim that commons-based practices tend to produce significant amounts of social value, are capable of resolving market failures in the management of strategic resources and, in certain respects, constitute a superior mode for the organisation of the social intellect in the contemporary techno-social context. The main objective of this approach is to unearth possible ways through which corporations can capture the immense social value that lies dormant within the intellectual commons, transform communally managed resources into commodities and, ultimately, enhance business profitability. On the basis of their potential for the generation of private profit, neoliberal thinkers claim that a relation of mutually beneficial co-existence between commodity markets and the intellectual commons is not only an attainable but also a desirable business and policy choice, on the grounds that it benefits social well-being. Their advocacy for such a choice thus opens the discourse for a more balanced intellectual property regime, which aims to reconstruct capitalist accumulation in knowledge-based economic sectors along rational lines. It is in this context that neoliberal thinkers consider that the commons could act as fix to capital and give birth to a more balanced economy, which would combine the best elements of both worlds. In Peter Barnes's words, '[t]he essence [...] is to fix capitalism's operating system by adding a commons sector to balance the corporate sector. The new sector [...] would offset the corporate sector's negative externalities with positive externalities of comparable magnitude' (Barnes 2006, 65–66).

In contradistinction, social democratic theories evaluate commons-based peer production as important in itself, because it promotes collective aims, such as democratic participation, human community, sociality and efficiency in intellectual production, distribution and sharing, without burdening individual freedom. As social democratic theorists see it, the intellectual commons have the potential to rebalance power in the networked information environment between civil society on the one hand and government and corporate power on the other, while, at the same time, offering the opportunity for a mutually beneficial relationship with the forces of the market by 'adding value' to one another (Bollier 2008, 251). In addition, political economists within the social democratic tradition hold that the circulation of value under the existing power co-relations between capital and the intellectual commons operate to the detriment of the latter. Therefore, such thinkers believe that a productive ecosystem between intellectual commons communities and for-profit corporations is only attainable through deliberate state policies inclined to circulate value back to the sphere of the intellectual commons and shift power to the hands of civil society (Kostakis and Bauwens 2014). For these reasons, social democratic theorists advocate radical institutional and legal reforms within the state apparatus, which will render its transformation from the withering welfare state form into a new form of state in partnership with the communities of the intellectual commons.

Accordingly, critical theories hold that commons-based practices are morally justified on political grounds owing to their potential for the displacement of forms of domination by social relations oriented towards freedom, equality and collective empowerment. Critical theorists examine the commons within the wider context of social antagonism as unified practices without the confines of separate categories, such as intellectual, social or material. According to the critical approach, the interrelation between the commons and capital is conceived as a dynamic process of both domination and resistance between the conflicting forces of commodification and commonification. Commencing from an understanding of the labour/capital antagonism as inherently irreconcilable, critical intellectuals reject any possibilities for the 'harmonious' interrelation between the commons and capital and, instead, project two possible states of sublation between the two. Whereas in the one case the commons are co-opted and subsumed under capital, such theorists favour the alternative prospect, in which the forces of commonification openly contend capitalist relations of production and proceed to the socialisation of the economy and the polity. Eventually, the centre of gravity from which social change is ultimately generated becomes not the state but rather the communities of the commons and the wider movements for social emancipation. When forces of commonification at the social base reach a certain stage of development, the revolutionary act of force shall give birth to the new commons-based society.

The interrelation of the intellectual commons with existing institutional arrangements, especially the dominant institutions of the state and commodity markets and the dominant social power of capital, as viewed from each of the four theoretical perspectives mentioned above is summarised in Table 10.2.

Historically, the cultural commons have evolved in strong interrelation with the law, mutually shaping and being shaped by one another. In

	Potential	Relation	Justification
Rational choice theories	Complement to markets and the state	Patch to capital	Consequentialist
Neoliberal theories	Component of capital accumulation	Fix to capital	Utilitarian
Social democratic theories	Substitute to the welfare state	Synergy with capital	Deontological
Critical theories	Non-domination	Alternative to capital	Political

Table 10.2: The potential of the intellectual commons and their interrelation with capital in literature.
Source: Author

this agonistic narrative, the intellectual commons and the law have been determined by the battles between owners and commoners over countervailing modes of sharing and enclosure, collaboration and competition, self-governance and domination. Art and culture have been terrains of contestation between forces of commonification and commodification in interaction with institutions, norms and law.

Creativity and sociality are essential aspects of the human being, manifested in patterns of sharing and modes of collaborative artistic creation in the historical periods examined by the book. Yet, these human characteristics have been determined to a large extent by the dominant ways that intellectual production, distribution and consumption were organised. In modernity and in our ages, socialised creativity and inventiveness have been framed and organised according to the rule of capital, which institutionalises the enclosure and commodification of information, knowledge and culture in order to safeguard, circulate and accumulate its social power. The conclusion drawn from this historical analysis is that legal institutions from the Renaissance to our ages have systematically disregarded the prominent role of sharing and collaboration in art and culture, thus suppressing the social potential of the intellectual commons, instead of accommodating it.

The current surge of the intellectual commons is the outcome of an evolutionary process, which ought to be taken into account by legislators and policymakers. This book offers a historical narrative of the regulation of art and culture from the standpoint of the intellectual commons. This narrative reveals the role of regulation in framing practices of sharing and collaboration among creators. Since the Renaissance and throughout modernity, communal practices of producing and sharing culture have been systematically marginalised by property-oriented systems of law. In the present historical conjuncture, the intellectual commons acquire again a central role in cultural production, distribution and consumption. In light of the lessons of the past, the law ought to recognise and accommodate commons-based practices, instead of suppressing their potential by framing them as incompatible with the current framework of intellectual property law.

The social research in this book provides empirical evidence about the existence of distinct sequences and circuits of social value circulating within and beyond the communities of the intellectual commons. The evidence further shows that these commons-based value circuits come into specific interrelations with monetary value circuits, resulting in value crises in the intellectual commons. In each social dimension, the circuits of commons-based value take two forms, i.e. one form in contestation with capitalist forms of value and one form co-opted by capitalist forms of value. Taking the foregoing into account, the circuits of commons-based value generally take the form of the following formulae shown in Table 10.3 (below).

Dimensions	Circuits	Formulae
Economic	Contested	Collaboration → Use value → Gift → Common pool resource → Gift (CL→UV→G→CPR→G)
	Co-opted	Competition → Exchange value → Commodity → Private appropriation → Commodity (CP→EV→C→PA→C)
Stricto sensu social	Contested	Productive contribution → Merit → Trust → Communal cohesion → Social cohesion (PP→MR→T→CC→SC)
	Co-opted	Financial contribution → Control of infrastructure → Monetary exchange → Social capital → No redistribution (F→MR→M→SCa→SC/N)
Cultural	Contested	Sharing → Mutual aid → Shared ethos → Communal identity → Mutuality ethics (S→MA→SE→CI→ME)
	Co-opted	N/A
Political	Contested	Participation → Self-empowerment → Collective empowerment → Community self-governance → Collective empowerment (P→SE→CE→CSG→CE)
	Co-opted	Deliberation → Self-empowerment → Collective empowerment → No accumulation → No redistribution (D→SE→CE)

Table 10.3: The formulae of commons-based value circulation.
Source: Author

Value flows show that the intellectual commons produce and redistribute to society immense amounts of value. In addition, the circuits of commons-based value constitute the intellectual commons as value spheres interdependent and, yet, distinct from the dominant value system of commodity markets. Interdependence is manifested in the penetration of intellectual commons communities by the universality of money as the general equivalent of social value. Transvestment of value between these two worlds is thus unilateral. Most forms of social value generated by commons-based practices are generally capable of being transformed into money and commodities, whereas the opposite conversion has not been observed in practice. Given that commodity markets are the dominant system of value circulation in our societies, the unilateral flow of social value from the communities of the intellectual commons towards society without the existence of any counter-balancing flows to compensate for the expenditure of productive communal activity leads to value crises. Such crises exert significant pressure upon commons-based practices and direct communities towards forms of commodification. Hence, depending on the quantity and quality of their penetration by monetary values, the communities of the intellectual commons evolve either in contested or co-opted form vis-à-vis the power of capital.

Rather than being mere economic mechanisms for the allocation of resources, commodity markets have strong ethical repercussions, since they are capable of distributing rewards and retributions in the form of monetary remuneration or monetary scarcity to individuals and communities. In the framework of commodity market dominance, lack of transvestment renders commons-based values invisible, monetary scarcity obstructs the reproduction of intellectual commons communities, and value crises discredit the intellectual commons as social practices worth protecting and promoting. Given that, as already stated, the intellectual commons yield enormous value to society, their artificial devaluation and consequent displacement from affirmative policy choices is a detrimental social construct accruing from the ideological fixation on the commodity market as the exclusive and most efficient human mechanism for the allocation of resources and values. The need to sustain commons-based value spheres thus justifies the enactment of proactive statutory rules in favour of the intellectual commons.

10.2. The Justification of an Intellectual Commons Law

The overall analysis of this book supports the general ethical and political argument that the intellectual commons are a social regime for the regulation of intellectual production, distribution and consumption, which bears moral significance.

At a meta-level of analysis, the moral justification of the intellectual commons in the book evolves from the ontological to the normative level of analysis in spiral form. In particular, the ethical argumentation of the book commences with ontological, epistemological and historical analyses, proceeds with social research and concludes with the normative perspective of the intellectual commons. The latter is constructed through a back-and-forth movement between morally significant aspects of the intellectual commons discovered at previous levels of analysis and ethical judgements stipulated in the ninth, normative, chapter. This cycle of moral justification is exhibited in the figure below:

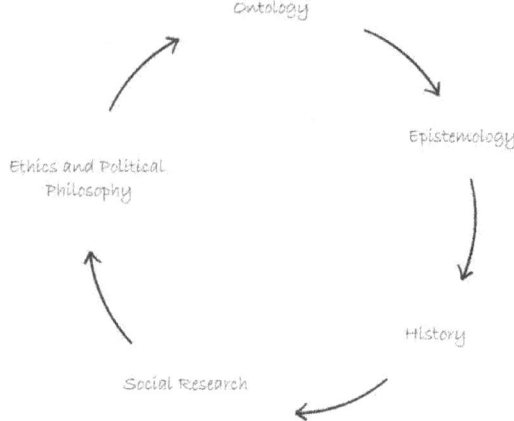

Figure 10.1: The cycle of moral justification.
Source: Author

In each level of analysis, the moral justification of the intellectual commons is conducted by adhering to the critical methodological choices stated below:

Level of analysis	Methodology
Ontological	Processual ontology
Epistemological	Critical theory
Historical	Critical history of law
Empirical	Critical realism and critical political economy
Ethical and political	Critical jurisprudence

Table 10.4: The methodology of moral justification.
Source: Author

The social potential of the intellectual commons is the overarching basis for their moral significance. Based on their potential, the intellectual commons are evaluated not on what they currently are but on what they are capable of becoming. The concept of the social potential is capable of encompassing deontological, consequentialist and political modes of moral justification in an all-inclusive manner. Hence, it renders possible the formulation of a holistic normative model of the intellectual commons, which benefits from all the foregoing modes of justification. Along these lines, the social potential of the intellectual commons constitutes the nexus for the connection of the research results of all levels of analysis featured in the study.

Level of analysis	Actuality of the intellectual commons	Potentiality of the intellectual commons
Ontological	Characteristics of commons-based peer production[76]	Tendencies of commonification[77]
Epistemological	• Addressing state and market failure • Increasing private profit • Democratising intellectual production • The real movement of communism within the current capitalist formation	• Complement to markets and the state • Component of capital accumulation • Partnership with the state • Alternative to capital
Historical	Alternative mode of contemporary intellectual production, distribution and consumption suppressed by intellectual property law	Main mode of intellectual production, distribution and consumption promoted by intellectual commons law
Empirical	• Contested and co-opted circuits of commons-based value • Value crises within the sphere of the intellectual commons	• Contested circuits of commons-based value • Transvestment of monetary into commons-based value
Ethical and political	Protection by the law through: • The principle of the exceptional nature of exclusivity • The principle of the lawfulness of exclusivity • The principle of the proportionality of exclusivity • The principle of the temporality of exclusivity • Statutory rules for the protection of the public domain	Promotion by the law through: • The principle of the freedom of non-commercial creativity and innovation • Statutory rules for the expansion of the public domain • Extensive rights to access, work upon and transform information, knowledge and culture for non-commercial purposes

Table 10.5: The social potential of the intellectual commons.
Source: Author

The contemporary formations of the intellectual commons feature elements of inherent moral value, produce outcomes of net social benefit and underpin freedom, justice and democracy in ways that justify their protection by the law. The aspects of commons-based personhood, work, value and community are realised in social practices with characteristics worthy of protection and promotion by an independent body of statutory rules.

Whereas the sets of arguments in relation to commons-based value follow a utilitarian line of justification, arguments related to personhood and work in the intellectual commons are primarily of a deontological nature. Finally, arguments related to communal practices within the intellectual commons highlight the political significance of the commons-based production, distribution and consumption of intangible resources. In combination, the foregoing argumentation forms a holistic normative model for the moral justification of the intellectual commons as a social totality.

Aspects	Characteristics	Justification
Personhood	Freedom of science and culture Human dignity Personal autonomy Self-development	Deontological
Work	Work/commons mix Joint authorship Collective work Inherent sociality of intellectual work No harm to others No spoilage of the commons	Deontological
Value	Static efficiency Dynamic efficiency Infrastructure as a commons Efficiency in production Quality in production Superiority of the mode of production Accommodation of multiple incentives Efficient allocation	Utilitarian
Community	Counter-enclosure Counter-domination Collective empowerment Social justice Fairness Freedom of expression Democratisation of intellectual production	Political

Table 10.6: The justification of an intellectual commons law.
Source: Author

In order to address the morality of the intellectual commons, the central argument of the book is that an intellectual commons law ought to be adopted in relative independence from intellectual property law. Such a field of law should embody statutory rules for the protection and promotion of the intellectual commons and effectively construct a non-commercial sphere of collaborative creativity and innovation in parallel to intellectual property-enabled commodity markets. The fundamentals of such a body of law would be as follows:

- The crucial first step is the reconstitution of the public domain as a common space of sharing, collaboration, innovation, and freedom of expression through policies for its protection, expansion and enrichment.
- Secondly, a commons-oriented legal framework ought to unconditionally recognise and protect the creative practices within commons-based peer production and guarantee the characteristics of societal constitutionalism encountered in intellectual commons communities.
- Finally, commons-oriented legal institutions ought to treat the freedom to take part in science and culture as the rule to the exception of private rights of exclusivity upon intellectual works, by introducing sets of extensive rights to access, work upon and transform information, knowledge and culture for non-commercial purposes.

10.3. Concluding Remarks and Political Implications

In contemporary societies, the powers of the social intellect are dominated by the actuality of capital, commodity markets of intangible goods, and intellectual property law. The effective enclosure and private ownership of intangible resources renders possible the imposition of commodity markets as the primal modes of regulation in our networked information economy. Intellectual property law conjoins the intellectual commons and the commodity markets into a unity of valorisation under the rule of capital. The ratio legis of intellectual property law reveals a delicate balance between private rights and the common interest. In particular, intellectual property law purports to strike an appropriate balance between the interests of authors, inventors or other rightholders in the exploitation of exclusive rights and society's opposing interest in the open access and free use of intellectual resources. The limited duration and the exceptions and limitations to intellectual property rights permit the incremental production of intangible resources. The doctrine of the public domain and the divide between exclusive rights and unprotected subject matter, such as ideas, discoveries and data, constitute a form of recognition of the intellectual commons by the law, albeit reduced to act as component to capital accumulation. From such a perspective, intellectual property law can be characterised as a semi-property/semi-commons institution, based on the recognition of both exclusive private rights and privileges of shared or common use upon intangible resources (Heverly 2003; Smith 2007).[78] Nevertheless, such commons-oriented institutional characteristics within the body of intellectual property law do not seem to provide a sufficient counterweight to its inherently property-oriented essence. The semi-property prevails over the semi-commons element.

On the other hand, the intellectual commons are a non-legal concept referring to any communal regime of shared use of intangible resources, which constructs common spaces of collective creativity and innovation. In contradistinction to the power of exclusion conferred by the institution of property, institutions of the intellectual commons deal with the management and equitable allocation of rights of usage over resources. In these institutional arrangements, the sharing of intangible resources among members of a community or among all members of society displaces private or state enclosure and communal decision-making displaces the accumulation of political power at singular points of agency. The concept of the intellectual commons is thus broad enough to include both the open access regime of the public domain and spaces of regulated use encountered in 'copyleft' licensing regimes. Rather than proposing reforms within the property-oriented framework of contemporary expansive intellectual property laws, the current book advances a normative line of argumentation in favour of an independent body of law for the regulation of the intellectual commons, i.e. both the open access commons of the public domain and any other type of regime oriented towards the shared use of intellectual works. The appropriate protection and promotion of these two sectors of our intellectual commonwealth aspires to construct a vibrant non-commercial zone of creativity and innovation in parallel to intellectual property-enabled commodity markets of intellectual works.

The compatibility of an intellectual commons law with contemporary intellectual property laws provides a hard reality-check for commons-oriented policymakers. Transnational and international intellectual property law treaties form a sophisticated framework of legal rules, which prevail over contradicting national laws. This framework entrenches the property-oriented regulation of intellectual production, distribution and consumption at the global level and leaves space for reform only on the sidelines of intellectual property law, let alone radical changes such as the enactment of independent commons-oriented rules. Hence, the ambitious aim for the establishment of an intellectual commons law inevitably entails shifts in transnational correlations of power, which render possible the reform of intellectual property laws towards their becoming compatible with the construction of the non-commercial sphere of the intellectual commons.

10.4. The Way Forward

This study builds upon previous theoretical and empirical work on the reform of intellectual property law and the protection of the public domain.[79] At the same time, it calls attention to the limitations of intellectual property law reformism, which remains confined within the property-oriented legal framework of the current condition. As an alternative, the current analysis supports the radicalisation of intellectual property law reformism though a shift in focus of the relevant discourse towards the intellectual commons as an independent source of moral value and object of law worth being affirmatively protected and promoted.

Of course, the approach described above has its own limitations. Debating on the morality of an imaginary body of law still to come in force in any jurisdiction in the world runs the risk of becoming wishful thinking, given the limited penetration of commons-oriented policymaking and the negative correlations of power in the relevant centres of decision-making. Yet, this study does not attempt to reinvent the wheel in the relevant field of law. Rather, its much more modest purpose is to reimagine the commons-based elements already present within intellectual property law, such as the public domain and the exceptions and limitations of exclusive rights, and reconstruct them in a novel and systematic way into an independent commons-oriented body of law with its own moral justification, general principles, ratio legis, doctrines of law and jurisprudence.

Given the immense extent of such a project, this study cannot but end far from fully describing what the law of the intellectual commons ought to look like. Future legal research ought to focus on the following fields of commons-oriented policymaking, as these have been stressed both in this study and in the relevant literature:

A. The affirmative recognition of the public domain by positive law as a common space for the exercise of the freedom of science and culture, encompassing all uses upon intellectual works not restricted by exclusive rights (Benkler 1999, 361).
B. The expansive definition of the public domain by positive law, encompassing all categories of intangible resources and all types of social uses, which are important for intellectual production, social justice and democracy owing to their infrastructural nature.
C. The protection and realisation of the freedom of the public to access and use the public domain, both as negative liberty and as social right vis-à-vis the state to ensure to everyone an adequate minimum of such access and use.
D. The specification of the freedom of science and culture in positive law through the enactment of new private rights to access, work upon and transform protected intellectual works to create derivative or new intellectual works for purposes of non-commercial creativity and innovation within and beyond the limitations of international intellectual property law treaties.
E. The institutionalisation of the balancing act between, on the one hand, the freedom to take part in science and culture and, on the other hand,

exclusive rights engraved in intellectual property laws, through the enactment of appropriate principles of law and institutional mechanisms, which will guarantee the exceptional nature of enclosures upon intangible resources.

F. The principled reform of intellectual property laws at the national and international level on the grounds of striking a fair balance and averting conflicts between the fundamental freedom of the public to take part in science and culture, as specified in affirmative statutory rules of an intellectual commons law, and the human rights of authors to their works.

Taking the foregoing into account, it is evident that a significant amount of further work is required to specify legal provisions compatible with existing international intellectual property law treaties and ready to be adopted by national parliaments and international organisations in the direction of an intellectual commons law. The role of this book is merely to spark off the relevant debate.

Notes

[1] The term 'commons-based peer production' was coined by Yochai Benkler (2002, 2004) to pinpoint the emergent phenomenon of collaborative production of intangible resources among multiple creators 'without relying on either market pricing or managerial hierarchies to coordinate their common enterprise' (Benkler and Nissenbaum 2006, 394).

[2] According to Marx, '[t]he crude materialism of the economists who regard as the natural properties of things what are social relations of production amongst people, and qualities which things obtain because they are subsumed under these relations [...] imputes social relations to things as inherent characteristics, and thus mystifies them (Marx 1973, 687). Hence, a reified perception of a social relation is a perception 'that a relation between people takes on the character of a thing and thus acquires "phantom objectivity", an autonomy that seems so strictly rational and all-embracing as to conceal every trace of its fundamental nature: the relation between people' (Lukács 1971, 83). Positivist ontologies of the intellectual commons tend to be fertile to such conceptual misunderstandings.

[3] 'What Des-Cartes [sic] did was a good step. You have added much several ways, and especially in taking the colors of thin plates into philosophical consideration. If I have seen further it is by standing on the shoulders of Giants' (Newton I., Letter to Robert Hooke, 1675).

[4] As a general rule, data and information do not per se fall within the scope of copyright or patentable subject matter or, instead, do not per se fulfil other criteria of copyright protection or patentability. Nonetheless, the commodification of information flows and the subsequent investment of time, money and effort for the compilation of databases have pushed for the introduction of statutory private monopolies over information, the most prominent of which is the European Union Directive on the Legal Protection of Databases (1996). By virtue of the latter, an exclusive 'sui generis' right for producers of non-original databases has been established throughout the European Economic Area, which, instead of protecting units of data per se, grants its holders the right to exclude others from the extraction and/or reutilisation of the whole or of a substantial part of the contents of the databases under protection.

5 According to the Berne Convention for the Protection of Literary and Artistic Works (1886), copyright applies only to expressions of ideas that have been fixed in a tangible medium and not to ideas themselves (article 2 § 1 of the Berne Convention). The Agreement on Trade-Related Aspects of Intellectual Property Rights (TRIPS) (1994) further clarifies the scope of copyright: '[c]opyright protection shall extend to expressions and not to ideas, procedures, methods of operation or mathematical concepts as such' (article 9 § 2 of the TRIPS Agreement). Along the same lines, US copyright law explicitly excludes ideas from its protective scope by providing that: '[i]n no case does copyright protection for an original work of authorship extend to any idea, procedure, process, system, method of operation, concept, principle, or discovery, regardless of the form in which it is described, explained, illustrated, or embodied in such work' (17 U.S.C., Sec. 102(b), 1982). In relation to patentability, article 27 § 1 of the TRIPS Agreement includes within the scope of patentable subject matter only inventions, whether products or processes of technology, that 'are new, involve an inventive step and are capable of industrial application'. In a more detailed manner, the European Patent Convention (1973) excludes from the scope of patentable subject matter (i) discoveries, scientific theories and mathematical methods, (ii) aesthetic creations, (iii) schemes, rules and methods for performing mental acts, playing games or doing business, and programmes for computers, and (iv) presentations of information (article 52 § 2 of the EPC).

6 Owing to the fact that patentability criteria apply only to technological applications of scientific knowledge, scientific advancements cannot in themselves be patented, except in their embodiment as useful/industrial applications. It is after all to this end that the publication of the knowledge underlying an invention as freely accessible is a prerequisite for the granting of private monopoly rights over technological applications in most patent systems.

7 According to an alternative approach, which focuses on the freedom to use intellectual works instead of intellectual works themselves, the public domain can be defined as 'the range of uses of information that any person is privileged to make absent individualized facts that make a particular use by a particular person unprivileged' (Benkler 1999, 362).

8 The use of 1968 reflects when Garrett Hardin published the article 'The Tragedy of the Commons' in the journal *Science*, which was bound from then on to become extremely popular in relevant scientific and political debates about the commons and their potential (Hardin 1968).

9 Data only concern the social sciences and arts and humanities research domains. Results have been refined to exclude articles regarding the topic 'House of Commons'.

10 Nevertheless, Benkler distances himself from the rational choice framework on the grounds that it fails to 'give a complete answer to the sustainability of

motivation and organization for the truly open, large-scale nonproprietary peer production projects' (Benkler 2002, 378).

[11] O'Reilly, T., and Battelle, J. 2004. Opening Welcome: State of the Internet Industry. San Francisco, California, 5 October.

[12] Based on an all-inclusive conception of labour, which extends to every aspect of social reproduction, this distinct form of social value appropriation is also defined by certain critical thinkers as exploited free labour (Hardt 1999, 93; Hardt and Negri 2004, 147). To the extent that the accumulation of social power by capital can take many forms, accumulation by exploitation being just one of them, the interpretation of all forms of value capture from the virtuous circle of the intellectual commons and their insertion in the circuits of capital circulation/accumulation as exploitation is ideologically framed, since it disregards the fact that the intellectual commons reproduce a form of life distinct from the reproduction of capital and are thus not a by-product of capitalist organisation and exploitation but, instead, an assemblage of alternative circuits of power circulation/accumulation.

[13] See Innocentive. 2015. Facts and Stats. Last accessed 1 January 2019, http://www.innocentive.com/about-innocentive/facts-stats.

[14] The idea that alternative social dynamics are constantly at work within existing social arrangements, though expressed through mass struggles, is as old as emancipatory social movements themselves. The Industrial Workers of the World close the preamble of their constitution with the phrase: '[b]y organizing industrially we are forming the structure of the new society within the shell of the old' (IWW, Preamble to the IWW Constitution. Last accessed 1 January 2019, http://www.iww.org/culture/official/preamble.shtml).

[15] De Angelis extends the Marxian 'law of value' so as to include, apart from the subsumption of labour by capital, all the ways in which capital co-opts facets of social reproduction (De Angelis 2007, 155–157).

[16] For a comic-book version of the argument across the history of music see Boyle and Jenkins 2017.

[17] An analysis of the origins and sources of Shakespearean inspiration is available at: http://www.shakespeare-online.com/sources. Last accessed 1 January 2019.

[18] According to Greek mythology, Prometheus was the Titan god of forethought who moulded humanity out of clay, gave fire to humans and invented the useful arts. Prometheus symbolises the beginnings of the creation of humanity and the birth of human order and logic out of chaos.

[19] More information about Picasso's African-influenced period – 1907 to 1909 – is available at: http://www.pablopicasso.org/africanperiod.jsp. Last accessed 1 January 2019.

[20] Between 250 and 4,000 French francs.

21 In the United Kingdom, public libraries surged after the 1850 Public Libraries Act (13 and 14 Vict c.65) gave local boroughs the power to establish openly accessible public libraries. In the United States, public libraries spread rapidly in the form of a social movement after the establishment of the American Library Association in 1876 and the engagement of wealthy businessmen, such as Andrew Carnegie. The public library system in Continental Europe was characterised by the central role of national libraries.

22 Titled 'A Bill for the Encouragement of Learning by Vesting the Copies of Printed Books in the Authors, or Purchasers, of such Copies, during the Times therein Mentioned' (8 Ann. c. 21).

23 Indicatively Defoe 1704, 21–22.

24 Titled 'An Act for preventing the frequent Abuses in printing seditious treasonable and unlicensed Bookes and Pamphlets and for regulating of Printing and Printing Presses' (14 Car. II. c. 33).

25 See the preamble to the statute.

26 The natural law conception of copyright as Blackstonian property was also later rejected by the English House of Lords in its 1774 judgment in *Donaldson v. Beckett* (Eng. Rep. 837 [H.L.]).

27 The amendment read '[t]o promote the Progress of Science and useful Arts, by securing for limited Times to Authors and Inventors the exclusive Right to their respective Writings and Discoveries' (US Constitution, article I, section 8, clause 8, enacted September 17, 1787).

28 In its generalisation, Marx described this contradiction as follows: 'Only in the eighteenth century, in "civil society", do the various forms of social connectedness confront the individual as a mere means towards his private purposes, as external necessity. But the epoch which produces this standpoint, that of the isolated individual, is also precisely that of the hitherto most developed social (from this standpoint, general) relations. The human being is in the most literal sense a political animal not merely a gregarious animal, but an animal which can individuate itself only in the midst of society' (Marx 1973, 223).

29 In its classic definition, détournement has been conceptualised as '[t]he integration of present or past artistic productions into a superior construction of a milieu' (Internationale Situationniste 1958). Debord and Wolman considered that 'Détournement not only leads to the discovery of new aspects of talent; in addition, clashing head-on with all social and legal conventions, it cannot fail to be a powerful cultural weapon in the service of a real class struggle. The cheapness of its products is the heavy artillery that breaks through all the Chinese walls of understanding. It is a real means of proletarian artistic education, the first step toward a literary communism' (Debord and Wolman 1956).

30 According to UNESCO, in the period 2004–2013 the global flows of cultural goods doubled, while consumption shifted to online services (UNESCO 2016).

31 World Intellectual Property Organization Copyright Treaty and Performances and Phonograms Treaty, adopted in 1996.
32 Especially Directive 96/9/EC of the European Parliament and of the Council of 11 March 1996 on the Legal Protection of Databases, Directive 2001/29/EC on the Harmonisation of Certain Aspects of Copyright and Related Rights in the Information Society and Directive (EU) 2019/790 on Copyright and Related Rights in the Digital Single Market.
33 447 U.S. 303 (1980).
34 The Agreement on Trade-Related Aspects of Intellectual Property Rights (TRIPS) was adopted in 1994. It was negotiated at the end of the Uruguay Round of the General Agreement on Tariffs and Trade (GATT) in 1994 and was signed as Annex 1C to the Agreement establishing the World Trade Organization. TRIPS entered into force on 1 January 1995. The WIPO Copyright Treaty (WCT) and WIPO Performances and Phonograms Treaty (WPPT) were both adopted in 1996. The WCT entered into force on 6 March 2002; the WPPT entered into force on 20 May 2002.
35 In relation, though, to the 'species' of intellectual property, the eighteenth-century jurist William Blackstone has taken a more ambivalent approach than in his writings regarding the archetypical legal form of property over material things: 'from the instant of publication, the exclusive right of an author or his assigns to the sole communication of his ideas immediately vanishes and evaporates; as being a right of too subtle and unsubstantial a nature to become the subject of property at the common law, and only capable of being guarded by positive statutes and special provisions of the magistrate' (Blackstone 1838, 326–327).
36 Enshrined in article 9 of the Berne Convention since 1967, the three-step test obliges member states to enact copyright limitations on the condition that (i) such limitations only refer to certain special cases, (ii) they do not conflict with a normal exploitation of the work, and (iii) they do not unreasonably prejudice the legitimate interests of the author. Since its enactment in the text of the Convention, the three-step test has been transposed in all major inter- and transnational legal instruments of copyright law, including the TRIPS Agreement, the WIPO internet treaties and the EU Copyright Directive.
37 See WIPO 2003; Geiger et al. 2010.
38 As De Angelis writes, interpreting Marx, '[a] tendency [...] is always the emergent property of clashes of forces'. (De Angelis 2007, 168).
39 More information about the Embros Theatre and its vibrant daily activities can be found at the community's website, available at: www.embros.gr. Last accessed 1 January 2019.
40 The self-description of the community is available at: https://www.hackerspace.gr. Last accessed 1 January 2019.
41 Available at: https://libre.space. Last accessed 1 January 2019.
42 The online transmission of the ERTOpen programme can be accessed at: http://www.ertopen.com/radio. Last accessed 1 January 2019.

43 More on the mission and activities of the Athens Impact Hub is available at: http://athens.impacthub.net/en/impact-making-unit. Last accessed 1 January 2019.
44 More information about CommonsFest can be found at: https://el.wikipedia.org/wiki/Φεστιβάλ_των_Κοινών-Commonsfest. Last accessed 1 January 2019.
45 See more at: http://www.p2plab.gr/en/archives/category/projects. Last accessed 1 January 2019.
46 De Angelis (2017, 192) and De Peuter and Dyer-Witheford (2010, 45) have also described the circulation of commons-based value in the form of abstract formulae.
47 This finding concurs with Jakob Rigi's assumption that peer-to-peer reciprocity does not generally follow the logic of quantifiable equivalence observed in conventional gift economies (Rigi 2013, 404).
48 For the notion of transvestment see Bauwens and Niaros 2017, 24.
49 See the conclusion of Chapter 4 for an elaboration of this argument in the contemporary social context of postmodern intellectual production, distribution and consumption.
50 See Chapter 3 for the role of sharing and collaboration in commons-based peer production.
51 See Chapters 5–8 for the influence of social structure upon individual commoners.
52 See Chapter 3 for the importance of the public domain as input in intellectual production.
53 See Chapter 4 for the historical significance of sharing and collaboration in cultural production, especially in the contemporary context.
54 According to Blackstone, property is 'that sole and despotic dominion which one man claims and exercises over the external things of the world, in total exclusion of the right of any other individual in the universe' (Blackstone 2001, 3).
55 See Chapter 4 for an analysis of the characteristics of the mode of contemporary cultural production.
56 See Chapter 4 for an analysis of the relevant argument.
57 In this context, Robert Nozick posited his famous philosophical enquiry as follows: 'If I own a can of tomato juice and spill it into the sea so that its molecules mingle […] do I thereby come to own the sea?' (Nozick 1974, 175).
58 As Edwin Hettinger points out, '[g]iven this vital dependence of a person's thoughts on the idea of those who came before her, intellectual products are fundamentally social products. Thus, even if one assumes that the value of these products is entirely the result of human labour, this value is not entirely attributed to any particular labourer (or small group of labourers)' (Hettinger 1989, 38).
59 Locke himself explicitly criticised the harm caused by the extensive duration of exclusive rights upon intellectual works in his essay 'Liberty of the

Press', demanding that 'nobody should have any peculiar right in any book which has been in print fifty years, but any one as well as another might have the liberty to print it, for by such titles as these which lie dormant and hinder others many good books come quite to be lost' (Locke 1997, 333).

[60] See Chapters 5–8 for an empirical analysis of the circulation and pooling of commons-based forms of value.

[61] In the words of Jessica Litman, '[t]he public domain should be understood [...] as a device that permits the rest of the system to work by leaving the raw material of authorship available for authors to use' (Litman 1990, 970–977).

[62] John Stuart Mill has written that law has 'made property of things which never ought to be property, and absolute property where only a qualified property ought to exist' (Mill 1909, 208).

[63] 'Human intelligence is like water, air and fire', exclaimed William Langland; 'it cannot be bought and sold, [it is] made to be shared on earth in common' (Langland 1370–90). In his letter to Henry Dearborn, Thomas Jefferson wrote that '[t]he field of knowledge is the common property of mankind, and any discoveries we can make in it will be for the benefit of yours and of every other nation, as well as our own' (Jefferson 1972).

[64] 'When something is noncommodifiable, market trading is a disallowed form of social organisation and allocation', writes Margaret Jane Radin. 'Some things are completely commodified – deemed suitable for trade in a laissez-faire market. Others are completely noncommodified – removed from the market altogether. But many things can be described as incompletely commodified – neither fully commodified nor fully removed from the market' (Radin 1987, 1855).

[65] In this context, Marella points out that 'property forms a continuum from individual to collective property and that alongside this continuum different bundles of rights exist in varying degrees [...] In the structure of legal entitlements associated with the commons, the right to exclude is strongly reduced and the right to access obviously expands' (Marella 2017, 74).

[66] Along these lines, Benkler asserts that '[g]overnment will not, in the first instance, prevent anyone from reading or using this part or that of the information environment. Information will, in this sense, be "free as the air to common use." Departures from this base-line must be limited to those instances where government has the kind of good reasons that would justify any other regulation of information production and exchange: necessity, reason, and a scope that is no broader than necessary' (Benkler 1999, 357).

[67] From such a perspective, Yochai Benkler comments that '[a] commercial information production system operating in a society such as ours [...] will tend to cause unequal distribution of private power over information flows. This raises two concerns. First, power over information flows that mirrors economic power in society will tend to prevent effective political challenge to the prevailing order, however inimical that order may be to a majority of

the polity [...] The second concern with the distributive effects of commercial concentration is that a lopsided distribution of private power in society can be "censorial." It can inhibit free exchange of information and ideas and prevent many people from expressing themselves' (Benkler 1999, 380).

[68] In this context, Séverine Dusollier writes that a healthy and thriving public domain is worthy of promotion because it 'plays an essential role for cultural and democratic participation, economic development, education and cultural heritage' (Dusollier 2011, 69).

[69] From such a standpoint, Peter Drahos asserts that 'the intellectual commons are a form of political expression that need to be defended as such' (Drahos 2006). In the particular context of free and open source software, Chris Kelty invites us to consider 'coding, hacking, patching, sharing, compiling, and modifying of software [as] forms of political action' that 'both express and 'implement' ideas about the social and moral order of society' (Kelty 2008, 10). These forms of political expression are reflected in the alternative cultures of repairing, making, hacking, open science and cultural mix, which thrive in intellectual commons communities.

[70] Bennoune, Karima. 2017. Report of the Special Rapporteur in the Field of Cultural Rights. United Nations (A/HRC/34/56), para. 43. Last accessed 1 January 2019, http://daccess-ods.un.org/access.nsf/Get?Open&DS=A/HRC/34/56&Lang=E.

[71] The institution of the public domain is a form of social regulation, which has different, if not contrasting, characteristics, function and purpose than commodity markets and operates as a means to ameliorate the detrimental consequences to intellectual production, distribution and consumption of extensive enclosures brought about by the latter.

[72] See World Conference on Human Rights. 2013. Vienna Declaration. Programme of Action. 25 June 1993, A/CONF, Vol. 157, p. 23, para. 8.

[73] In the words of Nancy Kranich, '[f]or democracy to flourish, citizens need free and open access to information [...] The commons elevates individuals to a role above mere consumers in the marketplace, shifting the focus to their rights, needs, and responsibilities as citizens' (Kranich and Schement 2008, 547–549).

[74] As Christophe Geiger writes, 'the term "exception" implies a hierarchy. If the use is not exactly covered by the definition of the exception, one must return to the principle of exclusivity. In order to illustrate this figuratively, one could say that an exception is a kind of an island in a sea of exclusivity. The term "limitation" implies a different grading. The scope of exclusivity is determined by its limitations. Beyond these borders, the author is no longer in control of his work. In order to use the same picture again, the right would then have to be considered as an island of exclusivity in a sea of freedom' (Geiger 2010, 521).

[75] See UNESCO 2005.

[76] As described in Table 2.2 of the book, the characteristics of commons-based peer production are non-excludability, non-rivalry and zero marginal costs of sharing, cumulative capacity, non-monetary incentives and voluntary participation, self-allocation of productive activity and consensus-based coordination, communal value spheres, and communal ownership of produced resources.

[77] As described in Table 2.2 of the book, the tendencies of commonification are open access, sharing, collaboration, self- and collective empowerment, circular reciprocity and self-governance.

[78] A semi-commons is a regime that combines exclusive and shared uses of a resource.

[79] Indicatively, see Benkler 2006; Bessen and Meurer 2008; Boldrin and Levine 2008; Boyle 1996, 2008; De Rosnay and De Martin 2012; Drahos 1996; Dusollier 2011; Fisher 1988, 2004; Geiger 2004, 2010, 2017; Guibault and Hugenholtz 2006; Koren 2017; Lessig 2004, 2008; Lemley 1997, 2015; Leval 1990; Litman 1990; Netanel 2008; Rose 1986, 1994, 2003; Samuelson 2003, 2017; Von Lohmann 2008; Woodmansee and Jaszi 1994.

Bibliography

Adorno, Theodor. 1991 [1958]. *Notes to Literature, Volume One*. New York: Columbia University Press.
Adorno, Theodor. 1992 [1958]. *Notes to Literature, Volume Two*. New York: Columbia University Press.
Adorno, Theodor. 2002 [1958]. *Essays on Music*. Berkeley, CA: University of California Press.
Adorno, Theodor, and Horkheimer, Max. 2002. *Dialectic of Enlightenment*, trans. Edmund Jephcott. Stanford, CA: Stanford University Press.
Agamben, Giorgio. 2000. *Means without End, Notes on Politics*. Minneapolis, MN: University of Minnesota Press.
Amabile, Teresa. 1996. *Creativity in Context*. Boulder, CO: Westview Press.
Amin, Ash, and Thrift, Nigel (Eds.). 2004. *The Blackwell Cultural Economy Reader*. Oxford: Blackwell.
Andrejevic, Mark. 2011. Social Network Exploitation. In Zizi Papacharissi (Ed.), *A Networked Self-Identity: Community, and Culture on Social Network Sites*, pp. 82–101. New York: Routledge.
Antal, Frederick. 1986. *Florentine Painting and Its Social Background*. Harvard, MA: Harvard University Press.
Appadurai, Arjun. 1988. Introduction: Commodities and the Politics of Value. In Arjun Appadurai (Ed.), *The Social Life of Things, Commodities in Cultural Perspective*, pp. 3–63. Cambridge: Cambridge University Press.
Archer, Margaret, Bhaskar, Roy, Collier, Andrew, Lawson, Tony, and Norrie, Alan. 1998. General Introduction. In Margaret Archer, Roy Bhaskar, Andrew Collier, Tony Lawson, and Alan Norrie (Eds.), *Critical Realism: Essential Readings*, pp. ix–xxiv. London: Routledge.
Aristotle. 1996 [335 BCE]. *Poetics*, trans. Malcolm Heath. London: Pengin.
Arrow, Kenneth. 1962. Economic Welfare and the Allocation of Resources for Invention. In Universities–National Bureau (Ed.), *The Rate and Direction of Inventive Activity: Economic and Social Factors*. National Bureau of Economic Research, Special Conference Series 13, pp. 609–626. Princeton, NJ: Princeton University Press. Last accessed 1 January 2019, http://www.nber.org/chapters/c2144.pdf?new_window=1.

Arthur, Sue, and Nazroo, James. 2003. Designing Fieldwork Strategies and Materials. In Jane Ritchie and Jane Lewis (Eds.), *Qualitative Research Practice*, pp. 109–137. Los Angeles, CA: Sage.

Arvidsson, Adam, and Peitersen, Nicolai. 2013. *The Ethical Economy: Rebuilding Value After the Crisis*. New York: Columbia University Press.

Aufderheide, Patricia, and Jaszi, Peter. 2004. *Untold Stories: Creative Consequences of the Rights Clearance Culture for Documentary Filmmakers*. Washington, DC: Center for Social Media. Last accessed 1 January 2019, http://cmsimpact.org/wp-content/uploads/2016/01/UNTOLDSTORIES _Report.pdf.

Bailey, Saki. 2012. Occupying the Commons – a Commonsense.it Project, An Interview with Saki Bailey. The Future of Occupy. Last accessed 1 January 2019, http://thefutureofoccupy.org/2012/03/occupying-the-commons-a -commonsense-it-project-an-interview-with-saki-bailey.

Bailey, Saki. 2013. The Architecture of Commons' Legal Institutions for Future Generations. In Saki Bailey, Gilda Farrell, and Ugo Mattei (Eds.), *Protecting Future Generations through Commons*, pp. 107–140. Strasbourg: Council of Europe Publishing.

Bardhan, Pranab, and Ray, Isha. 2006. Methodological Approaches to the Question of the Commons. *Economic Development and Cultural Change*, 54(3), 655–676.

Barnes, Peter. 2006. *Capitalism 3.0: A Guide to Reclaiming the Commons*. San Francisco, CA: Berrett-Koehler Publishers Inc.

Barthes, Roland. 1977. The Death of the Author. In *Image, Music, Text*, trans. Stephen Heath. London: Fontana Press.

Bauwens, Michel. 2005. P2P and Human Evolution: Placing Peer to Peer Theory in an Integral Framework. *Integral World*. Last accessed 1 January 2019, http://www.integralworld.net/bauwens2.html.

Bauwens, Michel. 2005. The Political Economy of Peer Production. *ctheory.net*. Last accessed 1 January 2019, http://www.ctheory.net/articles.aspx?id=499.

Bauwens, Michel. 2015. A Commons Transition Plan. In Michel Bauwens, George Dafermos, and John Restakis (Eds.), *Commons Transition: Policy Proposals for an Open Knowledge Society*, Foundation of Peer-to-Peer Alternatives, pp. 13–96. Last accessed 1 January 2019, http://commonstransition .org/commons-transition-the-book.

Bauwens, Michel, and Kostakis, Vassilis. 2015. Towards a New Reconfiguration Among the State, Civil Society and the Market. *Journal of Peer Production*, 7, 1–6. Last accessed 1 January 2019, http://peerproduction.net/issues /issue-7-policies-for-the-commons/peer-reviewed-papers/towards-a-new -reconfiguration-among-the-state-civil-society-and-the-market.

Bauwens, Michel, and Niaros, Vassilis. 2017. *Value in the Commons Economy: Developments in Open and Contributory Value Accounting*. Berlin: Heinrich Boell Stiftung. Last accessed 1 January 2019, https://www.boell.de/sites /default/files/value_in_the_commons_economy.pdf.

Baxandall, Michael. 1972. *Painting and Experience in Fifteenth Century Italy: A Primer in the Social History of Pictorial Style*. Oxford: Oxford University Press.

Beck, Ulrich. 2006. *Power in the Global Age*. Cambridge: Polity.

Becker, Howard. 2008. *Art Worlds*. Berkeley, CA: University of California Press.

Benkler, Yochai. 1999. Free as the Air to Common Use: First Amendment Constraints on Enclosure of the Public Domain. *New York University Law Review*, 74(2), 354–446.

Benkler, Yochai. 2002. Coase's Penguin, or, Linux and the Nature of the Firm. *Yale Law Journal*, 112(3), 369–446. Last accessed 1 January 2019, http://www.yalelawjournal.org/article/coases-penguin-or-linux-and-the-nature-of-the-firm.

Benkler, Yochai. 2003a. Freedom in the Commons: Towards a Political Economy of Information. *Duke Law Journal*, 55(6), 1245–1276.

Benkler, Yochai. 2003b. The Political Economy of Commons. *Upgrade IV*, 3, 6.

Benkler, Yochai. 2004. 'Sharing Nicely': On Shareable Goods and the Emergence of Sharing as a Modality of Economic Production. *Yale Law Journal*, 114, 273–358.

Benkler, Yochai. 2006. *The Wealth of Networks: How Social Production Transforms Markets and Freedom*. New Haven, CT: Yale University Press.

Benkler, Yochai. 2011. *The Penguin and the Leviathan: How Cooperation Triumphs over Self-Interest*. New York: Crown Business.

Benkler, Yochai. 2014. Between Spanish Huertas and the Open Road: A Tale of Two Commons? In B. Frischmann, M. Madison, and K. Strandburg (Eds.), *Governing Knowledge Commons*, pp. 69–98. Oxford: Oxford University Press.

Benkler, Yochai. 2016. Peer Production and Cooperation. In Johannes Bauer and Michael Latzer (Eds.), *Handbook on the Economics of the Internet*, pp. 91–119. Cheltenham: Edward Elgar.

Benkler, Yochai, and Nissenbaum, Helen. 2006. Commons-Based Peer Production and Virtue. *Journal of Political Philosophy*, 14(4), 394–419.

Bennett, Tony. 1995. *The Birth of the Museum: History, Theory, Politics*. London: Routledge.

Bentham, Jeremy. 1948 [1823]. *An Introduction to the Principles of Morals and Legislation*. Oxford: Blackwell.

Bessen, James, and Meurer, James. 2008. *Patent Failure: How Judges, Bureaucrats, and Lawyers Put Innovators at Risk*. Princeton, NJ: Princeton University Press.

Bhaskar, Roy. 1979. *The Possibility of Naturalism: A Philosophical Critique of the Contemporary Human Sciences*. Atlantic Highlands, NJ: Humanities Press.

Bhaskar, Roy. 2008. *A Realist Theory of Science*. London, New York: Routledge.

Bhaskar, Roy. 2008. *Dialectic: The Pulse of Freedom*. London: Routledge.

Bhaskar, Roy. 2014. Foreword. In Paul Edwards, Joe O'Mahoney, and Steve Vincent (Eds.), *Studying Organizations Using Critical Realism*, pp. v–xv. Oxford: Oxford University Press.

Bhaskar, Roy, and Lawson, Tony. 1998. Introduction, Basic Texts and Developments. In Margaret Archer, Roy Bhaskar, Andrew Collier, Tony Lawson, and Alan Norrie (Eds.), *Critical Realism: Essential Readings*, pp. 3–15. London: Routledge.

Blackstone, William. 1838. *Commentaries on the Laws of England*. vol. II. New York: W.E. Dean.

Blackstone, William. 2001 [1765–1769]. *Commentaries on the Laws of England, Volume 2*. London: Cavendish.

Boldrin, Michele, and Levine, David. 2008. *Against Intellectual Monopoly*. Cambridge: Cambridge University Press.

Boldrin, Michele, and Levine, David. 2013. The Case Against Patents. *Journal of Economic Perspectives*, 27(1), 3–22.

Bollier, David. 2007. The Growth of the Commons Paradigm. In Charlotte Hess and Elinor Ostrom (Eds.), *Understanding Knowledge as a Commons: From Theory to Practice*, pp. 27–40. Cambridge, MA: MIT Press.

Bollier, David. 2008. *Viral Spiral, How the Commoners Built a Digital Republic of their Own*. New York: The New Press.

Bollier, David, and Helfrich, Silke. 2015. Commons. In Giacomo D' Alisa, Federico Demaria, and Giorgios Kallis (Eds.), *Degrowth: A Vocabulary for a New Era*, pp. 75–78. Abingdon: Routledge.

Bollier, David, and Weston, Burns. 2013. *Green Governance: Ecological Survival, Human Rights and the Law of the Commons*. Cambridge: Cambridge University Press.

Bookchin, Murray. 1995. *The Philosophy of Social Ecology*. Montreal: Black Rose Books.

Botsman, Rachel. 2012. *The Currency of the New Economy is Trust*. TEDGlobal 2012. Last accessed 1 January 2019, http://www.ted.com/talks/rachel_botsman_the_currency_of_the_new_economy_is_trust.htm.

Botsman, Rachel, and Rogers, Roo. 2010. *What's Mine Is Yours: How Collaborative Consumption is Changing the Way We Live*. London: HarperCollins Publishers.

Bourdieu, Pierre. 1993. *The Field of Cultural Production: Essays on Art and Literature*. New York: Columbia University Press.

Bourdieu, Pierre. 1995. *The Rules of Art, Genesis and Structure of the Literary Field*. Stanford, CA: Stanford University Press.

Boyle, James. 1996. *Shamans, Software and Spleens: Law and the Construction of the Information Society*. Cambridge, MA: Harvard University Press.

Boyle, James. 1997. A Politics of Intellectual Property: Environmentalism for the Net? *Duke Law Journal*, 47, 87–116.

Boyle, James. 2003. The Second Enclosure Movement and the Construction of the Public Domain. *Law and Contemporary Problems*, 66, 33–74. Last accessed 1 January 2019, http://scholarship.law.duke.edu/lcp/vol66/iss1/2.

Boyle, James. 2008. *The Public Domain, Enclosing the Commons of the Intellect*. New Haven, CT: Yale University Press.

Boyle, James, and Jenkins, Jennifer. 2017. *Theft! A History of Music.* Duke Center for the Study of the Public Domain. Last accessed 1 January 2019, https://law.duke.edu/sites/default/files/centers/cspd/musiccomic/Theft.pdf.

Bracha, Oren. 2004. The Commodification of Patents 1600–1836: How Patents Became Rights and Why We Should Care. *Loyola of Los Angeles Law Review,* 38, 177–244. Last accessed 1 January 2019, http://digitalcommons.lmu.edu/llr/vol38/iss1/4.

Bracha, Oren. 2008. The Ideology of Authorship Revisited: Authors, Markets, and Liberal Values in Early American Copyright. *Yale Law Journal,* 118, 186–271.

Braun, Virginia, and Clarke, Victoria. 2006. Using Thematic Analysis in Psychology. *Qualitative Research in Psychology,* 3(2), 77–101.

Brinkman, Svent. 2014. Unstructured and Semi-Structured Interviewing. In Patricia Leavy (Ed.), *The Oxford Handbook of Qualitative Research,* pp. 277–299. Oxford: Oxford University Press.

Broumas, Antonios. 2013. Governing Media through Technology: The Empowerment Perspective. In Monroe Price, Stefaan Verhulst, and Libby Morgan (Eds.), *Routledge Handbook of Media Law,* pp. 419–437. Abingdon: Routledge.

Bryman, Alan. 2012. *Social Research Methods.* Oxford: Oxford University Press.

Bugbee, Bruce. 1967. *Genesis of American Patent and Copyright Law.* Washington, DC: Public Affairs Press.

Burke, Peter. 2008. *What is Cultural History?* Cambridge: Polity.

Buskirk, Martha. 2003. *The Contingent Object of Contemporary Art.* Cambridge, MA: MIT Press.

Caffentzis, George. 2008. Autonomous Universities and the Making of the Knowledge Commons. *The Commoner.* Last accessed 1 January 2019, http://www.commoner.org.uk/?p=66.

Caffentzis, George. 2010. The Future of 'The Commons': Neoliberalism's 'Plan B' or the Original Disaccumulation of Capital? *New Formations,* 69(1), 23–41.

Caffentzis, George. 2013. *In Letters of Blood and Fire: Work, Machines and the Crisis of Capitalism.* Oakland, CA: PM Press.

Caffentzis, George, and Federici, Silvia. 2014. Commons Against and Beyond Capitalism. *Community Development Journal: An International Forum,* 49(1), 92–105.

Cahir, John. 2007. The Public Domain: Right or Liberty? In Charlotte Waelde and Hector MacQueen (Eds.), *Intellectual Property: The Many Faces of the Public Domain,* pp. 35–53. Cheltenham: Edward Elgar.

Castells, Manuel. 2008. The New Public Sphere: Global Civil Society, Communication Networks, and Global Governance. *Annals, AAPSS,* 616, 78–93.

Castells, Manuel. 2009. *Communication Power.* Oxford: Oxford University Press.

Castells, Manuel. 2012. *Networks of Outrage and Hope, Social Movements in the Internet Age.* Cambridge: Polity Press.

Castelnuovo, Enrico. 1989. World Art: Themes of Unity in Diversity. In Irving Lavin (Ed.), *Acts of the XXVth International Congress of the History of Art*, pp. 43–48. University Park, PA: Penn State University Press:
Castoriadis, Cornelius. 1997. *The Imaginary Institution of Society*. Cambridge: Polity Press.
Cerny, Phillip. 1997. Paradoxes of the Competition State: The Dynamics of Political Globalisation. *Government and Opposition*, 22(2), 251–274.
Chang, Ha Joon. 2014. *Economics: The User's Guide*. New York: Bloomsbury Press.
Chesbrough, Henry. 2003. *Open Innovation: The New Imperative for Creating and Profiting from Technology*. Boston, MA: Harvard Business School Press.
Clippinger, John, and Bollier, David. 2005. A Renaissance of the Commons: How the New Sciences and Internet are Framing a New Global Identity and Order. In Rishab Ghosh (Ed.), *CODE: Collaborative Ownership and the Digital Economy*. Cambridge, MA: MIT Press.
Cohen, Julie. 2007. Creativity and Culture in Copyright Theory. *UC Davis Law Review*, 40, 1151–1205. Last accessed 1 January 2019, http://scholarship.law.georgetown.edu/facpub/58.
Coombe, Rosemary. 2011. Cultural Agencies: The Legal Construction of Community Subjects and Their Properties. In Mario Biagioli, Peter Jaszi, and Martha Woodmansee (Eds.), *Making and Unmaking Copyright Law: Creative Production in Legal and Cultural Perspective*, pp. 79–98. Chicago, IL: University of Chicago Press.
Cotter, Thomas. 2010. Transformative Use and Cognizable Harm. *Vanderbilt Journal of Entertainment and Technology Law*, 12(4), 701–753.
Crawford, Sue, and Ostrom, Elinor. 2005. A Grammar of Institutions. In Elinor Ostrom (Ed.), *Understanding Institutional Diversity*, pp. 137–174. Princeton, NJ: Princeton University Press.
Creswell, John, and Plano Clark, Vicki. 2011. *Designing and Conducting Mixed Methods Research*. Los Angeles, CA: Sage.
Cuche, Denys. 2001. *Η Έννοια της Κουλτούρας στις Κοινωνικές Επιστήμες*. trans. Fanis Siatistas. Athens: Typothito.
Danemark, Bert, Ekstrom, Mats, Jakobsen, Liselotte, Karlsson, Jan, and Bhaskar, Roy. 2002. *Explaining Society: Critical Realism in the Social Sciences*. London: Routledge.
Daskalothanasis, Nikos. 2004. *Ο Καλλιτέχνης ως Ιστορικό Υποκείμενο από τον 19ο στον 21ο Αιώνα*. Athens: Agra Publications.
David, Paul. 1993. Intellectual Property Institutions and the Panda's Thumb: Patents, Copyrights, and Trade Secrets in Economic Theory and History. In Mitchel Wallerstein, Mary Mogee, and Roberta Schoen (Eds.), *Global Dimensions of Intellectual Property Rights in Science and Technology*. Washington, DC: National Academy of Sciences. Last accessed 1 January 2019, http://www.nap.edu/catalog/2054.html.

David, Paul. 2005. From Keeping 'Nature Secret' to the Institutionalization of Open Source. In Rishab Ghosh (Ed.), *Code*, pp. 85–108. Cambridge, MA: MIT Press.

Davis, Natalie. 1983. Beyond the Market: Books as Gifts in Sixteenth-Century France. *Transactions of the Royal Historical Society*, 33, 69–88.

De Angelis, Massimo. 2007. *The Beginning of History: Value Struggles and Global Capital*. London: Pluto Press.

De Angelis, Massimo. 2009. The Tragedy of the Capitalist Commons. *Turbulence*, 5, 32–34. Last accessed 1 January 2019, http://turbulence.org.uk/turbulence-5/capitalist-commons.

De Angelis, Massimo. 2012. Crises, Capital and Cooptation: Does Capital Need a Commons Fix? In David Bollier and Silke Helfrich (Eds.), *The Wealth of the Commons: A World Beyond Market and State*, pp. 184–191. Amherst, MA: Levellers Press.

De Angelis, Massimo. 2017. *Omnia Sunt Communia: Principles for the Transition to Postcapitalism*. London: Zed Books.

De Angelis, Massimo, and Harvie, David. 2014. The Commons. In Martin Parker, George Cheney, Valerie Fournier, and Chris Land (Eds.), *The Routledge Companion to Alternative Organization*, pp. 280–294. Abingdon: Routledge.

De Moor, Tine. 2013. Co-operating for the Future: Inspiration from the European Past to Develop Public–Collective Partnerships and Transgenerational Co-operatives. In Saki Bailey, Gilda Farrell, and Ugo Mattei (Eds.), *Protecting Future Generations through Commons*, pp. 81–104. Strasbourg: Council of Europe Publishing.

De Peuter, Greig, and Dyer-Witheford, Nick. 2010. Commons and Cooperatives. *Affinities: A Journal of Radical Theory. Culture, and Action*, 4(1), 30–56.

De Sola Pool, Ithiel. 1983. *Technologies of Freedom*. Cambridge, MA: Belknap Press.

De Sousa Santos, Boaventura. 2002. *Toward a New Legal Common Sense*. Cambridge: Cambridge University Press.

Deazley, Ronan. 2004. *On the Origin of the Right to Copy: Charting the Movement of Copyright Law in Eighteenth-Century Britain (1695–1775)*. Oxford: Hart Publishing.

Debord, Guy, and Wolman, Gil. 1956. A User's Guide to Détournement, trans. Ken Knabb, *Les Lèvres Nues*. 8. Last accessed 1 January 2019, http://www.cddc.vt.edu/sionline/presitu/usersguide.html.

Defoe, Daniel. 1704. *An Essay on the Regulation of the Press*. London.

Dery, Mark. 2010. *Culture Jamming: Hacking, Slashing, and Sniping in the Empire of Signs*. Last accessed 1 January 2019, http://markdery.com/?page_id=154.

Ditzion, Sidney. 1947. *Arsenals of a Democratic Culture: A Social History of the American Public Library Movement in New England and the Middle States from 1850 to 1900*. Chicago, IL: American Library Association. Last accessed 1 January 2019, https://archive.org/details/arsenalsofademoc006465mbp.

Doctorow, Cory. 2014. *Information Doesn't Want to Be Free: Laws for the Internet Age*. San Francisco, CA: McSweeney's.

Drahos, Peter. 2016 [1996]. *A Philosophy of Intellectual Property*. Aldershot: Dartmouth.

Drahos, Peter, and Braithwaite, John. 2002. *Information Feudalism: Who Owns the Knowledge Economy?* London: Earthscan.

Dulong De Rosnay, Melanie, and Carlos De Martin, Juan (Eds.). 2012. *The Digital Public Domain: Foundations for an Open Culture*. Cambridge: Open Book Publishers.

Dusollier, Séverine. 2011. *Scoping Study on Copyright and Related Rights and the Public Domain*, WIPO Study, CDIP/4/3/REV./STUDY/INF/1. Last accessed 1 January 2019, http://www.wipo.int/edocs/mdocs/mdocs/en/cdip_4/cdip_4_3_rev_study_inf_1.pdf.

Dyer-Witheford, Nick. 1999. *Cyber-Marx, Cycles and Circuits of Struggle in High-Technology Capitalism*. Urbana, IL: University of Illinois Press.

Dyer-Witheford, Nick. 2006. The Circulation of the Common. Paper presented at: *Immaterial Labour, Multitudes and New Social Subjects: Class Composition in Cognitive Capitalism*. Cambridge University.

Eagleton, Terry. 1986. *Against the Grain: Essays 1975–1985*. London: Verso.

Edgerton, David. 1999. From Innovation to Use: Ten Eclectic Theses on the Historiography of Technology. *History and Technology: An International Journal*, 16(2), 111–136.

Evans, David. 2009. *Appropriation*. Cambridge, MA: MIT Press.

Fattori, Tommaso. 2013. Commons and Commonification of Public Services. In Saki Bailey, Gilda Farrell, and Ugo Mattei (Eds.), *Protecting Future Generations through Commons*, pp. 257–277. Strasbourg: Council of Europe Publishing.

Feather, John. 1988. Authors, Publishers and Politicians: The History of Copyright and the Book Trade. *European Intellectual Property Review*, 12, 377–380.

Featherstone, Mike. 2007. *Consumer Culture and Postmodernism*. London: Sage Publications.

Febvre, Lucien, and Jean-Martin, Henri. 2010. *The Coming of the Book: The Impact of Printing, 1450–1800*. London: Verso.

Fisher, William. 1988. Reconstructing the Fair Use Doctrine. *Harvard Law Review*, 101, 1661–1795.

Fisher, William. 1999. The Growth of Intellectual Property: A History of the Ownership of Ideas in the United States. In Hannes Siegrist (Ed.), *Eigentum im Internationalen Vergleich*. Gottingen: Vandenhoeck and Ruprecht. Last accessed 1 January 2019, http://chnm.gmu.edu/digitalhistory/links/pdf/chapter7/7.4.pdf.

Fisher, William. 2001. Theories of Intellectual Property. In Stephen Munzer (Ed.), *New Essays in the Legal and Political Theory of Property*, pp. 169–173. Cambridge: Cambridge University Press.

Fisher, William. 2004. *Promises to Keep: Technology, Law, and the Future of Entertainment*. Stanford, CA: Stanford University Press.

Fletcher, Amber. 2017. Applying Critical Realism in Qualitative Research: Methodology Meets Method. *International Journal of Social Research Methodology*, 20(2), 181–194.

Floridi, Luciano. 2010. *Information: A Very Short Introduction*. Oxford: Oxford University Press.

Foray, David. 2004. *The Economics of Knowledge*. Cambridge, MA: MIT Press.

Foucault, Michel. 1979. What Is an Author? In Josue Harari (Ed.), *Textual Strategies: Perspectives in Post-Structuralist Criticism*, pp. 141–160. Ithaca, NY: Cornell University Press.

Freeland, Cynthia. 2001. *But Is It Art? An Introduction to Art Theory*. Oxford: Oxford University Press.

Frischmann, Brett. 2009. The Pull of Patents. *Fordham Law Review*, 77, 2143–2167.

Frischmann, Brett. 2012. *Infrastructure: The Social Value of Shared Resources*. Oxford: Oxford University Press.

Frischmann, Brett, Madison, Michael, and Strandburg, Katherine. 2014. Introduction. In Brett Frischmann, Michael Madison, and Katherine Strandburg (Eds.), *Governing Knowledge Commons*, pp. ix–xv. New York: Oxford University Press.

Fuchs, Christian. 2008. *Internet and Society: Social Theory for the Information Age*. New York: Routledge.

Fuchs, Christian. 2011. *Foundations of Critical Media and Information Studies*. Abingdon: Routledge.

Fuchs, Christian. 2014. *Digital Labour and Karl Marx*. New York: Routledge.

Fuchs, Christian. 2016. *Reading Marx in the Information Age, A Media and Communication Studies Perspective on Capital*. vol. I. New York: Routledge.

Fuchs, Christian, and Hofkirchner, Wolfgang. 2005. Self-Organization, Knowledge and Responsibility. *Kybernetes*, 1–2, 241–260.

Fumagalli, Andrea, Giuliani, Alfonso, Lucarelli, Stefano, and Vercellone, Carlo. 2019. *Cognitive Capitalism, Welfare and Labour: The Commonfare Hypothesis*. Abingdon: Routledge.

Fuster Morell, Mayo. 2010. *Governance of Online Creation Communities: Provision of Infrastructure for the Building of Digital Commons*. Florence: European University Institute.

Fuster Morell, Mayo. 2014. Governance of Online Creation Communities for the Building of Digital Commons: Viewed through the Framework of Institutional Analysis and Development. In Brett Frischmann; Michael Madison; Katherine Strandburg (Eds.), *Governing Knowledge Commons*, pp. 281–311. Oxford: Oxford University Press.

Garnham, Nicholas. 1990. *Capitalism and Communication: Global Culture and the Economics of Information*. London: Sage.

Geiger, Christophe. 2004. Fundamental Rights, a Safeguard for the Coherence of Intellectual Property Law? *IIC – International Review of Intellectual Property and Competition Law*, 35(3), 268–280.

Geiger, Christophe. 2010. Promoting Creativity through Copyright Limitations: Reflections on the Concept of Exclusivity in Copyright Law. *Vanderbilt Journal of Entertainment and Technology Law*, 12(3), 515–548.

Geiger, Christophe. 2018. Freedom of Artistic Creativity and Copyright Law: A Compatible Combination? *UC Irvine Law Review*, 8(3), 413–458. Last accessed 1 January 2019, https://www.law.uci.edu/lawreview/vol8/no3/Online_Geiger.pdf.

Geiger, Christophe, Hilty, Reto, Griffiths, Jonathan, and Suthersanen, Uma. 2010. Declaration, A Balanced Interpretation of the 'Three-Step Test' In Copyright Law. *Jipitec*, 1. Last accessed 1 January 2019, http://www.ip.mpg.de/fileadmin/ipmpg/content/forschung_aktuell/01_balanced/declaration_three_step_test_final_english1.pdf.

Ghosh, Shubha. 2007. How to Build a Commons: Is Intellectual Property Constrictive, Facilitating, or Irrelevant? In Charlotte Hess and Elinor Ostrom (Eds.), *Understanding Knowledge as a Commons: From Theory to Practice*, pp. 209–245. Cambridge, MA: MIT Press.

Giddens, Anthony. 1984. *The Constitution of Society*. Berkeley, CA: University of California Press.

Goldstein, Peter. 1991. Copyright. *Journal of the Copyright Society of the U.S.A.*, 38, 109–122.

Goldstein, Peter. 2003. *Copyright's Highway, From Gutenberg to the Celestial Jukebox*. Stanford, CA: Stanford University Press.

Graeber, David. 2001. *Toward an Anthropological Theory of Value, the False Coin of Our Own Dreams*. New York: Palgrave.

Greenfeld, Liah. 1989. *Different Worlds: A Sociological Study of Taste, Choice and Success in Art*. Cambridge: Cambridge University Press.

Greenwald, Bruce, and Stiglitz, Joseph. 2015. *Creating a Learning Society: A New Approach to Growth, Development, and Social Progress*. New York: Columbia University Press.

Gregory, Chris. 2000. Value Switching and the Commodity-Free Zone. In Antoon Vandervelde (Ed.), *Gifts and Interests*, pp. 95–113. Leuven: Peeters.

Guest, Greg, MacQueen, Kathleen, and Namey, Emily. 2012. *Applied Thematic Analysis*. Thousand Oaks, CA: Sage.

Guibault, Lucie, and Hugenholtz, Bernt (Eds.). 2004. *The Future of the Public Domain: Identifying the Commons in Information Law*. AH Alphen aan den Rijn: Kluwer Law International.

Habermas, Jurgen. 1989 [1962]. *The Structural Transformation of the Public Sphere*. Cambridge: Polity Press.

Habermas, Jurgen. 1966. Knowledge and Interest. *Inquiry*, 9(1-4), 285-300.
Habermas, Jurgen. 1996. *Between Facts and Norms: Contributions to a Discourse Theory of Law and Democracy*, trans. William Rehg. Cambridge, MA: MIT Press.
Hardin, Garrett. 1968. The Tragedy of the Commons. *Science*, 162(3859), 1243-1248.
Hardt, Michael. 1999. Affective Labor. *Boundary*, 2(2), 89-100.
Hardt, Michael. 2010. The Common in Communism. In Costas Douzinas and Slavoj Žižek (Eds.), *The Idea of Communism*, pp. 131-144. London: Verso.
Hardt, Michael, and Negri, Antonio. 1994. *Labor of Dionysus, A Critique of the State-Form*. Minneapolis, MN: University of Minnesota Press.
Hardt, Michael, and Negri, Antonio. 2000. *Empire*. Cambridge, MA: Harvard University Press.
Hardt, Michael, and Negri, Antonio. 2004. *Multitude, War and Democracy in the Age of Empire*. London: Penguin.
Hardt, Michael, and Negri, Antonio. 2009. *Commonwealth*. Cambridge, MA: Belknap Press.
Hardt, Michael, and Negri, Antonio. 2012. *Declaration*. New York: Argo Navis.
Hardt, Michael, and Negri, Antonio. 2017. *Assembly*. New York: Oxford University Press.
Hargreaves, Ian. 2011. *Digital Opportunity: Review of Intellectual Property and Growth. An Independent Report*. Last accessed 1 January 2019, http://www.ipo.gov.uk/ipreview-finalreport.pdf.
Harvey, David. 1989. *The Condition of Postmodernity: An Enquiry into the Origins of Cultural Change*. Oxford: Blackwell.
Harvey, David. 2003. *The New Imperialism*. Oxford: Oxford University Press.
Hauser, Arnold. 1999 [1951]. *The Social History of Art*. vol. II. London: Routledge.
Hayek, Friedrich. 1945. The Use of Knowledge in Society. *American Economic Review*, XXXV(4), 519-530.
Hayek, Friedrich. 1948. *Individualism and Economic Order*. London: University of Chicago Press.
Hayek, Friedrich. 1955. *The Counter-Revolution of Science*. London: Collier-Macmillan.
Hayek, Friedrich. 2013 [1982]. *Law, Legislation and Liberty*. Abingdon: Routledge.
Hebdige, Dick. 2003. *Subculture: The Meaning of Style*. London: Routledge.
Heinich, Nathalie. 2005. *Η Κοινωνιολογία της Τέχνης*. Athens: Plethron.
Helfrich, Silke, and Haas, Jorg. 2009. The Commons: A New Narrative for Our Times. In Silke Helfrich (Ed.), *Emissions: To Whom Does the World Belong*. Berlin: Heinrich Boll Foundation. Last accessed 1 January 2019, https://us.boell.org/sites/default/files/downloads/CommonsBook_Helfrich_-_Haas-neu.pdf.

Heller, Michael. 1998. The Tragedy of the Anticommons: Property in the Transition from Marx to Markets. *Harvard Law Review*, 111(3), 621–688.
Heller, Michael. 2008. *The Gridlock Economy: How Too Much Ownership Wrecks Markets, Stops Innovation and Costs Lives*. New York: Basic Books.
Heller, Michael, and Eisenberg, Rebecca. 1998. Can Patents Deter Innovation? The Anticommons in Biomedical Research. *Science*, 280(5364), 698–701. Last accessed 1 January 2019, https://www.sciencemag.org/content/280/5364/698.full.
Hesmondhalgh, David. 2002. *The Cultural Industries*. London: Sage.
Hess, Charlotte. 2008. Mapping New Commons. In *12th Biennial Conference of the International Association for the Study of the Commons*, Cheltenham, UK. Last accessed 1 January 2019, http://dlc.dlib.indiana.edu/dlc/bitstream/handle/10535/304/Mapping_the_NewCommons.pdf.
Hess, Charlotte, and Ostrom, Elinor. 2003. Ideas, Artifacts, and Facilities: Information as a Common-Pool Resource. *Law and Contemporary Problems*, 66(1&2), 111–145.
Hess, Charlotte, and Ostrom, Elinor. 2007a. Introduction: An Overview of the Knowledge Commons. In Charlotte Hess and Elinor Ostrom (Eds.), *Understanding Knowledge as a Commons, From Theory to Practice*, pp. 3–26. Cambridge, MA: MIT Press.
Hess, Charlotte, and Ostrom, Elinor. 2007b. A Framework for Analyzing the Knowledge Commons. In Charlotte Hess and Elinor Ostrom (Eds.), *Understanding Knowledge as a Commons, From Theory to Practice*, pp. 41–81. Cambridge, MA: MIT Press.
Hesse, Carla. 1990. Enlightenment Epistemology and the Laws of Authorship in Revolutionary France, 1777–1793. *Representations*, 30, 109–137.
Heverly, Robert. 2003. The Information Semicommons. *Berkeley Technology Law Journal*, 18(4), 1127–1189.
Hobsbawm, Eric. 1961. *The Jazz Scene*. London: Penguin.
Hooper-Greenhill, Eilean. 1992. *Museums and the Shaping of Knowledge*. London: Routledge.
Howe, Jeff. 2006. *Crowdsourcing: A Definition*. Last accessed 1 January 2019, http://crowdsourcing.typepad.com/cs/2006/06/crowdsourcing_a.html.
Hugenholtz, Bernt, and Senftleben, Martin. 2011. *Fair Use in Europe: In Search of Flexibilities*. iVIR. Last accessed 1 January 2019, https://ssrn.com/abstract=1959554.
Hunter, Dan. 2003. Cyberspace as Place and the Tragedy of the Digital Anticommons. *California Law Review*, 91(2), 439–520. Last accessed 1 January 2019, http://scholarship.law.berkeley.edu/californialawreview/vol91/iss2/4.
Hyde, Lewis. 2007. *The Gift, Creativity and the Artist in the Modern World*. New York: Vintage.
Hyde, Lewis. 2010. *Common as Air*. New York: Farrar, Straus and Giroux.
Internationale Situationniste. 1958. Definitions. *Central Bulletin 1*. Last accessed 1 January 2019, http://www.cddc.vt.edu/sionline///si/definitions.html.

International Federation of Library Associations and Institutions; Technology and Social Change Group. 2017. Development and Access to Information 2017. Last accessed 1 January 2019, https://da2i.ifla.org/wp-content/uploads/da2i-2017-full-report.pdf.

International Federation of Library Associations and Institutions; Technology and Social Change Group. 2019. Development and Access to Information 2019. Last accessed 1 January 2019, https://da2i.ifla.org/wp-content/uploads/da2i-2019-full-report.pdf.

Jacobs, Lewis. 1930. *The Rise of the American Film*. New York: Harcourt Brace.

James, Louis. 1976. *Print and the People, 1819–1851*. London: Allen Lane.

Jameson, Fredric. 1991. *Postmodernism or The Cultural Logic of Late Capitalism*. Durham, NC: Duke University Press.

Jaszi, Peter. 1991. Toward a Theory of Copyright: Metamorphoses of 'Authorship'. *Duke Law Journal*, 40(2), 455–502.

Jefferson, Thomas. 1972 [1807]. Letter to Henry Dearborn. In Adrienne Koch and William Peden (Eds.), *The Life and Selected Writings of Thomas Jefferson*. New York: The Modem Library.

Jencks, Charles. 1990. *Post-Modernism: The New Classicism in Art and Architecture*. New York: Rizzoli.

Jenkins, Henry. 2006. *Convergence Culture: Where Old and New Media Collide*. New York: New York University Press.

Jenkins, Henry, Purushotma, Ravi, Weigel, Margaret, Clinton, Katie, and Robison, Alice. 2009. *Confronting the Challenges of Participatory Culture: Media Education for the 21st Century*. Cambridge, MA: MIT Press.

Juris, Jeffrey. 2008. *Networking Futures: The Movements against Corporate Globalization*. Durham, NC: Duke University Press.

Kapczynski, Amy. 2010. Access to Knowledge: A Conceptual Genealogy. In Gaelle Krikorian and Amy Kapczynksi (Eds.), *Access to Knowledge in the Age of Intellectual Property*, pp. 17–56. New York: Zone Books.

Kaufmann, Thomas. 2004. *Toward a Geography of Art*. Chicago, IL: University of Chicago Press.

Kaul, Inge, and Mendoza, Ronald. 2003. Advancing the Concept of Public Goods. In Inge Kaul, Pedro Conceicao, Katell Le Goulven, and Ronald Mendoza (Eds.), *Providing Global Public Goods, Managing Globalization*, pp. 78–111. Oxford, New York: Oxford University Press.

Kealy, Edward. 1979. From Craft to Art: The Case of Sound Mixers and Popular Music. *Sociology of Work and Occupations*, 6, 3–29.

Kelty, Christopher (2008). *Two Bits: The Cultural Significance of Free Software*. Durham, NC: Duke University Press.

Klingender, Francis. 1947. *Art and the Industrial Revolution*. London: Paladin.

Koren, Niva-Elkin. 2017. Copyright in a Digital Ecosystem: A User-Rights Approach. In Ruth Okediji (Ed.), *Copyright Law in an Age of Limitations and Exception*, pp. 132–168. Cambridge: Cambridge University Press.

Kostakis, Vassilis, and Bauwens, Michel. 2014. *Network Society and Future Scenarios for a Collaborative Economy*. Basingstoke: Palgrave Macmillan.

Kostakis, Vassilis, Niaros, Vassilis Dafermos, George, and Bauwens, Michel. 2015. Design Global, Manufacture Local: Exploring the Contours of an Emerging Productive Model. *Futures*, 73, 126–135.

Kranich, Nancy and Schement, Jorge. 2008. Information Commons: Annual Review of Information, Science and Technology, 42(1), 546–591.

Kubler, George. 1962. *The Shape of Time: Remarks on the History of Things*. New Haven, CT: Yale University Press.

Kuhn, Thomas. 1970. *The Structure of Scientific Revolutions*. Chicago, IL: Chicago University Press.

Laclau, Ernesto, and Mouffe, Chantal. 1985. *Hegemony and Socialist Strategy: Towards a Radical Democratic Politics*. London: Verso.

Lakhani, Karim, and Panetta, Jill. 2007. The Principles of Distributed Innovation. *Innovations: Technology, Governance, Globalization*, 2(3), 97–112.

Lange, David. 1981. Recognizing the Public Domain. *Law and Contemporary Problems*, 44, 147–178. Last accessed 1 January 2019, https://scholarship.law.duke.edu/faculty_scholarship/824.

Langland, William. (1370–1390). *Piers Plowman*.

Lash, Scott, and Lury, Celia. 2007. *Global Culture Industry*. Cambridge: Polity Press.

Lawson, Tony. 1998. Economic Science Without Experimentation. In Margaret Archer, Roy Bhaskar, Andrew Collier, Tony Lawson, and Alan Norrie (Eds.), *Critical Realism: Essential Readings*, pp. 144–169. London: Routledge.

Lazzarato, Maurizio. 2014. *Signs and Machines: Capitalism and the Production of Subjectivity*. Los Angeles, CA: Semiotexte.

Leadbeater, Charles. 2008. *We-Think: Mass Innovation, not Mass Production*. London: Profile Books.

Lemley, Mark. 1996. Romantic Authorship and the Rhetoric of Property. *Texas Law Review*, 75, 873–906.

Lemley, Mark. 1997. Dealing with Overlapping Copyrights on the Internet. *University of Dayton Law Review*, 22, 547–585.

Lemley, Mark. 1997. The Economics of Improvement in Intellectual Property Law. *Texas Law Review*, 75, 989–1094.

Lemley, Mark. 2015. Faith-Based Intellectual Property. *UCLA Law Review*, 62, 1328–1347.

Lessig, Lawrence. 2002a. *The Future of Ideas: The Fate of the Commons in a Connected World*. New York: Vintage Books.

Lessig, Lawrence. 2002b. The Architecture of Innovation. *Duke Law Journal*, 51, 1783–1801.

Lessig, Lawrence. 2004. *Free Culture: The Nature and Future of Creativity*. New York: Penguin Press.

Lessig, Lawrence. 2006. Re-crafting a Public Domain. *Yale Journal of Law and the Humanities*, 18(3), 56–83. Last accessed 1 January 2019, http://digital commons.law.yale.edu/yjlh/vol18/iss3/4.
Lessig, Lawrence. 2008. *Remix: Making Art and Commerce Thrive in the Hybrid Economy*. New York: Penguin.
Leval, Pierre. 1990. Toward a Fair Use Standard. *Harvard Law Review*, 103(5), 1105–1136.
Levin, Richard, Klevorick, Alvin, Nelson, Richard, and Winter, Sidney. 1987. Appropriating the Returns from Industrial Research and Development. *Brookings Papers on Economic Activity*, 3, 783–831.
Lévi-Strauss, Claude. 1966. *The Savage Mind*. Chicago, IL: University of Chicago Press.
Levy, Pierre. 1997. *Collective Intelligence: Mankind's Emerging World in Cyberspace*. Cambridge: Perseus Books.
Lievrouw, Leah. 2011. *Alternative and Activist New Media*. Cambridge: Polity.
Linebaugh, Peter. 2008. *The Magna Carta Manifesto: Liberties and Commons for All*. Berkeley, CA: University of California Press.
Litman, Jessica. 1990. The Public Domain. *Emory Law Journal*, 39, 965–1023.
Livorni, Ernesto. 2009. The Giubbe Rosse Café in Florence: A Literary and Political Alcove from Futurism to Anti-Fascist Resistance. *Italica*, 86(4), 602–622.
Locke, John. 1997 [1695]. Liberty of the Press. In Mark Goldie (Ed.), *Locke: Political Essays*, pp. 329–338. Cambridge: Cambridge University Press.
Locke, John. 1988. [1689]. *Two Treatises of Government*. Cambridge: Cambridge University Press.
Lucie-Smith, Edward. 1986. *Lives of the Great Twentieth Century Artists*. New York: Rizzoli.
Lukács, Georg. 1971 [1923]. *History and Class Consciousness: Studies in Marxist Dialectics*, trans. Rodney Livingstone. Cambridge, MA: MIT Press.
Lukács, Georg. 1974 [1914]. *The Theory of the Novel*. Cambridge, MA: MIT Press.
Lunney, Glynn. 2001. The Death of Copyright: Digital Technology, Private Copying, and the DMCA. *Virginia Law Review*, 87, 813–920.
Lury, Celia. 2004. *Brands: The Logos of the Global Economy*. Abingdon: Routledge.
Luxemburg, Rosa. 2003 [1913]. *The Accumulation of Capital*. London: Routledge.
Macey, Gregg. 2010. Cooperative Institutions in Cultural Commons. *Cornell Law Review*, 95, 757–792.
Machlup, Fritz. 1983. Semantic Quirks in Studies of Information. In Fritz Machlup and Una Mansfield (Eds.), *The Study of Information: Interdisciplinary Message*, pp. 641–671. New York: Wiley.
MacKinnon, Rebecca. 2012. *Consent of the Networked, The Worldwide Struggle for Internet Freedom*. New York: Basic Books.

Macpherson, Crawford Brough. 1964. *The Political Theory of Possessive Individualism*. Oxford: Oxford University Press.
Macpherson, Crawford Brough. 1973. *Democratic Theory: Essays in Retrieval*. Oxford: Oxford University Press.
Madison, Michael. 2003. Rights of Access and the Shape of the Internet. *Boston College Law Review*, 44, 433–508.
Madison, Michael, Frischmann, Brett, and Strandburg, Katherine. 2010a. Reply: The Complexity of the Commons. *Cornell Law Review*, 95, 839–850.
Madison, Michael, Frischmann, Brett, and Strandburg, Katherine. 2010b. Constructing Commons in the Cultural Environment. *Cornell Law Review*, 95, 657–710.
Mandich, Giulio. 1960. Venetian Origins of Inventors' Rights. *Journal of the Patent Office Society*, 42, 378–382.
Mankiw, Gregory. 2014. *Principles of Economics*. Cincinatti, OH: South-Western College Pub.
Mann, Michael. 2012. *The Sources of Social Power: Volume 4, Globalizations, 1945–2011*. Cambridge: Cambridge University Press.
Marx, Karl. 1844. *On the Jewish Question*. Last accessed 1 January 2019, https://www.marxists.org/archive/marx/works/1844/jewish-question/.
Marx, Karl. 1970 [1845]. *The German Ideology*. New York: International Publishers Co.
Marx, Karl. 1973. *Grundrisse: Foundations of the Critique of Political Economy*. London: Penguin.
Marx, Karl. 1988 [1844]. Economic and Philosophic Manuscripts of 1844. In *Economic and Philosophic Manuscripts of 1844 and the Communist Manifesto*, 13–168. Amherst, MA: Prometheus.
Marx, Karl. 1990 [1867]. *Capital: A Critique of Political Economy*. vol. I. London: Penguin.
Marx, Karl. 1992 [1894]. *Capital: A Critique of Political Economy*. vol. III. London: Penguin.
Marx, Karl. 1997 [1843–1844]. Toward the Critique of Hegel's Philosophy of Law: Introduction. In Loyd D. Easton and Kurt H. Guddat (Eds.), *Writings of the Young Marx on Philosophy and Society*. Indianapolis, IN: Hackett.
Mauss, Marcel. 1973. Techniques of the Body. *Economy and Society*, 2(1), 70–88.
Mauss, Marcel. 1990. *The Gift: The Form and Reason for Exchange in Archaic Societies*. London: Routledge.
May, Chris. 2010. *The Global Political Economy of Intellectual Property Rights: The New Enclosures*. Abingdon: Routledge.
May, Chris, and Sell, Susan. 2006. *Intellectual Property Rights: A Critical History*. Boulder, CO: Lynne Rienner Publishers.
Meconi, Honey (Ed.). 2004. *Early Musical Borrowing*. London: Routledge.
Merges, Robert. 2004a. A New Dynamism in the Public Domain. *University of Chicago Law Review*, 71, 183–203. Last accessed 1 January 2019, http://ssrn.com/abstract=558751.

Merges, Robert. 2004b. From Medieval Guilds to Open Source Software: Informal Norms, Appropriability Institutions, and Innovation. *Conference on the Legal History of Intellectual Property*. Last accessed 1 January 2019, http://works.bepress.com/robert_merges/76/.

Merleau-Ponty, Maurice. 1993. Cézanne's Doubt. In Galen Johnson and Michael Smith (Eds.), *The Merleau-Ponty Aesthetics Reader*, pp. 59–75. Evanston, IL: Northwestern University Press.

Merton, Robert. 1979. *The Sociology of Science: Theoretical and Empirical Investigations*. Chicago, IL: Chicago University Press.

Merton, Robert, Lowenthal, Marjorie, and Kendal, Patricia. 1956. *The Focused Interview: A Manual of Problems and Procedures*. New York: Free Press.

Miege, Bernard. 1979. The Cultural Commodity. *Media Culture and Society*, 1, 297–311.

Miege, Bernard. 1989. *The Capitalisation of Cultural Production*. New York: International General.

Miles, Matthew, and Huberman, Michael. 1994. *Qualitative Data Analysis*. Los Angeles, CA: Sage.

Mill, John Stuart. 1858. *A System of Logic, Ratiocinative and Inductive*. New York: Harper and Brothers.

Mill, John Stuart. 1909 [1848]. 'Of Property', in *Principles of Political Economy, with some of their Applications to Social Philosophy*, pp. 208–209. London: Longmans, Green, & Co.

Mosco, Vincent. 2009. *The Political Economy of Communication*. Los Angeles, CA: Sage.

Mueller, Milton. 2012. Property and Commons in Internet Governance. In Eric Brousseau, Meriem Marzouki, and Cecile Meadel (Eds.), *Governance, Regulations and Powers on the Internet*, pp. 39–62. Cambridge: Cambridge University Press.

Narotzky, Susana. 1997. *New Directions in Economic Anthropology*. London: Pluto Press.

Nesbit, Molly. 1987. What Was an Author? *Yale French Studies*, 73, 229–257.

Netanel, Neil. 1996. Copyright and a Democratic Civil Society. *Yale Law Journal*, 106, 283–387.

Netanel, Neil. 2008. *Copyright's Paradox*. Oxford: Oxford University Press.

Newman, Karen. 2009. *Cultural Capitals: Early Modern London and Paris*. Princeton, NJ: Princeton University Press.

Nozick, Robert. 1974. *Anarchy, State and Utopia*. New York: Basic Books.

O'Connor, Justin. 2011. *The Arts and Creative Industries*. Sydney: Australian Council for the Arts. Last accessed 1 January 2019, http://eprints.qut.edu.au/43834/1/Arts_and_creative_industries.pdf.

O'Mahoney, Joe, and Vincent, Steve. 2014. Critical Realism as an Empirical Project, a Beginner's Guide. In Paul Edwards, Joe O'Mahoney, and Steve Vincent (Eds.), *Studying Organizations Using Critical Realism*, pp. 1–20. Oxford: Oxford University Press.

O'Reilly, Tim. 2005. *What Is Web 2.0*. O'Reilly Network. Last accessed 1 January 2019, http://www.oreilly.com/pub/a/web2/archive/what-is-web-20.html.

OECD. 2013. *Competition Policy and Knowledge-Based Capital: Key Findings*. Last accessed 1 January 2019, https://www.oecd.org/daf/competition/Knowledge-based-capital-%20KeyFindings2013.pdf.

Offe, Claus. 2015. *Europe Entrapped*. Cambridge: Polity.

Orsi, Cosma. 2005. *The Political Economy of Solidarity. Federico Caffè Centre Research Report 5*. Roskilde: Roskilde University.

Orsi, Cosma. 2009. Knowledge-Based Society, Peer Production and the Common Good. *Capital and Class*, 33, 31–51.

Ostrom, Elinor. 1990. *Governing the Commons: The Evolution of Institutions for Collective Action*. Cambridge: Cambridge University Press.

Ostrom, Elinor. 1998. A Behavioral Approach to the Rational Choice Theory of Collective Action. Presidential Address to the American Political Science Association. *American Political Science Review*, 92(1), 1–22.

Ostrom, Elinor, and Hess, Charlotte. 2008. Private and Common Property Rights. In Boudewijn Bouckaert and Gerrit De Geest (Eds.), *Encyclopedia of Law and Economics*, pp. 332–379. Northampton: Edward Elgar. Last accessed 1 January 2019, http://papers.ssrn.com/sol3/papers.cfm?abstract_id=1304699.

Ostrom, Vincent, and Ostrom, Elinor. 1977. Public Goods and Public Choices. In Emanuel Savas (Ed.), *Alternatives for Delivering Public Services: Toward Improved Performance*, pp. 7–49. Boulder, CO: Westview Press.

Pagano, Ugo. 2014. The Crisis of Intellectual Monopoly Capitalism. *Cambridge Journal of Economics*, 38(6), 1409–1429.

Pashukanis, Evgeny. 1978. *Law and Marxism: A General Theory*. London: Ink Links.

Patry, William. 2009. *Moral Panics and the Copyright Wars*. Oxford: Oxford University Press.

Patterson, Lyman. 1968. *Copyright in Historical Perspective*. Nashville, TN: Vanderbilt University Press.

Peifer, Karl-Nikolaus. 2010. The Return of the Commons, Copyright History as a Common Source. In Ronan Deazley, Martin Kretschmer, and Lionel Bently (Eds.), *Privilege and Property, Essays on the History of Copyright*, pp. 347–357. Cambridge: Open Book Publishers.

Pevsner, Nikolaus. 2014. *Academies of Art, Past and Present*. Cambridge: Cambridge University Press.

Picasso, Pablo. 1993. *His Words*, ed. Hiro Clark. San Francisco, CA: Collins.

Pliny. 77 ad. *Naturalis Historia*, Vol. IX–X. Books 33–37.

Poggioli, Renato. 1968. *The Theory of the Avant-Garde*. Cambridge, MA: Harvard Belknap Press.

Polanyi, Karl. 2001 [1944]. *The Great Transformation: The Political and Economic Origins of Our Time*. Boston, MA: Beacon Press.

Popper, Karl. 1961. *The Poverty of Historicism*. London: Routledge and Kegan Paul.
Popper, Karl. 1963. *Conjectures and Refutations: The Growth of Scientific Knowledge*. London: Routledge and Kegan Paul.
Poster, Mark. 2006. *Information Please: Culture and Politics in the Age of Digital Machines*. Durham, NC: Duke University Press.
Power, Dominic, and Scott, Allen. 2004. A Prelude to Cultural Industries and the Production of Culture. In Dominic Power and Allen Scott (Eds.), *Cultural Industries and the Production of Culture*, pp. 3–16. London: Routledge.
Prahalad, Coimbatore, and Ramaswamy, Venkat. 2004. Co-Creation Experiences: The Next Practice in Value Creation. *Journal of Interactive Marketing*, 18(3), 5–14.
Psillos, Stathis. 2007. Causality. In Mervyn Hartwig (Ed.), *Dictionary of Critical Realism*, pp. 57–61. London: Routledge.
Puchta, Claudia, and Potter, Jonathan. 2004. *Focus Group Practice*. Los Angeles, CA: Sage.
Radin, Margaret 1982. Property and Personhood. *Stanford Law Review*, 34(5), 957–1015.
Radin, Margaret Jane 1987. Market Inalienability. *Harvard Law Review*, 100, 1849–1937.
Rawls, John 2005. *Political Liberalism*. New York: Columbia University Press.
Rawls, John 2009. *A Theory of Justice: Revised Edition*. Cambridge, MA: Harvard University Press.
Raymond, Eric. 1999. *The Cathedral and the Bazaar: Musings on Linux and Open Source by an Accidental Revolutionary*. Beijing: O'Reilly.
Restakis, John. 2010. *Humanizing the Economy: Co-operatives in the Age of Capital*. Gabriola Island: New Society Publishers.
Restakis, John. 2015. Public Policy for a Social Economy. In Michel Bauwens, George Dafermos, and John Restakis (Eds.), *Commons Transition: Policy Proposals for an Open Knowledge Society*, pp. 97–162. Foundation of Peer-to-Peer Alternatives. Last accessed 1 January 2019, http://commonstransition.org/commons-transition-the-book.
Riegl, Alois. 1893. *Stilfragen, Grundlegungen zu einer Geschichte der Ornamentik*. Berlin: G. Siemers.
Rifkin, Jeremy. 2014. *The Zero Marginal Cost Society: The Internet of Things, the Collaborative Commons, and the Eclipse of Capitalism*. New York: St Martin's Press.
Rigi, Jakob. 2013. Peer Production and Marxian Communism: Contours of a New Emerging Mode of Production. *Capital and Class*, 37(3), 397–416.
Rittner, Leona, Scott, Haine, and Jackson, Jeffrey. 2016. *The Thinking Space: The Café as a Cultural Institution in Paris, Italy and Vienna*. Abingdon: Routledge.
Rose, Carol. 1986. The Comedy of the Commons: Custom, Commerce, and Inherently Public Property. *University of Chicago Law Review*, 53(3), 711–781.

Rose, Carol. 1994. *Property and Persuasion: Essays on the History, Theory, and Rhetoric of Ownership*. Boulder, CO: Westview.

Rose, Carol. 2003. Romans, Roads and Romantic Creators: Traditions of Public Property in the Information Age. *Law and Contemporary Problems*, 66(1–2), 89–110.

Rose, Mark. 1993. *Authors and Owners: The Invention of Copyright*. Cambridge, MA: Harvard University Press.

Russell, Bertrand. 1945. *A History of Western Philosophy*. New York: Simon and Schuster.

Sacks, Danielle. 2011. The Sharing Economy. *Fast Company Magazine*, May 2011. Last accessed 1 January 2019, https://www.fastcompany.com/1747551/sharing-economy.

Sahlins, Marshal. 2013. *Islands of History*. Chicago, IL: University of Chicago Press.

Samuelson, Paul. 1954. The Pure Theory of Public Expenditure. *Review of Economics and Statistics*, 36(4), 387–389.

Samuelson, Pamela. 2003. Mapping the Digital Public Domain: Threats and Opportunities. *Law and Contemporary Problems*, 66(1–2), 147–171.

Samuelson, Pamela. 2017. Justifications for Copyright Limitations and Exceptions. In Ruth Okediji (Ed.), *Copyright Law in an Age of Limitations and Exceptions*, pp. 12–59. Cambridge: Cambridge University Press.

Sandqvist, Tom. 2006. *Dada East: The Romanians of Cabaret Voltaire*. Cambridge, MA: MIT Press.

Saussure, Ferdinand de. 1966. *Course in General Linguistics*. New York: McGraw Hill.

Sayer, Andrew. 2010. *Method in Science: A Realist Approach*. London: Routledge.

Schapiro, Meyer. 1999. Philosophy and Worldview in Painting. In Meyer Schapiro (Ed.), *Worldview in Painting – Art and Society: Selected Papers*. New York: George Braziller.

Schumpeter, Joseph. 1994 [1942]. *Capitalism, Socialism and Democracy*. London: Routledge.

Schweik, Charles. 2007. Free/Open Source Software as a Framework for Establishing Commons in Science. In Charlotte Hess and Elinor Ostrom (Eds.), *Understanding Knowledge as a Commons: From Theory to Practice*, pp. 277–309. Cambridge, MA: MIT Press.

Schweik, Charles, and English, Robert. 2012. *Internet Success: A Study of Open-Source Software Commons*. Cambridge, MA: MIT Press.

Seeger, Pete. 1993. *Where Have All the Flowers Gone: A Singer's Stories, Songs, Seeds, Robberies*. Bethlehem, PA: Sing Out Corporation.

Shaver, Lea, and Sganga, Caterina. 2009. The Right to Take Part in Cultural Life: On Copyright and Human Rights. *Wisconsin International Law Journal*, 27, 637–662.

Simmel, Georg. 2011 [1978]. *The Philosophy of Money*, trans. Tom Bottomore and David Frisby. London: Routledge.
Smith, Henry. 2007. Intellectual Property as Property: Delineating Entitlements in Information. *Yale Law Journal*, 116, 1742–1822.
Smythe, Dallas. 1984. New Directions for Critical Communications Research. *Media Culture and Society*, 6(3), 205–217.
Soderberg, Johan, and O'Neil, Mathieu. 2014. Introduction. In Johan Soderberg and Maxigas (Eds.), *Book of Peer Production*, pp. 2–3. Aarhus: NSU Press.
Stewart, David, and Shamdasani, Prem. 2015. *Focus Groups: Theory and Practice*. Los Angeles, CA: Sage.
Stiglitz, Joseph. 1991. *The Invisible Hand and Modern Welfare Economics*. NBER Working Paper No. 3641. Cambridge, MA: National Bureau of Economic Research. Last accessed 1 January 2019, http://www.nber.org/papers/w3641.pdf.
Tapscott, Don, and Williams, Anthony. 2006. *Wikinomics: How Mass Collaboration Changes Everything*. New York: Penguin.
Teubner, Gunther. 2013. Societal Constitutionalism and the Politics of the Common. In *Finnish Yearbook of International Law*, vol. 21, pp. 111–124. Oxford: Hart Publishing.
Tinterow, Gary, and Loyrette, Henri. 1994. *Origins of Impressionism*. New York: The Metropolitan Museum of Art.
Toffler, Alvin. 1980. *The Third Wave: The Classic Study of Tomorrow*. New York: Bantam Books.
Tronti, Mario. 1972. Workers and Capital. *Telos*, 14, 25–62.
Tummers, Anna. 2008. 'By His Hand': The Paradox of Seventeenth-Century Connoisseurship. In Anna Tummers and Koenraad Jonckheere (Eds.), *Art Market and Connoisseurship: A Closer Look at Paintings by Rembrandt, Rubens and their Contemporaries*, pp. 31–66. Amsterdam: Amsterdam University Press.
UNESCO. 2005. *The 2005 Convention on the Protection and Promotion of the Diversity of Cultural Expressions*. Paris, 20 October 2005. Last accessed 1 January 2019, http://en.unesco.org/creativity/sites/creativity/files/passeport-convention2005-web2.pdf.
UNESCO. 2016. *The Globalisation of Cultural Trade: A Shift in Consumption, International Flows of Cultural Goods and Services 2004–2013*. Last accessed 1 January 2019, https://en.unesco.org/creativity/sites/creativity/files/pdf globalisation_of_cultural_trade_a_shift_in_consumption.pdf.
Valguarnera, Filippo. 2013. Access to Nature and Intergenerational Justice. In Saki Bailey, Gilda Farrell, and Ugo Mattei (Eds.), *Protecting Future Generations through Commons*, pp. 189–213. Strasbourg: Council of Europe Publishing.
Vazquez, Adolfo. 1973. *Art and Society: Essays in Marxist Aesthetics*. London: Merlin Press.

Virno, Paulo. 1996. Notes on the General Intellect. In Saree Makdisi, Cesare Casarino, and Rebecca Karl (Eds.), *Marxism Beyond Marxism*, pp. 265–272. London: Routledge.
Von Hippel, Eric. 2005. *Democratizing Innovation*. Cambridge, MA: MIT Press.
Von Lohmann, Fred. 2008. Fair Use as Innovative Polity. *Berkeley Technology Law Journal*, 23(2), 829–865.
Voorhoof, Dirk. 2015. Freedom of Expression and the Right to Information: Implications for Copyright. In Christophe Geiger (Ed.), *Research Handbook on Human Rights and Intellectual Property*, pp. 331–353. Cheltenham: Edward Elgar.
Wackernagel, Martin. 1938. *The World of the Florentine Renaissance Artist: Projects and Patrons, Workshop and Art Market*. Princeton, NJ: Princeton University Press.
Wall, Derek. 2014. *The Commons in History: Culture, Conflict and Ecology*. Cambridge, MA: MIT Press.
Walzer, Michael. 2002. Equality and Civil Society. In Simone Chambers and Will Kymlicka (Eds.), *Alternative Conceptions of Civil Society*, pp. 34–49. Princeton, NJ: Princeton University Press.
Watson, Steven. 2003. *Factory Made: Warhol and the Sixties*. New York: Pantheon Books.
Weber, Max. 1958. *The Rational and Social Foundations of Music*, trans. Don Martindale, Johannes Riedel, and Gertrude Neuwirth. Carbondale, IL: Southern Illinois University Press.
Weber, Max. 1978. *Economy and Society: An Outline of Interpretive Sociology*. vol. II. Berkeley, CA: University of California Press.
White, Harrison, and White, Cynthia. 1965. *Canvases and Careers: Institutional Change in French Painting World*. New York: John Wiley.
Williams, Raymond. 1983. *Keywords*. London: Fontana.
Williams, Raymond. 1989. *What I Came to Say*. London: Hutchinson Radius.
WIPO. 2003. *Study on Limitations and Exceptions of Copyright and Related Rights in the Digital Environment*. SCCR/9/7. Last accessed 1 January 2019, http://www.wipo.int/edocs/mdocs/copyright/en/sccr_9/sccr_9_7.pdf.
WIPO. 2012. *Report on an Analysis of the Economic/Legal Literature on Intellectual Property (IP) Rights: A Barrier to Entry?* CDIP/8/INF/6 CORR. Last accessed 1 January 2019, http://www.wipo.int/edocs/mdocs/mdocs/en/cdip_8/cdip_8_inf_6_corr.pdf.
WIPO. 2012. *Traditional Knowledge and Intellectual Property*. Background Brief No 1. Last accessed 1 January 2019, https://www.wipo.int/pressroom/en/briefs/tk_ip.html.
Woodmansee, Martha. 1984. The Genius and the Copyright: Economic and Legal Conditions of the Emergence of the Author. *Eighteenth-Century Studies*, 17, 425–448.
Woodmansee, Martha. 1994. On the Author Effect: Recovering Collectivity. In Martha Woodmansee and Peter Jaszi (Eds.), *The Construction of Authorship:*

Textual Appropriation in Law and Literature, pp. 18–25. Durham, NC: Duke University Press.
Woodmansee, Martha, and Jaszi, Peter (Eds.). 1994. *The Construction of Authorship: Textual Appropriation in Law and Literature*. Durham, NC: Duke University Press.
Wright, Eric Olin. 2008. Commentary 2: Sociologists and Economists on the Commons. In Pranab Bardhan and Isha Ray (Eds.), *Contested Commons: Conversations between Economists and Anthropologists*. Oxford: Blackwell.
Wu, Tim. 2002. Network Neutrality, Broadband Discrimination. *Journal on Telecommunications and High Technology Law*, 2(2), 141–79.
Wu, Tim. 2010. *The Master Switch: The Rise and Fall of Information Empires*. New York: Alfred A. Knopf.
Zheng, Yu, Santaeulalia, Raul, and Koh, Dongya. 2015. Labor Share Decline and the Capitalization of Intellectual Property Products. *Society for Economic Dynamics, Meeting Papers 844*.
Zilsel, Edgar. 2003. *The Social Origins of Modern Science*, eds. Diederick Raven and Wolfgang Krohn, Berlin: Springer Science and Business Media.
Žižek, Slavoj. 2008. *In Defense of Lost Causes*. London: Verso.
Žižek, Slavoj. 2010. How to Begin from the Beginning. In Costas Douzinas and Slavoj Žižek (Eds.), *The Idea of Communism*, pp. 209–226. London: Verso.
Zukerfeld, Mariano, and Yansen, Guillermina. 2016. Access, Resources, and Classes in the History of Capitalism: A Theory of Social Stratification from a Cognitive Materialist Perspective. *tripleC*, 14(1), 208–231.
Zwick, Detlev, Bonsu, Samuel, and Darmody, Aron. 2008. Putting Consumers to Work. *Journal of Consumer Culture*, 8(2), 163–196.

Index

A

agency 7, 14–15, 29–30, 33, 44–45, 50, 53, 58, 60–61, 91–92, 129–130
alternative to capital 52–59, 60, 157
authorship 64–68, 74, 75
  individualistic notion 64–68, 83, 135
  romantic notion 70, 72
autonomy 37, 46, 66, 86, 95, 126, 133–134, 156

B

Barnes, Peter 157
Bauwens, Michel 45, 49, 127
Benkler, Yochai 47, 51, 147, 169n1
Blackstone, William 76, 83, 136, 173n35
Botsman, Rachel 38
Boyle, James 12, 86

C

Caffentzis, George 56
capital
  accumulation 36–39
  alternative to capital 52–59, 60, 157
  fix to capital 35–44, 60
  industrial 71, 74, 76
  mercantile 65–68, 71
  patch to capital 29–35, 60, 157
Castells, Manuel 48
Castoriadis, Cornelius 120
co-optation 43, 51, 60, 93, 94, 97, 105–112, 115–117, 123, 125, 160–161
co-opted sphere 5, 18, 93, 103–105, 110–111
collaborative consumption 38, 42
collective empowerment 3, 19–20, 35, 45–47, 107–109, 146, 156
commodification 3, 51

co-opted sphere 5, 18, 93, 103–105, 110–111
contested sphere 5, 18, 93, 103–105, 110–111
forces of 11, 19, 51, 66, 74, 76, 82, 90, 111, 112, 124, 158
historical perspective 6
see also commonification
common pool resources 4–5, 12, 13, 15, 30, 63, 144–145
commonification 2–5
co-opted sphere 5, 18, 93, 103–105, 110–111
contested sphere 5, 18, 93, 103–105, 110–111
forces of 4, 19, 20, 25, 58, 64, 90, 91, 112, 117–118, 124
see also commodification
commons
natural 30–31
as substitute to welfare state 44–45, 50, 60, 159
tragedy of anti-commons 40–41
see also intellectual commons; knowledge commons
commons based values
circulation 89, 92–93, 103–112, 160
cultural dimension 107, 121, 160
economic dimension 103–105, 121, 160
forms 121–122
general dimensions 110–112
mode of circulation 122–125
monetary value dialectics 113–118
moral significance 139–140
political dimension 107–109, 121, 160
social dimension 105–106, 119–120, 121, 160
see also co-opted sphere; contested sphere
commons-based peer production 1–2, 4–5, 7–8, 14, 79, 140–141, 169n1, 177n76
morality 5–8

communication commons 24
communities
intellectual commons 91–98
productive communal activity 120–121
see also co-optation; contestation
consequentialism 7–8, 10, 32–33, 130
contemporary theories 5–6
contestation 43, 51, 60, 93, 94, 97, 105–112, 115–117, 123, 125, 160–161
contested sphere 5, 18, 93, 103–105, 110–111
copyleft licensing 32, 123
copyright law 6, 63–87, 170n5
creativity
collaboration 135–138
commodification of art and culture 64–65
role of author in artistic production 64–65, 135–138
critical theories 6, 27, 52–59, 60, 158, 159
crowdsourcing 38
cultural commons 6–7, 9, 20, 23–24, 47–48, 158–159
globalisation 81
modernity 69–77, 85
postmodernity 77–85
Renaissance period 64–69, 85, 159
role of author in artistic production 64
culture
folk 47, 65, 149–150
popular 71–72

D

De Angelis, Massimo 25, 56
decentralisation 141–142, 144–145
democratisation 2–3, 45–47, 50–52, 78, 144–150

deontological 7–8, 10, 32–33, 50, 60, 130
dialectics 3–4, 9–10, 18–19, 52, 76, 86–87, 113–118
dignity 132–134, 156, 164
Dougherty, Dale 37
Drahos, Peter 176n69
Dusollier, Séverine 176n68
Dyer-Witheford, Nick 55–56

E

empowerment *see* collective empowerment; self-empowerment
enclosing power of industrial capital 76
ethics 7–8, 34, 49–50, 107–108, 143, 144, 150–151, 153

F

Fattori, Tommaso 45
Federici, Silvia 56
fix to capital 35–44, 60
folk culture 47, 65, 149–150
free software 1–2, 4, 39
free-riders 29, 34, 151
freedom 134
  of expression 148–149
  of speech 148–149
Frischmann, Brett 140

G

Geiger, Christophe 176n74
gift 82, 104–105, 160, 174n47
globalisation 52, 81
Goldstein, Paul 68
Gregory, Chris 124
guild system 65–69, 85

H

Haas, Jorg 12
Hardin, Garrett 170n8
Hardt, Michael 55, 58, 126

Harvey, David 125–126
Hayek, Friedrich 41
Helfrich, Silke 12
Hess, Charlotte 12, 32–33
Hettinger, Edwin 174n58
Howe, Jeff 38
human dignity 132–134, 156, 164

I

IAD (institutional analysis and development) 30–32, 34
ideology 33, 79–83
industrial capital 71, 74, 76
information commons *see* intellectual commons
institutional analysis and development (IAD) 30–32, 34
intellectual commons 1–10, 25
  characteristics 5–6, 8, 15–17
  commodification 82–85
  commons based and monetary value dialectics 113–118
  communities 91–98
  concepts 31–33
  elements 7, 8, 14–17
  future reform 166–168
  immanence 17, 155
  independent body of law 150–152, 161–165
  manifestations 22–24, 156
  moral dimension 155–161
  normative theories 2–3, 6, 7, 25, 129–153
  online and offline community comparison 117–118
  ontology 11–25
  ownership and access 17, 18, 139–140
  political implications 165–166
  social value research 89–101, 103–112, 119–127, 163
  tendencies 18–21, 156, 177n76
  see also theories

J

Jefferson, Thomas 16, 175n63

K

Kelty, Chris 176n69
knowledge commons *see* intellectual commons
knowledge-based economies 2
Kostakis, Vassilis 49

L

law
  commons-oriented 8–10
  intellectual property law 2–3
  normative approach 2–3, 8–10
Leadbeater, Charles 36–37, 42
Levy, Pierre 41
Linebaugh, Peter 12
Litman, Jessica 12, 175n61
Locke, John 138, 174–175n59
Luxemburg, Rosa 125

M

market
  capitalisation 1
  intellectual property-enabled 6–7, 25, 27, 39–42, 44–45, 90, 92
  logic 20
  restructuring 39–42
Marx, Karl 52–54, 91, 125, 144, 169n2, 172n28
mercantile capital 65–68, 71
merit 105–106, 121, 160
monetary value, circulation 114–117
morality
  commons-based peer production 5–8
  cycle of moral justification 161–165
  intellectual commons 3, 8–10, 143–146

Mueller, Milton 39
mutuality 17, 49–50, 107–108, 160

N

Negri, Antonio 55, 58, 126
neoliberal theories 6, 27, 35–44, 60, 157, 159
Newton, Isaac 16
Niaros, Vassilis 127
non-commercial 31–32, 46
non-excludability 15–18, 31
non-rivalry 15–18, 31, 138
non-subtractability 12, 138, 144–145
normative theories 2–3, 6, 7, 129–153
  community 143–150, 164
  normative model 153
  personhood 132–135, 164
  value 139–143, 164
  work 135–139, 164
Nozick, Robert 174n57

O

open hardware design 1–2, 4, 142
open licensing 2–3, 4
open scientific publishing 1–2, 4
O'Reilly, Tim 37
Orsi, Cosma 49
Ostrom, Elinor 5–6, 11–12, 27, 30, 32–33
  Governing the Commons 28

P

partner state 48–52
patch to capital 29–35, 60, 157
Picasso, Pablo 69–70
popular culture 71–72
post-operaist 55, 56
Promethean artist 6, 69–70, 74, 75, 77, 78, 85, 135, 171n18
prosumption 37, 38

public domain 3, 12, 24, 86, 138, 148, 149, 166–167, 170n7, 175n61
public good 15, 34, 140
public sphere 45, 47–48, 130, 148, 149

R

Radin, Margaret Jane 175n64
rational choice theories 27–32, 60, 157, 159, 170–171n10
Rawls, John 147
Raymond, Eric 142
reciprocity 17, 21, 30, 45, 49–50, 61, 110, 156
Rogers, Roo 38

S

self-empowerment 35, 46, 107–108, 111, 121, 156, 160
self-governance 2, 16–17, 18, 35, 107–108, 156
social democratic theories 6, 27, 44–52, 60, 157–158, 159
state
  partner 48–52
  welfare 44, 50, 60, 158, 159

T

Tapscott, Dan 36, 39, 41
technology corporation 1

theories 27–62
  growth of academic interest in commons concept 28–29
  see also critical theories; neoliberal theories; rational choice theories; social democratic theories
Toffler, Alvin 37
trust 105–106, 160

U

utilitarianism 7–8, 34–35, 43, 60, 159

V

values
  circulation 112
  crises 125–127
  pooling 112, 124

W

Wall, Derek 12
Warhol, Andy 79
welfare state 44, 50, 60, 158, 159
Williams, Anthony 36, 39, 41
work 135–139, 164

Z

zero marginal cost 15, 16, 19, 20, 31
Žižek, Slavoj 57

Printed by BoD™in Norderstedt, Germany